DÂMO

The Writings of a Hindû Chela

Compiled by SVEN EEK

THEOSOPHICAL UNIVERSITY PRESS
POINT LOMA, CALIFORNIA
1940

THEOSOPHICAL UNIVERSITY PRESS
POINT LOMA, CALIFORNIA

PRINTED IN THE UNITED STATES OF AMERICA

Preface

THIS volume is not a history of the early days of the Theosophical Society. No attempt has been made to produce a highly documented and exhaustive record, but by a careful selection of valuable material from the archives of the Theosophical Society (Point Loma), and from the magazine, *The Theosophist,* as well as from other sources, the aim has been to recreate for the reader the atmosphere of zeal and of devotion to the Masters and the T. S. which inspired the whole life of one of the outstanding characters in the early days of the Theosophical Society, Dâmodar K. Mâvalankar. Unimportant matters, such as official notes and formal reports which contain nothing of permanent interest, though signed by Dâmodar, have been omitted.

No doubt many Theosophists have entertained the thought of compiling the writings of Dâmodar, but as far as we know, this is the only book of its kind that is at present available. It was some years ago that consideration was first given to the preparation of a book on Dâmodar, but it was not until this summer of 1940 that the Literary Executive Committee felt that our Press could undertake this additional work, the compilation of which has been done by Mr. Sven Eek, Manager of the Publications Department of Theosophical University Press.

Particular help was given to the Editorial Board by Professor C. J. Ryan, who has contributed the valuable Biographical Notes. Professor Ryan is well known to Theosophists as the author of *H. P. Blavatsky and the Theosophical Movement* and of innumerable articles in Theosophical periodicals during more than forty years.

The material for this present volume has been taken from original sources, and is literally transcribed with the exception of obvious typographical errors which have been corrected. In certain instances such corrections appear in square brackets for the sake of absolute clarity. The Editors of this book are responsible only for those footnotes enclosed in square brackets and signed EDS.

Acknowledgment is due to A. Trevor Barker, Editor of *The Mahatma Letters to A. P. Sinnett* and *The Letters of H. P. Blavatsky to A. P. Sinnett,* for permission to include extracts from these two books.

— THE EDITORS

International Theosophical Headquarters,
 Point Loma, California.
  September 6, 1940.

Contents

IV — HISTORICAL

V — PERSONAL LETTERS

CONTENTS ix

VI — REFERENCES TO DÂMODAR BY THE MAHÂTMANS AND H. P. BLAVATSKY

Part I: Quotations from *The Mahatma Letters to A. P. Sinnett* 291

Part II: Quotations from *The Letters of H. P. Blavatsky to A. P. Sinnett* 298

APPENDIX

Notes on "A Hindu Chela's Diary" 311
A Hindu Chela's Diary 313

Those whom we desire to know us will find us at the very frontiers. Those who have set against themselves the Chohans . . . — would not find us were they to go [to] L'hassa with an army.

— THE MASTER K. H.

I

Biographical Notes

[As the title of this chapter shows, no attempt is here made to present either a highly documented and detailed Biography of Dâmodar, or a critical study of his literary output. The facts of his life as here stated are all derived from authoritative sources. — Eds.]

BIOGRAPHICAL NOTES

"TOOK *bhât* [rice] in the morning, and proceeded on from Kabi alone, sending back my things with the coolies to Darjiling."

These were the last words written by Dâmodar K. Mâvalankar that have been made public. They were penned in a small pocket diary which was sent back to his friends as he set out on the last lap from Darjiling in British India on his pilgrimage to the lands beyond the giant crests of Kanchanjunga which tower 28,000 feet into the blue. Shigatse, the seat of the Tashi Lama, is twenty-five days march from Darjiling, and it was toward this goal that Dâmodar went in company with a party sent to meet him. We learn from Colonel H. S. Olcott that Dâmodar's record:

since joining H. P. B. and myself at Bombay is one of unbroken energy and unfaltering zeal in the cause of humanity. A nobler heart never beat in a human breast, and his departure was one of the hardest blows we ever received. As above remarked, he had almost broken down his constitution by incessant official work, and when leaving Adyar had begun to spit blood and show signs of a rapid decline. Yet, with undaunted courage, he undertook the hard journey across the Himalayas, indifferent to the biting cold, the drifted snow, the lack of shelter and food, intent upon reaching the Guru whom he had first seen in his youth when lying on a sick-bed, of whom he had lost sight for many years, but whom he had recovered soon after joining the Theosophical Society, as his spiritual faculties developed and he was able to seek him in the *sûkśma śarîra*. What made him so devotedly attached and unswervingly loyal to H. P. B. was the discovery that this Guru was one of the Adepts behind our movement, the intimate associate of "Upasika," as he always subsequently called H. P. B. From the chief coolie of his escort I [Colonel Olcott] got particulars about him of great interest. . . . Damodar would not keep any more clothes than the ascetic costume he was wearing, nor any of the rice, meal, pulse, or other dry provisions with which his friends had supplied him. The most he would do was to let the chief coolie bake him a dozen *chapaties,* or unleavened pancakes. The last that was seen of him by the coolies was when, with face turned towards the Tibetan frontier, he trudged painfully on and disappeared behind a turning of the road.

— *Old Diary Leaves,* Vol. III, pp. 265-6

Without further explanation this description in Col. Olcott's *Old Diary Leaves* of Dâmodar's departure for the mysterious land of Tibet might leave the casual reader puzzled and wondering why anyone should wish to abandon relatives, friends, and the duties incumbent upon every responsible man, for a goal which promised little that the world holds dear. The old monastic idea of shutting oneself away from the world in order to pursue a life of devotion and spiritual exercises has lost its appeal in the West, and it would be no exaggeration to include a large portion of the East as well. But the case of Dâmodar throws a different light on the subject.

Dâmodar K. Mâvalankar must have become a 'chela' or pledged disciple of one of the great Oriental Mahâtmans or Masters of Wisdom very early in life, and it is clear that this was not the first incarnation in which he had stepped on the Path of Enlightenment. H. P. Blavatsky says:

Damodar was ready from his last birth to enter the highest

PATH and suspected it. He had long been waiting for the expected permission to go to Tibet before the expiration of the 7 years; . . . — *The Theosophist*, August, 1932, pp. 623-4

In Dr. G. de Purucker's *Occult Glossary* we read:

The chela-life, or chela-path, is a beautiful one, full of joy to its very end; but also it calls forth and needs everything noble and high in the learner or disciple himself or herself; for the powers or faculties of the Higher Self must be brought into activity in order to attain and to hold those summits of intellectual and spiritual grandeur where our Masters themselves live. For that, Masterhood, is the end of discipleship; . . . The more mystical meanings attached to this term "Chela" can be given only to those who have irrevocably pledged themselves to the esoteric life — to Esotericism and its School.

Dâmodar's significance in the Theosophical Movement lies largely in the fact that he became a high exemplar of the Theosophical life in spite of extraordinary difficulties, and that almost alone among hundreds of other earnest aspirants was he found qualified to proceed to the Tibetan mountain-home of the Founders of the Theosophical Society, the Mahâtmans Koot Hoomi and Morya. These members of the Great Lodge of spiritual Adepts, one a Brahman from Kashmir, the other a Râjput, decided to launch the Theosophical Movement at a critical period when the sands of spiritual life were running low in the West, and when even the ancient home of Âryâvarta showed signs of degeneration and decay. The glorious age of the Vedas, when inspired lawgivers stirred the souls of the people of India and a truly mystic civilization was in flower, was gone, seemingly for ever; and a caste-ridden people held in thrall by

rigid forms and superstitious fancies needed a new
impetus, a new inspiration, to re-create their lives.
But the main purpose of the Theosophical Movement
was to reawaken the spiritual intuitions and to promote the idea of universal brotherhood in the pro-
gressive nations of the West, where the need was
great in that materialistic period.　But the Orient
was not overlooked, and Dâmodar, a patriotic Hindû,
as well as a natural-born occultist and Theosophist
found in *Isis Unveiled*, H. P. Blavatsky's first book,
a glorious picture of ancient India which filled his
breast with a longing to lead his countrymen to a
worthier mode of living so as to restore Âryâvarta
to its one-time splendor.　After reading *Isis* he discovered the Theosophical Society and immediately became an active member.

Dâmodar belonged to a wealthy family of the
Karhâda Mahârâshtra Brahman caste.　On August 3,
1879, he joined the Society at Bombay; several of his
relatives, including his father and his uncle, also became members.

Little is known of his early life, but since the age
of seven he had felt an urge to give himself to a life
of devotion, and once, when he was brought near to
death by fever, he had a vision of his future Teacher,
the Master Koot Hoomi.　This Master assured him
that he would not die but would live to do a much
needed work in the world.　As already mentioned,
Dâmodar afterwards recognised in one of H. P. Blavatsky's Adept Teachers the wonderful man who had
awakened his inner vision when a child, and this for

ever sealed his devotion to the cause of Theosophy. In H. P. Blavatsky he found one who was closely in touch with the Master in whom he trusted, and an older and more experienced chela than himself. He never wavered in his obedience to her.

Dâmodar joined the Theosophical Society nearly six months after H. P. Blavatsky's arrival in India in February, 1879, and he was soon ready to serve on her journal, *The Theosophist,* which was established in October, 1879. According to Brahmânical customs, he had to get his father's permission to live at the Theosophical Headquarters and to adopt the mode of life of a Sannyâsin — one who abandons worldly bonds and attractions in the service of the spiritual nature. This he was allowed to do, but he went farther and abandoned his caste,* no trifling matter, as can be realized by reading an article that appeared in *The Theosophist,* and which is included in this volume (see "Castes In India," Chapter II). According to the Hindû custom he had been betrothed in his childhood, of course without his consent, and the time had arrived when he was expected to assume the responsibilities of married life. This would have seriously interfered with the realization of his hope of preparing under his

---

*The Mahâtman Morya, referring to difficulties facing certain Hindû Theosophists, wrote: ". . . unless a man is prepared to become a thorough theosophist *i. e.* to do as D. Mavalankar did,— give up entirely caste, his old superstitions and show himself a true reformer . . . he will remain simply a member of the Society with no hope whatever of ever hearing from us."

— *The Mahatma Letters to A. P. Sinnett,* p. 462

Master in Tibet for self-mastery (the chela discipline)
which must be undergone by those who aspire to become
saviors of humanity. The higher degrees require
a complete self-dedication. His father, a man of gener-
ous feelings, sympathized with Dâmodar's aspirations
and consented to the abandoning of the marriage
obligations, a proceeding recognised in India as perfectly honorable in the case of a Sannyâsin. Dâmodar
assigned his share of the ancestral estate to his family
under the understanding that his wife should be properly cared for. She fully agreed to this arrangement
and took up her residence in her father-in-law's home.

Unfortunately, however, when Dâmodar, along with
H. P. Blavatsky and Col. Olcott, was formally received
into the Buddhist communion during their tour in
Ceylon in 1880, his orthodox Hindû relatives were
greatly disturbed and they demanded that he return
to his caste. As he absolutely refused, they left the
Theosophical Society and became its open enemies.
Of course, neither H. P. Blavatsky, Olcott nor Dâmodar
accepted the notion that sectarian Buddhism was the
only true religion. Their action was chiefly an outer
expression of kindly support to the Buddhists in Ceylon
who were struggling to preserve their national faith,
as well as a demonstration that Theosophists believe
that every religion contains the same spiritual teaching,
more or less hidden by the obscuring veils of dogma.
Col. Olcott wrote his highly successful *Buddhist Catechism* soon after this Ceylon journey, and through his
efforts the Buddhists in that island were given complete
protection by the British Government. Dâmodar was

very busy during the tour with his duties as Assistant Recording Secretary in connexion with the new Branches and other activities that were being started, but at the same time his occult development was being assisted by the Masters as we learn from 'A Hindu Chela's Diary' and four letters to W. Q. Judge dated Jan. 24, 1880, and June 14, 21, and 28, 1881, printed in this volume. The few occult experiences he was permitted to mention in those letters are exceedingly interesting as they throw a vivid light on the method by which an accepted chela may receive personal instruction and spiritual benefits from the Masters even while he is working hard at the ordinary duties of everyday life.

It will be seen by the letter to W. Q. Judge, in January, 1880, that even then valuable opportunities for learning had been provided for the young aspirant. He had already entered upon the intensive spiritual discipline prescribed for chelas of his degree who have to live in the outer world. He observed some simple rules of diet and meditation, but above all he proved his sincerity and love for humanity by tireless work for Theosophy. He threw up a Government appointment and other interests to labor literally from dawn to midnight for the Cause, in his official capacity as Assistant Recording Secretary of the Theosophical Society and in many other ways, especially in helping H. P. Blavatsky to get out *The Theosophist* under the greatest difficulties. For the magazine he wrote many book reviews, 'open letters,' long and thoughtful comments on letters from contributors, reports of activities, and,

of course, original articles. For some time before he
left for Tibet he held the responsible place of Manager.
The Master Koot Hoomi said he was "indispensably
necessary at Headquarters" and that for his unselfish
labor and devotion he was receiving their help, "silent
though it be." In regard to the difficulties in producing *The Theosophist* with such a small staff, H. P.
Blavatsky wrote to A. P. Sinnett, her friend and the
editor of an important and flourishing Anglo-Indian
journal, in reply to some criticism he made:

> Do you forget that you are addressing two European beggars
> with two Hindu other beggars to help them in the management
> and not the rich *Pioneer* with lakhs behind it? I would like
> to see you undertake the management and editing of *Phoenix*
> with two pence in your pocket; with a host of enemies around;
> no friends to help you; yourself — the editor, manager, clerk,
> and even *peon* very often, with a poor half-broken down Damo-
> dar to help you alone for three years, one who was a boy right
> from the school bench, having no idea of business any more
> than I have, and Olcott always — 7 months in the year —
> away! . . . please remember that while you in the midst of all
> your arduous labours as the editor of the *Pioneer* used to leave
> your work regularly at 4 after beginning it at 10 a.m. — and
> went away either to lawn tennis or a drive, Olcott and I begin
> ours at *five* in the morning with candle light, and end it some-
> times at 2 a.m. We have no time for lawn tennis as you had,
> and clubs and theatres and social intercourse. We have no
> time hardly to eat and drink.
> — *The Letters of H. P. Blavatsky to A. P. Sinnett,* p. 57

It must not be forgotten that Dâmodar had a very
fragile physical body and suffered from chronic ill-
health, but he never let up on that account. The spirit
of unselfish devotion that inspired him brought about

a rapid spiritual and even psychic unfolding. His intellect was already well developed as is seen by his writings. Without forcing, occult powers began to appear quite naturally as they should in such cases, according to Theosophy. He soon became able to transmit astral messages on his Master's business and even to take astral journeys at will when called upon in the line of duty. He was occasionally instructed to heal the sick, and at such times he was endowed with the necessary 'magnetism.' Some of the communications from the Mahâtmans, published in *The Mahatma Letters to A. P. Sinnett,* in 1923, were transmitted through Dâmodar.

The ignorant and prejudiced critics who denied H. P. Blavatsky's ability to transmit or 'precipitate' letters, etc., from the Masters by occult methods because the proceedings were not conducted under what they called 'test conditions' such as they would dictate to a paid medium, were utterly unaware of the special conditions necessary before an 'astral mail service' could be inaugurated or sustained. Harmonious surroundings were the first requisite, and a unified 'magnetism' in the auras of transmitter and receiver had to exist. The process bears some resemblance to radio transmission, but the likeness must not be pushed too far; it is, however, equally 'scientific.'

Dâmodar, like H. P. Blavatsky, possessed a 'magnetic' aura congenitally sympathetic with that of the Masters, and so he could be employed as a focus of energy for astral transmission, but such phenomenal activities cannot be forced when disharmony prevails.

The periods of stress and bitter controversy in India seriously interfered with them, and so far as India was concerned they ceased when H. P. Blavatsky and Dâmodar left the country in 1885.

Col. Olcott relates several striking instances of Dâmodar's awakening powers, but, probably owing to his weak health, he was rarely employed to produce the so-called 'phenomena.' We quote in part two interesting accounts of his activities on the inner planes in November, 1883, during his tour with Olcott and others in Northern India when his occult powers were rapidly developing. According to Col. Olcott:

> . . . Damodar gave me another proof of his acquired power of travelling in the astral "double." He went to Adyar, conversed with H. P. B., heard the voice of a Master speak a message to me, and asked H. P. B. to telegraph me the substance of it so as to satisfy me of his veracity in these matters. On reporting the facts to me, he dictated the message as he heard it, and all present in my room signed a certificate as to the facts. The next morning the expected telegram from H. P. B. was delivered to me by the postman, this being the rule in India as to the class of "Deferred" messages. The despatch corroborated Damodar's dictated and certificated message, and again the witnesses who were present signed their names on the back of the Government despatch. — *Old Diary Leaves*, Vol. III, pp. 29-30

Here is the other case. Olcott writes:

> On putting his body to sleep as usual, he made a dash for the home of the Master among the Himalayas, but found, on arriving, that he too was away in the astral body; and, by the power of his attraction for his pupil, the latter was swept away as powerfully and instantaneously as though he had ventured into a deep and impetuous river current and been carried off his footing. The next minute Damodar found himself at Adyar,

in the presence of both his Master and H. P. B. On going to sleep he had held Mr. Ward's letter in his hand, and it had, it seems, gone along with him on the astral plane — itself, of course, changed from ponderable into astral, or etheric, matter. On telling the Master about the letter, he perceived it in his hand, gave it over to him, and was bidden to return to his place. By the radical power of the occult chemistry or physics, the astralized letter was restored to its solid state, taken by H. P. B., and the next day duly posted to my Aligarh address; the sequel is known. — *Op. cit.*, p. 31

Col. Olcott describes another astral visit by Dâmodar to H. P. Blavatsky which took place a week or so later in the train on the way to Lahore, and before long while Dâmodar and Olcott were in Lahore they both had the privilege of meeting and conversing with the Mahâtman Koot Hoomi in his *physical* body. W. T. Brown also saw him.

The time was approaching when Dâmodar's period of probation, considerably shortened because of his rapid advance, would end, and he would be allowed to begin his training in Tibet. On November 25, 1883, shortly after the meeting with the Mahâtman at Lahore, and when Olcott and Dâmodar were spending a few days at Jammu in Kashmir, as guests of the Mahârâja, the Masters called Dâmodar to one of their forest retreats (âśramas) which was not far away. Dâmodar instantly departed without notifying Olcott, who was alarmed by his disappearance until H. P. Blavatsky telegraphed from Adyar that the Master told her he would return. In less than three days he came back, a changed man, "seemingly robust, tough, and wiry, bold and energetic in manner: we could scarcely realize that he was the same person," writes Olcott.

Dâmodar's experience at the Master's âsrama was evidently a preparation for his journey to Tibet, which has already been mentioned, but before he could be granted this inestimable opportunity he had to be tested in a new and quite unexpected way in connexion with the disgraceful attacks on the Theosophical Society by Mme. Coulomb.

After Dâmodar's visit to the Master's âsrama near Jammu, mentioned above, he returned to Adyar and took up his arduous duties again. H. P. Blavatsky and Col. Olcott departed for Europe on February 20, 1884, and stayed away till December. During this time the Headquarters was left in charge of a Council which contained many discordant elements, and in a few months the Indian section was in the midst of the turmoil of the 'Coulomb affair,' details of which first reached Olcott when he was in Germany with H. P. Blavatsky in September, 1884, through a letter from the ever-faithful Dâmodar. Owing to the opposition Dâmodar had to meet from more or less disaffected members and owing to the complications of the Coulomb trouble, his health broke down again.

It would be out of place to consider the Coulomb-Hodgson case here except in so far as it concerns Dâmodar. Mme. Coulomb charged him with supporting in public the claim that the Mahâtmans are real persons, living men, while privately not believing it; and that he had conspired with her to deceive the members of the Society and the public in this matter. Of course there was no basis for this preposterous accusation, and the absurdity of her case was exposed when the illogical and self-contradictory nature of its contents was revealed. For example, she admitted that she and her husband tried to deceive *Dâmodar himself* by methods that would have been utterly useless and unreasonable if they really thought that he disbelieved in the Masters!*

In view of this Hindû Chela's intense devotion to the Master Koot Hoomi, the glorious ideal of his childhood vision, and the great help he had received from him and the other Mahâtmans, Mme. Coulomb's charges are so ridiculous that an apology for mentioning them is almost called for! The purity of Dâmodar's life, the flavor of his writings, his sacrifice of all the world holds dear — family, wealth, high social position, country, etc. — to work indefatigably for Theosophy (in which the existence of Mahâtmans is an indispensable factor) make the charges actually grotesque.

When the names and personalities of the Mahâtmans Morya and Koot Hoomi began to be disrespectfully treated by the Coulombs and other enemies of the Theosophical Movement, Dâmodar and the other chelas suffered far more acutely than from the personal charges against themselves. They found that the affair was very difficult to handle, not from any lack of evidence but for a reason not easily appreciated outside India or certain other Oriental countries. Ac-

*For information on this subject see *H. P. Blavatsky and the Theosophical Movement* by C. J. Ryan; or *Defence of H. P. Blavatsky*, and *The New Universe* by Beatrice Hastings.

cording to the unwritten code of the Indian Occult
Schools the honored names of the *Gurus* or spiritual
Teachers are never dragged into any kind of controversy; in fact, few if any true chelas will mention the
name or dwelling place of the Master to outsiders, or
even admit their connexion with a Guru.* Therefore,
when the prospect arose of having to give evidence
concerning the existence of such Teachers, statements
which might break this immemorial and wise tradition,
the situation became critical and tragical. Handi-
capped by this difficulty the defence was naturally
weakened, and through the excessive zeal of Dâmodar
and others in protecting their trust from profanation,
as they regarded it, serious errors of judgment were
committed. These are referred to by H. P. Blavatsky
in Letter L, quoted in Chapter VI of this volume where
she says that the Master was seriously displeased by
the mistaken methods of Dâmodar and other chelas in
handling the case.

In June, 1886, about a year after Dâmodar had

---

*H. P. Blavatsky says that "as in the case of Subba Row
(the well known writer, a learned chela of the Mahâtman M.)
they will sooner die than speak of their Masters." It may be
asked: How could H. P. Blavatsky, a high chela, or Dâmodar,
speak of the Masters and give out information hitherto preserved
with great secrecy, without breaking the rules? She explained
that at this critical period in human history the Masters had
decided that it was time to open the door a little wider, and
therefore she was given authority to reveal certain matters that
were formerly forbidden. But far more, of course, is reserved
until mankind is ready, mentally and morally, to understand it
and to employ it wisely.

reached Tibet and affairs were settling down again at Adyar, the Master K. H. wrote to Col. Olcott giving him the reason why Dâmodar had suffered so deeply. He says:

> The poor boy has had his *fall*. Before he could stand in the presence of the "Masters" he had to undergo the severest trials that a neophyte ever passed through, to atone for the many questionable doings in which he had over-zealously taken part, bringing disgrace upon the sacred science and its adepts. The mental and physical suffering was too much for his weak frame, which has been quite prostrated, but he will recover in course of time. This ought to be a warning to you all. You have believed "not wisely but too well." . . . *— Did H. P. Blavatsky Forge The Mahatma Letters?* by C. Jinarâjadâsa

H. P. Blavatsky knew of this, for she wrote, shortly after he reached Tibet: "The poor boy . . . has no happy times now since he is on probation and this is terrible."

Dâmodar's errors, however, did not arise from wrong or selfish motives — quite the reverse, but his Master well knew that even the most promising candidates for initiation must take the consequences of their acts, wise or foolish, just like anyone else. Before the Coulomb troubles the Master had spoken of the misunderstandings that Dâmodar aroused by his excessive zeal, but for all that he was found worthy of the high training of the Tibetan Mystery School, a rare distinction.

H. P. Blavatsky and Col. Olcott had the greatest respect and affection for him, and the high estimation in which the Masters held him is proved by a remark in a letter from Olcott to Miss Francesca Arundale

dated February 9, 1885. He says Dâmodar is starting
for Tibet and that the Master has arranged that if
H. P. Blavatsky, who was very ill, should die *before
Dâmodar returned to take her place as the link between
the Masters and the Society,* he, Olcott, would have to
fill the gap for the time being. Modestly he adds,
"These are His orders, but I should be a sorry substi-
tute." Olcott said that he loved Dâmodar as a son, and
he was terribly missed by both H. P. Blavatsky and
Olcott when he was called to Tibet.

William Q. Judge corresponded frequently with
Dâmodar and thought highly of him. In one letter to
Dâmodar he writes: "And as to having made greater
progress than you, I think I have some positive knowledge on that point. At one time I *may* have been
further than you, but not now." Judge was inclined
to think him "too humble" in contrast to some of his
critics who considered him too plain-speaking!

On March 31, 1885, H. P. Blavatsky sailed for
Europe in order to write her great work, *The Secret
Doctrine,* in relative peace. Dâmodar left Adyar on
February 23 on the first stage of his longed-for journey
to the Mystery School of his Master in Tibet. He
stayed, on his way, at Calcutta, Benares, Darjiling,
and Sikkim. At Benares he had long talks with the
woman ascetic, Mâji, a highly respected friend and
almost, we might say, colleague, of H. P. Blavatsky.
She is mentioned in one or more of Dâmodar's letters.
Dâmodar had to wait at Benares for about a fortnight
until the decision came that he was to start immediately
for Sikkim, where he would meet the distinguished per-

sonage under whose protection he was to travel to the
'Forbidden Land.' On April 23, 1885, they began the
perilous crossing of the Himâlayas.

For a considerable time no news was received from
Dâmodar, and many thought that he had not survived
the hardships of the journey. Olcott writes to Miss
F. Arundale on July 8, 1885, that in the absence of
authentic information rumors had arrived that he had
perished, but Olcott is certain that this is false. H. P.
Blavatsky had good reason to believe he was alive.
He had told her that he would arrange so that no one
would search for him, and it would appear certain that
he was lost. She gave him a few things to throw away
on his journey as if he were overcome by fatigue. His
object was to give no further cause, so far as he was
concerned, for any discussion about the Masters whose
names had been so desecrated.

From time to time, during H. P. Blavatsky's stay
at Würzburg in 1885-6, the Masters and some of their
chelas would visit her in the astral. Countess Wacht-
meister, herself a remarkable clairvoyant, also saw
them. On January 4-6, 1886, H. P. Blavatsky wrote to
A. P. Sinnett, "I saw Damodar last night. . . ."
About the same time she wrote to Dr. Franz Hartmann
that she knew Dâmodar was alive and probably in
Tibet at that moment. Evidently thinking of the
persecution she was still enduring and of her longing
to go "Home," she cried to Sinnett, "Happy Damodar!
He went to the land of Bliss, to Tibet and must now
be far away in the regions of our Masters." Mâji
reported, from statements made by pilgrims returning

from Tibet, that Dâmodar was there, and in *The Theosophist,* July, 1886, Supplement, a notice was issued, signed by H. S. Olcott and T. Subba Row, that news had arrived as recently as June 7 that Dâmodar was safely "under the guardianship of the friends he had sought" but that his return would probably be uncertain for a long time to come.

Another very interesting reference which settles the matter occurs in a letter from H. P. Blavatsky to her old friend Khan Bahadur N. D. Khandalavala, dated London, November, 1889, more than four years after Dâmodar's departure. She writes:

. . . Damodar *is not dead,* and Olcott knows it as well as I do. I had a letter from him not more than 3 months ago, and *his* opinion of his countrymen at the present juncture is a caution. . . . It is a *base falsehood* that he was driven away from Adyar. *I was* driven away, by the cowardice of those for whom I had risked my whole life, reputation and honour, and he was the only true, devoted friend I had in all India, the *only one* who having the Masters' and my secret, knew the *whole* truth and therefore knew that whatever people thought being blinded by appearance I had never deceived anyone — though I was bound on my oath and pledge to conceal much from everyone, even Olcott. Damodar was ready from his last birth to enter the highest PATH and suspected it. . . .

                    — *The Theosophist,* August, 1932, pp. 623-4

Among the host of members who have enrolled in the Theosophical Society since 1875, few have exemplified the true Theosophical life so well as Dâmodar, but he was also equipped with 'technical Theosophy' without which the highest ethics lack the philosophic and scientific foundation which answers the question of Why and Wherefore.

Dâmodar could express his ideas clearly in writing. His literary output was not large but it is valuable. It did not wander from the 'Original Lines' as laid down by the Masters, and therefore it is as 'modern' today as it was sixty or so years ago, for true Theosophy does not grow old. Dâmodar's range was wide, as the reader will find on perusing the contents of this volume. Of special interest are his lively but not exaggerated accounts of 'historical' events in which he took part, particularly those which reveal, within permitted bounds, his personal experiences with the Mahâtmans. Having received a good training in English he wrote the language with ease, and if his style lacked polish in his earlier period it quickly improved, and when occasion required it eloquently proclaimed the intensity of his belief and trust in the saving message of Theosophy.

Dâmodar was only one of a group of Indian and Tibetan chelas who helped H. P. Blavatsky in India, but none of them worked so closely beside her, and with the exception of Dâmodar and Subba Row we know little of their personal lives. Dâmodar's story arouses a vivid impression of the early days of the Theosophical Society in India, permeated with the enthusiasm and devotion of the few sincere workers who carried the Movement safely over apparently unsurmountable obstacles, from attacks by open enemies, and from the more dangerous onslaughts from within by the disappointed ambition, jealousy, cowardice and plain treachery for selfish ends of fairweather friends. Though the guidance of the Masters was naturally more apparent in the early days when the Society was in its infancy, the same inspiration has never failed throughout the sixty-five years of its checkered history, and today Theosophy, the Light from the East, is widely recognised as a powerful factor in the thought of the age.

— C. J. RYAN

II

Articles: Metaphysical and Occult

[This chapter contains the main body of Dâmodar's writings on metaphysical and occult subjects, written between the years 1880 and 1884. Very little of his appeared in *The Theosophist* in the ensuing months, before his departure to Tibet in February, 1885. The chronological order of publication has been preserved except where a secondary article continues a subject already under discussion. In such cases, articles bearing on the same subject are grouped together. — EDS.]

THE SWAMI OF AKALKOT

[From *The Theosophist*, January, 1880.]

A BOOK entitled "Swámi Charitra" (The life of Swámi) has just been published in Maráthi, in two parts, by one Náráyan Hári Bhágvat. It contains the life of one of the most remarkable among modern Hindus, the Swámi of Akalkot, from the time he became known under the name of Digámbar Báwa, in a town called Mangalvede near Akalkot. Nothing is known of this wonderful man before that time. Neither did any body dare question him about his antecedents. One named Bábájipant, who was one of those who had lived with the Swámi since the time his public career as an ascetic began, urged him once to give information about his name, native place, and family. Swámi gave no direct answer, but simply said "Datta Nagar," and "Chief person" — "the Vata tree." No other attempt to elicit information was made. The reason that led the author to commence this biography is very astonishing. He says that one night he went to bed as usual, but could not sleep for a long time, being oppressed with various thoughts. In this frame of mind he at last fell asleep, but was startled by a most unexpected dream. He saw a Sannyási approach his bed. This reverend man, unlike persons of his avocation, wore clothes, had "kun-

dala"* in his ears and carried with him a "dand"†
and kam andalu.‡ A man who accompanied him asked
the author to get up and see the Swámi. He seemed
to obey and Swámi then said:—"It is a well-known
fact that I took Samadhi§ at Akalkot. Write my
biography as will suit the present times, in accordance with my instructions. I now disappear." This
seen, the author awoke, got up, and was at a great
loss what to do, especially as he had never seen the
Swámi, and was consequently unable to obey the instructions conveyed to him in the dream. Neither
had he ever felt any sincere desire to see the Swámi
during his lifetime. Unlike many, he had never regarded him as an incarnation of God. While in this
state of mind he slept for the second time, and again
in his dream saw the same person in the same dress
and with the same marks about him, who said "get
up, why are you thus puzzled? Begin writing and
you will have the necessary materials." The author
thereupon resolved to at least make the attempt, and
wrote to all the persons who knew the Swámi well,
to supply as much information as they could. The

---

*A sort of ring usually worn by the Sannyasis in the lower
part of their ears.

†A three or seven knotted bamboo of the wonder-working
ascetics.

‡The gourd which Brahmacharies, Sannyasis and others use
for holding water.

§When a great Sadhu is dead, this phrase is usually used.
Samádhi is the highest stage of Yog training, and when a Yogi
is in that state he loses consciousness of this world and sees
nothing but his own Divine Spirit.

facts mentioned in the book are therefore authenticated. They are moreover credible, because the author
says he got many of these from persons he had never
written to.   Moreover it is not likely that a person
like Mr. Govind Vishnu Bhide, who is well informed
and experienced, would talk at random without considering well upon the matter. He says that once
when he went to see the Swámi in fulfilment of a vow
made by him, he had also a desire that Swámi should
advise him in regard to spiritual matters. No sooner
did he stand before the Swámi than the latter turned
his face towards him, and repeated the following verse
in Marathi:—

उपासनलो दृढ चालवावें ॥ सत्कर्मयोगें वय घालवावें ॥

भूदेवसंतांसि सदा लवावें ॥ सवीं मूर्खीं मंगल बालवावें ॥

No less credible is the fact mentioned by Mr. Vishnu
Chintamon Bhopatkar, Sheriff of the Sessions Court
at Poona. Some ten years ago, when he served as
Sheristedar of the District Judge, his wife suffered
from a very severe attack of fever. Every day the
sickness increased and the doctors pronounced her
incurable. He was therefore ready to try any remedy
suggested to him. He saw a friend of his who advised
him to make a vow that he would take his wife to
the Swámi of Akalkot, if she should improve, and
in the mean time to keep her under the treatment of
a native doctor named Gunesh Shastri Sakurdikar.
He accordingly prayed to the Swámi, and promised
to offer a cocoanut to his idol on his behalf. But
unfortunately he forgot his promise when he went

to bed. And although this fact was known to nobody, his brother-in-law saw in a dream the Swámi rebuking him for having forgotten his promise to offer a cocoanut on Swámi's account. As he was not aware of the promise made by Mr. Bhopatkar, he was at a loss as to what his dream meant, and consequently communicated the fact to all the family, in great astonishment. When Mr. Bhopatkar heard this, he repented having forgotten his promise, but immediately after taking a bath he offered the cocoanut on Swámi's account, and made a vow that if his wife was cured he would go with her in the month of January to Akalkot to see the Swámi. Then he sent for the native doctor mentioned to him by his friend, but found that he had left for his Inám village and was not in Poona. But nevertheless, to the great surprise of Mr. Bhopatkar, it happened that while he was returning home from the office he met on his way the very native doctor whom he was searching for. He then took him home and the latter gladly undertook to treat Mr. Bhopatkar's wife. The medicine administered proved a success, and she went on improving gradually. And, although she was pretty well by the month of January, Mr. Bhopatkar did not think it advisable for her to travel as she was still very weak, and consequently did not take her with him when he left Poona. But he had no sooner left Poona without her, than her sickness recurred so seriously that the next day he was telegraphed to return. Since she had been all right at the time of his departure the sudden receipt of this telegram made him

suspect that all this was due to his not having fulfilled his vow to take his wife with him to Akalkot.
He then invoked the Swámi, asked his pardon, and
promised to go with her to Akalkot in the month of
July if she should recover. She at once began to
mend so rapidly that by the time he reached home
he found her all right. In the month of July, although she had recovered, she was in too feeble a
state to face the cold of the season. He however
resolved to abide by his vow this time, and accordingly went to Akalkot with his wife and the doctor
under whose treatment she was. When they reached
their place of destination it was raining very hard,
and the place where they had put up was very
damp. Her constitution however received no shock,
but on the contrary she continued to improve. When
they all went to the Swámi he ordered a certain book
to be brought him, and after finding a certain chapter
gave it first to the doctor and then to Mr. Bhopatkar,
thereby intimating without speaking a word, that their
object in coming was gained.

There are many such facts as the above mentioned in the book, all going to confirm the Swámi's
claim to the knowledge of Yog Vidya. He was a practical example to show what a man *can* do, if he *will*.
If any body had taken advantage of the opportunity
thus offered to him and gone to the Swámi purely
with the intention of studying philosophy, how much
good might he not have done himself and his country!
During the twenty years or more that the Swámi was
at Akalkot, no less than 500,000 persons must have

gone to see him. But of this large number it would
seem that scarcely any had within them an honest
desire to study philosophy. Almost all were actuated
merely by selfish worldly desires. If they had gone
to him with a sincere aspiration to learn how to obtain control over bodily passions, he would have bestowed favours on them, of which no robber in the
world could have deprived them. But they sought
but these worldly enjoyments with which fools are
satisfied. They had never given a moment's consideration to the thought of what their state would be
after the death of their physical bodies. In the whole
book under notice are given but two or three instances of persons who went to the Swâmi with a
desire to obtain knowledge. The course which he
adopted to fulfil the desires of such persons is very
curious. One named Narsappa, an inhabitant of Mysore, had gone to Akalkot with a view to receive
some instructions on spiritual matters. He was at
a great loss how to explain his intentions to the Swâmi, as he knew neither Marathi nor Hindustâni. He
however would regularly go and sit silently by the
Sannyâsi. Once while he was sitting near a Purânik,*
Swâmi made him a sign to approach and upon his
obeying, Swâmi took a blank book that was lying by
him, and, after turning many of its leaves, gave him
a certain page to read. He there found, to his great
astonishment and joy, an injunction printed in Kanarese characters, that he should read Bhagvat Gita

---

*A person who reads any of the 18 works of Puran and ex-
plains the meaning.

if he would have his desires fulfilled. He then gladly communicated the fact to a Puránik friend and
asked him to read the book to him. The Puránik
approached the place where the Swámi was sitting,
and taking the blank book which had been placed in
the hands of Narsappa, looked for the page on which
Narsappa said he saw Kanarese characters. He also
examined all the other books, as well as all the papers
lying there, but nowhere could he find Kanarese characters. This fact is an illustration to show that this
singular being communicated his instructions only to
those who sincerely desired them.

The book teems with facts illustrative of the power
obtained by a Yogi. There are very few persons in
this country, who being in search of the ancient Aryan
Philosophy, have obtained control over the bodily
passions which trouble ordinary men beyond measure.
Fewer still who like one now living in India, whom
I dare not mention, are known. Almost all who have
thoroughly studied or are studying that ennobling
philosophy, keep themselves out of the public view
in compliance with wise and inexorable rules. It is
not through selfishness, as too many imagine. Though
unseen, they none the less are continually working
for the good of humanity. In thousands of cases what
they effect is ascribed to Providence. And whenever
they find anyone who, like themselves, has an ambition above the mere pleasures of this world, and is
in search of that Vidya which alone can make man wise
in this as well and [as] happy in the next, they stand
ready by his side, take him up in their hands as soon

as he shows his worthiness, and put in his way the
opportunities to learn that philosophy, the study of
which has made them masters of themselves, of nature's forces, and of this world. It is apparent that
the Swámi of Akalkot was one of such persons. A
man peculiarly oracular and sparing of speech, and
eccentric to a degree, he nevertheless did a world of
good, and his life was crowded with marvels. Many
facts might be quoted that would tend to show the
great knowledge possessed by him, but the few above
related will suffice to introduce him to the reader,
and to indicate his familiarity with the occult side
of nature. While he was alive, very few learnt the
Vidya from him; now that he is gone for ever, his
death is lamented, as is usually the case with the sons
of India. Their eyes are at last opened to the injury
they have inflicted upon themselves by neglecting a
golden opportunity.

The account of his death given in the biography
is pathetic, and worth repetition. On the last day
of the first fortnight of the month of Chaitra,* in
the year 1800 of the Shálivándn Era, people suspected
that the health of the Swámi had begun to fail. While
he was sleeping in the afternoon of that day, at the
place of Tatya Sáheb Subhedár he suddenly got up,
and ordered a square earthen tile which was lying
there to be placed on somebody's head. He then went
to a tank outside the skirts of the town, followed by
a large crowd, as well as by the person who had the

---

*The first month of the Hindu year according to the Sháli-
ván Era.

earthen tile on his head, and seated himself on the steps of the tank. He afterwards ordered the man to place the earthen tile in water without injuring it, and asked the crowd to make a loud noise.* He then removed to the temple of Murlidhar in the evening until which time he was all right. But at about 9 in the night he had a severe attack of cold and fever. But without communicating the fact to any body he got up early in the morning and went to the burning ground where he showed two or three funeral piles to some of his followers and asked them to remember them. He then directed his footsteps towards the village of Nagannhalli which is about two miles from where he was. And although it was past noon he had taken neither his bath nor meals, but nobody dared ask him do any thing. On his way he rested in a shed reserved for cows. His followers as usual began to prepare him a bed, when he said — "Henceforward I do not require any bed. Burn it on that tree opposite to me." This startled some of his followers, but they did not even suspect that the Swámi thereby meant any thing in regard to himself. The next day he returned to Akalkot and stopped under a Vata tree behind the palace of Karjalkar. And notwithstanding that he then suffered from fever, he carried on his conversation in his usual tone. Neither did he show any change in his actions. Short-

---

*According to the Hindu custom when any body loses his nearest relation or one he dearly loves, he turns round the dead body and makes a loud noise by pressing his hand against his mouth; such a noise is here meant.

ly afterwards he had an attack of diarrhœa, and
his appetite failed him. But he did not omit his customary bath, and if any body raised objection to his
doing so, on account of his sickness, he answered,
"What will your father lose if I die?" He was cured
of diarrhœa by Hanmantráo Ghorpade, the doctor
of the dispensary at Akalkot, but continued to suffer
from fever and shortly afterwards had paroxysm of
coughing. He was then placed under the treatment
of a native doctor named Nána Vaidya, all of whose
attempts to cure him failed. If asked not to bathe
or expose himself to air, he would pay no attention.
Neither could he be persuaded to take the medicine
prescribed for him. Two or three days afterwards
he began to breathe very hard, and he sank rapidly.
But still he made no complaint and he did not permit
his outward appearance to show any symptoms of what
he internally suffered. When his sickness was at last
too apparent to be concealed some of his respectable
friends thought it advisable for him to distribute alms
before his death. This he did most willingly, himself
repeating all the necessary mantrams. He gave, with
his hands, his own embroidered shawl to Ramáchárya.
As his cough increased every moment, he was advised
to remove from an open place into the inner part of
the house. But all the entreaties of his friends proved
in vain. The same answer was repeated to them.
At noon on the 13th day of the latter fortnight of the
month of Chaitra, he ordered his cows and other
animals to be brought before him. He then gave away
all the food and clothes offered to him. Seeing that

by that time his voice was almost gone, one of his
good disciples asked him if he had any instructions
to communicate. In reply he repeated the following
verse from the Gita:—

अनन्याश्चिन्तयन्तो मां ये जनाः पर्युपासते ।

तेषां नित्याभियुक्तानां योगक्षेमं वहाम्यहं ॥

He then turned from the left to the right side and
ordered himself to be seated. No sooner was the
order obeyed than he was...!

Now, as was above remarked, people have begun
to appreciate his greatness. They have erected a sort
of a temple on the spot where he breathed his last, to
commemorate his memory. But if they had held him
fast in their hearts while he was alive, and if they
had studied the Vidya with him, then they would have
raised themselves above base passions and the pursuit
of pleasures, and obtained that kingdom from which
the gainer is never dethroned. To such as may ask
how he could have assisted them in making themselves
masters of self, let the author speak. —"As all the
facts mentioned in the book relate to others, it is quite
plain that readers would have the author say what may
have happened to himself. It would be unjust for him
to shrink from relating his own experience in deference
to unworthy fears. It is thirteen months since he saw
the Swámi in his dream, and he does not now feel
the infirmities of age. All his senses are in proper
order and not decayed by age. By degrees he gains
possession of the secret that enables him to control
practically the passions which trouble ordinary men.

And whenever he cannot, with all his efforts, check
any improper desire, he sees, in an inexpressible way,
some event which shows that the Swámi is determined
upon driving all improper thoughts from the author's
mind by bringing him face to face with strange events.
This is the only experience which the author has had
until now of Swámi's greatness." — But it suffices to
show that the author is in the right path.

CASTES IN INDIA

[From *The Theosophist*, May, 1880.]

NO MAN of sincerity and moral courage can read Mr. G. C. Whitworth's Profession of Faith, as reviewed in the April THEOSOPHIST, without feeling himself challenged to be worthy of the respect of one who professes such honourable sentiments. I, too, am called upon to make my statement of personal belief. It is due to my family and caste-fellows that they should know why I have deliberately abandoned my caste and other worldly considerations. If, henceforth, there is to be a chasm between them and myself, I owe it to myself to declare that this alienation is of my own choosing, and I am not cut off for bad conduct. I would be glad to take with me, if possible, into my new career, the affectionate good wishes of my kinsmen. But, if this cannot be done, I must bear their displeasure, as I may, for I am obeying a paramount conviction of duty.

I was born in the family of the Karháda Maháráshtra caste of Brahmins, as my surname will indicate. My father carefully educated me in the tenets of our religion, and, in addition, gave me every facility for acquiring an English education. From the age of ten until I was about fourteen, I was very much exercised in mind upon the subject of religion and devoted myself with great ardour to our orthodox religious practices. Then my ritualistic observances

were crowded aside by my scholastic studies, but
until about nine months ago, my religious thoughts
and aspirations were entirely unchanged. At this time,
I had the inestimable good fortune to read "Isis Unveiled; a Key to the Mysteries of Ancient and Modern
Religion and Science," and to join the Theosophical
Society. It is no exaggeration to say that I have
been a really living man only these few months; for
between life as it appears to me now and life as I comprehended it before, there is an unfathomable abyss.
I feel that now for the first time I have a glimpse
of what man and life are — the nature and powers
of the one, the possibilities, duties, and joys of the
other. Before, though ardently ritualistic, I was not
really enjoying happiness and peace of mind. I simply practised my religion without understanding it.
The world bore just as hard upon me as upon others,
and I could get no clear view of the future. The only
real thing to me seemed the day's routine; at best
the horizon before me extended only to the rounding
of a busy life with the burning of my body and the
obsequial ceremonies rendered to me by friends. My
aspirations were only for more Zamindáries, social
position and the gratification of whims and appetites.
But my later reading and thinking have shown me
that all these are but the vapours of a dream and
that he only is worthy of being called man, who has
made caprice his slave and the perfection of his spiritual self a grand object of his efforts. As I could
not enjoy these convictions and my freedom of action
within my caste, I am stepping outside it.

In making this profession, let it be understood that I have taken this step, not because I am a Theosophist, but because in studying Theosophy I have learnt and heard of the ancient splendour and glory of my country — the highly esteemed land of Aryávarta. Joining the Theosophical Society does not interfere with the social, political, or religious relations of any person. All have an equal right in the Society to hold their opinions. So far from persuading me to do what I have, Mme. Blavatsky and Col. Olcott have strongly urged me to wait until some future time, when I might have had ampler time to reflect. But the glimpse I have got into the former greatness of my country makes me feel sadly for her degeneration. I feel it, therefore, my bounden duty to devote all my humble powers to her restoration. Besides, histories of various nations furnish to us many examples of young persons having given up everything for the sake of their country and having ultimately succeeded in gaining their aims. Without patriots, no country can rise. This feeling of patriotism by degrees grew so strong in me that it has now prepared my mind to stamp every personal consideration under my feet for the sake of my motherland. In this, I am neither a revolutionist nor a politician, but simply an advocate of good morals and principles as practised in ancient times. The study of Theosophy has thrown a light over me in regard to my country, my religion, my duty. I have become a better Aryan than I ever was. I have similarly heard my Parsi brothers say that they have

been better Zoroastrians since they joined the Theosophical Society. I have also seen the Buddhists write
often to the Society that the study of Theosophy has
enabled them to appreciate their religion the more.
And thus this study makes every man respect his
religion the more. It furnishes to him a sight that
can pierce through the dead letter and see clearly
the spirit. He can read all his religious books between the lines. If we view all the religions in their
popular sense, they appear strongly antagonistic to
each other in various details. None agrees with the
other. And yet the representatives of those faiths
say that the study of Theosophy explains to them all
that has been said in their religion and makes them
feel a greater respect for it. There must, therefore,
be one common ground on which all the religious
systems are built. And this ground which lies at
the bottom of all, is truth. There can be but one
absolute truth, but different persons have different
perceptions of that truth. And this truth is morality.
If we separate the dogmas that cling to the principles
set forth in any religion, we shall find that morality
is preached in every one of them. By religion I do
not mean all the minor sects that prevail to an innumerable extent all over the world, but the principal
ones from which have sprung up these different sects.
It is, therefore, proper for every person to abide by
the principles of morality. And, according to them,
I consider it every man's duty to do what he can
to make the world better and happier. This can proceed from a love for humanity. But how can a man

love the whole of humanity if he has no love for his countrymen? Can he love the whole, who does not love a part? If I, therefore, wish to place my humble services at the disposal of the world, I must first begin by working for my country. And this I could not do by remaining in my caste. I found that instead of a love for his countrymen, the observance of caste distinction leads one to hate even his neighbour, because he happens to be of another caste. I could not bear this injustice. What fault is it of anyone that he is born in a particular caste? I respect a man for his qualities and not for his birth. That is to say, that man is superior in my eyes, whose *inner* man has been developed or is in the state of development. This body, wealth, friends, relations and all other worldly enjoyments that men hold near and dear to their hearts, are to pass away sooner or later. But the record of our actions is ever to remain to be handed down from generation to generation. Our actions must, therefore, be such as will make us worthy of our existence in this world, as long as we are here as well as after death. I could not do this by observing the customs of caste. It made me selfish and unmindful of the requirements of my fellow-brothers. I weighed all these circumstances in my mind, and found that I believed in caste as a religious necessity no more than in the palm-tree yielding mangoes. I saw that if it were not for this distinction, India would not have been so degraded, for this distinction engendered hatred among her sons. It made them hate and quarrel with one another. The peace of the land was disturbed.

People could not unite with one another for good purposes. They waged war with one another, instead
of devoting all their combined energies to the cause
of ameliorating the condition of the country. The
foundation of immorality was thus laid, until it has
reached now so low a point that unless this mischief
is stopped, the tottering pillars of India will soon give
way. I do not by this mean to blame my ancestors
who originally instituted this system. To me their
object seems to be quite a different one. It was based
in my opinion on the qualities of every person. The
caste was not then hereditary as it is now. This will
be seen from the various ancient sacred books which
are full of instances in which Kshatriyas and even
Máhárs and Chámbhárs who are considered the lowest
of all, were not only made and regarded as Brahmins,
but almost worshipped as demi-gods simply for their
qualities. If such is the case why should we still
stick to that custom which we now find not only
impracticable but injurious? I again saw that if I were
to observe outwardly what I did not really believe
inwardly, I was practising hypocrisy. I found that I
was thus making myself a slave, by not enjoying the
freedom of conscience. I was thus acting immorally.
But Theosophy has taught me that to enjoy peace of
mind and self-respect, I must be honest, candid,
peaceful and regard all men as equally my brothers,
irrespective of caste, colour, race or creed. This, I see,
is an essential part of religion. I must try to put these
theoretical problems into practice. These are the
convictions that finally hurried me out of my caste.

I would at the same time ask my fellow countrymen who are of my opinion, to come out boldly for their country. I understand the apparent sacrifices one is required to make in adopting such a course, for I myself had to make them, but these are sacrifices only in the eyes of one who has regard for this world of matter. When a man has once extricated himself from this regard and when the sense of the duty he owes to his country and to himself reigns paramount in his heart, these are no sacrifices at all for him. Let us, therefore, leave off this distinction which separates us from one another, join in one common accord, and combine all our energies for the good of our country. Let us feel that we are Aryans, and prove ourselves worthy of our ancestors. I may be told that I am making a foolish and useless sacrifice; that I cut myself off from all social intercourse and even risk losing the decent disposal of my body by those upon whom our customs impose that duty; and that none but a visionary would imagine that he, even though chiefest among Brahmins, could restore his country's greatness and the enlightenment of a whole nation, so great as ours. But these are the arguments of selfishness and moral cowardice. Single men have saved nations before, and though my vanity does not make me even dream that so glorious a result is within my humble grasp, yet a good example is never valueless, and it can be set even by the most insignificant. Certain it is that without examples and self-sacrifices there can be no reform. The world, as I see it, imposes on me a duty, and I think the most powerful and the only permanent cause of happiness is the consciousness that I am trying to do that duty.

I wish it understood — in case what has preceded has not made this perfectly clear — that I have neither become a Materialist nor a Christian. I am an Aryan in religion as all else, follow the Ved, and believe it to be the parent of all religions among men. As Theosophy explains the secondary human religions, so does it make plain the meaning of the Ved. The teachings of the Rishis acquire a new splendour and majesty, and I revere them a hundred times more than ever before.

THE VEDANTASARA*

[From *The Theosophist*, September, 1883.]

THIS journal owes an apology to the publisher of the *Vedantasara* for not noticing the book earlier, although it has been lying on the office table for over four months. But a sufficient excuse will be found in the fact that as the work begins with an undue personal praise of the Founders of the Theosophical Society individually, and admittedly contains some ideas taken from the *Theosophist*, it was a puzzling question how to review this able and useful work in these columns, without being forthwith accused by our "well-wishers" of labouring in a "mutual admiration club." But that the silence of this magazine may not be mistaken for discourtesy, I now hasten to acknowledge receipt, by the Editor, of, and to thank sincerely Babu Heeralal Dhole for the copy he has kindly sent us.

---

*THE VEDANTASARA in Sanskrit with the commentary of Nrishingha Saraswatee, and with English, Hindi and Bengali Translations, Price Rs. 6-4 in India, and Rs. 7 in Foreign countries. THE PANCHADASI in English embodying the Vedanta and explaining the Aryan views of Cosmos, the Soul and the Parabrahma. In monthly parts. Annual subscription Rs. 6 in India; Rs. 7 in Ceylon, Straits Settlements, China, Japan and Australia; 14 Shillings in Africa, Europe, and U. S. America. *Cash to accompany orders invariably.* Drafts, hundis, and postal orders to credit of H. DHOLE, 127 Musjid Bari Street, Calcutta. Discounts of stamps must be remitted also.

The work is in three languages and bound together in one volume. Each might be made to form a separate work, and it is to be regretted that the idea should not have struck the able Authors or the Editor, to place it thus before the public. It seems unfair to charge people acquainted with only one tongue for the other two languages they neither know, nor perhaps care to know, anything about. Had our learned colleague, Babu Dhole, issued each part separately, charging for it Rupees two, or so, for a copy in each language, no ground for complaint and dissatisfaction would have arisen in any quarter, as it has now in more than one. The views,— at any rate in its first English part,— being avowedly those expressed in the columns of our magazine, very little has to be said of this portion, except that the author has made uncommon good use of it and elaborated very cleverly the whole. One point, however, may be noticed, as it is found to be constantly contradicted and picked holes into, by the theists as well as by all the supporters of independent creation — viz., the "definition of matter."

"Kapila defines matter to be eternal and co-existent with Spirit. It was never in a state of non-being, but always in a state of constant change, it is subtle and sentient," &c., &c., (p. 2.)

This is what the Editor of this Journal has all along maintained and can hardly repeat too often. The article: "What is Matter and what is Force?"* in the

---

*[See *The Complete Works of H. P. Blavatsky*, Vol. IV, pp. 82-95. See also *The Letters of H. P. Blavatsky to A. P. Sinnett*, p. 8, for authorship.   — EDS.]

Theosophist for September 1882, is sufficiently lucid in reference to this question. It is at the time pleasant to find that our learned friend and brother, Mr. T. Subba Row Garu, the great Adwaitee scholar, shares entirely with all of us these views, which every intuitional scholar, who comprehends the true spirit of the *Sankhya* philosophy, will ever maintain. This may be proved by the perusal of a recent work on *"Yoga Philosophy"* by the learned Sanskritist, Dr. Rajendra Lala Mittra, the *Introduction* to which has just appeared, showing clearly how every genuine scholar comprehends the *Sankhya* in the same spirit as we do.* The ONE LIFE of the Buddhists, or the Parabrahm of the

---

*In his *Introduction* to the above named work, the able Orientalist shows plainly the nearly perfect identity of Kapila's *Sankhya*, Patanjali's *Yoga,* Buddhism and, by indirect inference, of the Adwaitee or Upanishad philosophy. Moreover the author corroborates in it that which we have ever maintained, even against such a learned but rather too bigoted theist as the Pundit Dayanund — namely, that Kapila recognized no personal god, no more than did Patanjali. Says Dr. Rajendra Lala Mitra, L. L. D., C. I. E., . . . "Patanjali has contented himself by tacking a theistic appendage of no direct utility to a positively atheistic model (Kapila). . . . Hence it is that the Hindus call it *Sés'vara Sankhya* or *Sankhya cum deo* (with god), as opposed to the former which is *Nirisvara Sankhya,* or *Sankhya sine deo* (without god)" (p. xxii). "And we have enough in these facts to infer that the Yoga text-book is posterior to the Sankhya text-book, and that both the text-books are later than Buddha; but that the doctrines of both are very old, and now these (*Sankhya* and *Yoga* philosophies) are the immediate ancient Hindu archetypes of the nihilist theory of Buddha, and indirectly of the Pessimism of Schopenhauer and Hartmann." (p. xxiii. *Preface.*)

Vedantins, is omnipresent and eternal. Spirit and matter are but its manifestations. As the energising force —Purush of Kapila—it is Spirit—as undifferentiated cosmic matter, it is *Mulaprakriti*. As differentiated cosmic matter, the basis of phenomenal evolution, it is *Prakriti*. In its aspect of being the field of cosmic ideation, it is *Chidakasam;* as the germ of cosmic ideation it is *Chinmatra;* while in its characteristic of perception it is *Pragna*. Whoever presumes to deny these points denies the main basis of Hindu Philosophy and clings but to its exoteric, weather-beaten, fast fading out *shell*. The main point of the work under review seems to be to indicate how in this basic doctrine, upon which the whole structure of philosophy rests, both the Aryan and the Arhat tenets meet and are identical, in all, except in forms of expression, and how again Kapila's *Sankhya* supports it. The author has in this respect admirably succeeded in condensing the whole spirit of the philosophy in a few short pages. And a close study of the same is sufficient to bring the intelligent reader to the same sense of perception. For a superficial reader, Dr. N. Dhole, the English translator, seems to hold that Spirit is something quite apart and distinct from Matter, and quite a different substance or no-substance, if you please. But such readers can only be referred to the following extract:—

". . . . And since the recognition of this *First Principle,* call it *Prakriti, Purush, Parabrahma,* or Matter, Spirit, the Absolute, or the Unknowable, clashes not with the cherished ideas of the most inveterate Freethinker.". . .

The above passage clearly proves that like all true *Adwaitees*, the learned Doctor holds Spirit and Matter to be but different phases or aspects of the ONE LIFE which is every thing or NO *thing*, if you prefer. It would be a pertinent question to ask, how it is then that the author expresses himself a Dualist? The simple explanation will be found in the consideration that so far as the *phenomenal*, or the *manifested* world is concerned, the idea of duality is launched into the discussion to indicate the two aspects of THE ONE ETERNAL WHOLE, which together set the machinery of evolution into working order. But once turn from the manifested into the *noumenal*, the unmanifested LIFE and the erudite author will most probably cease to call himself a dualist, as is made very clear from the above quoted extract from his work. The article "What is Matter and what is Force?" already referred to above, will fit in here most appropriately. It is therefore inexplicable how a certain class of people presume to call the *Vedantasara* "a theistic book," when it is far more:— a philosophical treatise. Before, however, pronouncing a final judgment, the terms *theism, atheism, pantheism, materialism,* must be clearly defined, every person understanding them in his own way. Some call themselves believers in an Impersonal deity, which, no sooner are their views analyzed, seems to grow into a gigantic human being with every thing of good in him, and when still further dissected every thing bad in him. It would be interesting to know their doctrine concerning the origin of evil in a universe under the control of a perfect, conscious, omniscient, omni-

potent and omnipresent intelligent *Creator*. Whatever
is illogical or unmathematical will have to be entirely
rejected some day, since truth can never be opposed to
logic or to mathematics — the only two *exact* sciences.
The next question put in connection with the work
under notice by its theistic reviewers in *The Arya* is
as follows:—

"Nor do we see what analogy can there exist between Buddhism and Vedantism. We know that the
great Shankarya was an implacable enemy of Buddhistic; and he, being the great propounder of Vedantic
Advaitism, would not have supported the claims of
Buddhism."

A Daniel come to judgment! I challenge the ir-
responsible writer of the above lines to point out in
what respect the *esoteric doctrines* of Gautama Buddha
and Sankaracharya differ. It is hard to explain on any
other ground but theological unscrupulous cunning the
origin of the current false belief that Sankaracharya
was an enemy of Buddhism. This is a separate line of
study for one who devotes his special attention to the
historical development of occultism. This point, however, does in no way detract from the value and importance of the fact that Sankaracharya throughout his
works keeps wisely silent about the esoteric doctrine
taught by *Gautama* Buddha. He who studies *and reads
between the lines* the *Brahmasutra Bhashyam* of the
former, will practically find for himself that Vedantic
Adwaitism *is identical with esoteric Buddhistic Arhatism*. In my turn, I moreover ask the writer of the above

extract to show wherein lies the difference between Buddhism and Advaitism, and then it can be shown that this difference exists but in the imagination of a few wise-acres who do not care to study the subject thoroughly for themselves but depend upon the testimony of a few interested parties. Once that it is shown that there is no difference, the analogy is clearly established. The same writer promises us to prove further on that Adwaitism is the result of the *distorted interpretations of the sacred* VEDAS! As however the promised contribution has not yet appeared, I may just as well retort by reminding him of the fact that there are far wiser and abler persons who can prove that his interpretations will never stand the test of the "recognised Sciences of the day" as will what he calls the "distortions" of the *Adwaitees*. It must be remembered that these so called "distortions," antedating as they do by innumerable ages the discoveries of the "recognised Sciences of the day," cannot be said to have been copied from the latter to suit the times. We cannot however dismiss the writer without showing to our readers his ignorance of Adwaitism — a subject he so confidently presumes to criticize. Our (Adwaitees') fourth argument, he says, (naming the so called *Mahavakyams* in order) rests upon the authority of the sentence *Ekmevadvitiyam*. He seems to be ignorant of the *Atharvanaveda Mahavakya*. "Ayam Atma Brahma" is the Mahavakyam in question which the writer very prudently refrains from interpreting from his own *Dwaitee* standpoint. The translations of our texts given in the *Arya* are equally absurd and extravagant.

Pragnanam (प्रज्ञानम्) he interprets to mean "intellect"!
Our readers who have studied carefully the learned
articles on this subject by Mr. T. Subba Row, need no
telling how grossly misunderstood and misrepresented
are the *Adwaitee* tenets by this theistic self-called
"Aryan" reviewer of the *Vedanta-sara*. It was necessary to answer here that Review since on the whole
the philosophy of the work under notice, is in main
what we consider to be Vedantic Adwaitism, which
is precisely the same as Buddhistic Arhatism.

These somewhat lengthy remarks may be concluded
with a hope that Babu Heera Lal Dhole will act up to
the suggestion herein made to divide the work by issuing
each text in a separate volume, thus making it within
the easy means of all, as the present price is prohibi-
tive for many. At the same time it is to be regretted
that the learned author should have limited his re-
searches mainly to the *Theosophist.* Had he searched
more deeply into the lore of the ancient Aryan Literature, he would have increased immensely the value and
the influence of his book and made our own case
stronger too, since we could then have shown more for-
cibly that our doctrines are not the phantoms of our
imagination, but are directly drawn from, and supported by, the ancient writings, within the reach of him
who would search for them diligently and with necessary qualifications. It is needless to say again that
every student of Adwaitism ought to possess himself
of a copy of the work under review.

VEDANTISM AND BUDDHISM*

[From *The Theosophist*, August, 1884.]

IN the review of the *Vedantasara* on page 318 of Vol. IV of the *Theosophist*, I find the reviewer asserting that Sankaracharya's Adwaita teaching is identical with the Buddhistic exposition of Gautama Buddha, and that Sankaracharya "throughout his works keeps wisely silent about the esoteric doctrine taught by *Gautama* Buddha." He further challenges the *Arya* to disprove his statements. I now beg to draw the attention of the reviewer to page 76 of the *Arya* for this month, where a translation of Sankaracharya's remarks against Buddhism is given, and would like to know how he can reconcile this with his assertions.

9th June 1884.   AN ENQUIRER.

Note. — The translation in the *Arya* is of Sankaracharya's *Commentary* on the *Brahma Sutras of Vyasa*. The *Bouddhas*, therefore, referred to therein, could not have been the followers of *Gautama* Buddha who lived only about twenty-five hundred years ago, while *Vyasa*, who mentions the *Bouddhas* in his *Sutras* — against whom only does Sankaracharya argue — preceded him by several thousand years. Consequently the fact that Sankaracharya remains silent throughout his works about the esoteric doctrine taught by *Gautama* Buddha, remains perfectly sound and unassailed.

---

*[Comment by "An Enquirer" on "The Vedantasara" with Dâmodar's Note appended.   — EDS.]

Probably the so-called "Buddhist" religion in the time
of Vyasa, the writer of the *Brahma Sutras,* was degen-
erated as we find the Vedic Religion in our times.
Gautama was one of the reformers, and although his
followers may have been known by the same name, it
does not follow that the opposition to a religion called
Buddhistic necessarily means antagonism to the teachings of *Gautama.* If that were the case, Gautama
himself might be called an opponent of Buddhism, for
he went against its abuses, and thus against the de-
generated system known as Buddhism before his time.
We maintain that the Arhat Doctrine of which the
latest public expounder was Gautama Buddha, is
identical with the Adwaitee Philosophy, whose *latest*
public exponent was Sankaracharya. Hence the latter
Philosopher's silence about the former's teaching. The
objections urged by "An Enquirer" were already anticipated and answered by Mr. Subba Row in his article
on "Sankara's Date and Philosophy." (See Vol. IV,
Theosophist, page 306.)*   — D. K. M.

---

*[Republished in *Five Years of Theosophy,* pp. 278-308.
See also footnote (*infra*) p. 114.   — EDS.]

KAVYA DOSHA VIVECHANA*

[From *The Theosophist*, October, 1883.]

WE have to thank Mr. Simeon Benjamin, the author, for a copy of his *Kavya Dosha Vivechana*. This is an essay read by him before a meeting of the *Arya Samaj*, and subsequently republished by him at the request of its leaders. The work before us purports to point out the faults in Marathi poems taught in Government Vernacular and Anglo-Vernacular schools. The subject being of some importance, we shall, with the author's permission, examine minutely his analysis of the poems. His main contention is that some of these verses being unfit to be taught to children, should be eliminated from the Government school text-books. It is therefore necessary to examine carefully his reason in support of the contention. The first verse he takes objection to, is in the *Marathi* primer, which reads:—

मुके आंधळें पांगळ आणि थोंटे ॥

अशद्गुर्बळठांला करा साह्य मोठं ॥

जरीत्यांसहांसाल होतील तोटे ॥

तुम्हांलाचहोतां तसें जाल कोठं ॥

This he translates as meaning that if we were to

---

*An exposition of faults in the Marathi poems taught in Government Schools. By Simeon Benjamin. Price seven annas. Can be had from the Author; House No. 26, Payadhooni, Bombay.

laugh at the dumb, the blind and the cripple, we
would ourselves become like them, &c., &c. Thereupon he argues the falsity of this teaching and shows
how it frustrates the chief aim of bringing children
to a correct mode of action and thought. When the
children, he tells us, do actually laugh at such unfortunate creatures and find no such threatened retali-
ation, then they naturally lose all faith in, and regard for, such a teaching; and the principal object
of giving them sound instruction is foiled. There
would be a good deal of truth in this reasoning, were
the verses to really mean what the above translation
indicates. With every deference, however, to the profound learning and scholarship which the author
seems to possess, we submit that the verse yields
quite a different meaning, or, at least, another meaning might more appropriately be attached to the verse
than the one given by the erudite author. May we
not translate the poem in question to mean that we
should assist the invalids therein mentioned, not because such an act would recoil on us by making us
like them, but because we would in the end be the
sufferers: and for the second consideration that,
should such a misery befall us, we may find no sym-
pathisers. Or may it not also mean that in case we
should be the sufferers in that way, there would be
no one to look up to, we having estranged the sympathies of good people by laughing and scoffing at
the poor unfortunates when we were in good circumstances. This is not, of course, the literal translation:
but neither is that of Mr. Benjamin. In our humble

opinion, however, this interpretation is more warranted by the words of the poem than the other. Our first rendering would teach the doctrine of *Karma*, a scientific and axiomatic truth. The latter construction would be a check upon untrained minds from doing anything wrong. Where then lies the harm? The next verse to which objection is taken, is:—

विद्या नमें ज्या पुरुषास कांहीं ॥ विचार निती तिळठमात्र नाहीं ॥

अशा नरा काय अहो हिणाबें   ॥   पशूमध्यें सत्य तया गणावें ॥

This is interpreted in two different ways by the author. The first meaning, however, he sets aside. As to the second, he says, it is not fit to be taught to children, its meaning being:— "One who has no *Vidya* (knowledge) and is neither considerate nor moral (in the broadest sense of the term), should not be styled as *Aho* (you) but as *Aray* (thou) and reckoned among beasts." We think, however, that the word *Aho* is not correctly rendered. It does not refer to the man "without learning," &c., &c., since there is no such word as *Aray* (अरे) in the verse to point the distinction as shown by the translator, and that it rather refers to the reader, or the person to whom the lines are made to refer. What the poet says is:— "Oh! You (addressing his readers)! What shall we call a man without learning, morals and consideration! Surely he ought to be classed with the brutes." The exception taken by the critic thus falls to the ground, for there is no direct insult implied in the above application. The student is not advised to *insult* the man by calling him *"thou,"* but to avoid him rather, as one below the

rank of average humanity.   And we leave it to our
readers to decide whether the advice to avoid a man
without learning, *morals and consideration* (mark the
italicized portion) is justifiable or not.   The third
verse, found fault with, is from the third book:—

नाम रूप हें तूजला नसे ॥ त्य वंतुला मूर्खें वर्णवे कसें ॥

आदि अंत ना म्यही तुला ॥ तूंच दाविशी मार्ग आपुला ॥

In this poem, in talking of what is loosely termed
God, the poet says:— "Thou who hast no beginning,
no end, and no middle."   Our author is shocked at
such a conception.   The word *middle* has upset his
ideas! We would however humbly enquire if an infinite
something (and it *must be infinite* if it has no beginning
and no end), according to Geometry, is divisible?   If
it is *indivisible*, it can have *no* middle. We beg to
suggest to our learned author that if the Marathi poems
under review are not meant to be taught only in sectarian, and purely theistic schools but are used in colleges
where there may be as many Vedantins as Hindus of
other denominations, and the term being perfectly
applicable to Parabrahm, it has nothing either disrespectful or offensive in it; hence that it is quite fit to
be taught to children. We might go on in this wise,
and take exception to nearly every objection of the
critic of the pamphlet before us; but we regret having
neither the space nor time for it.   The instances,
however, here given are, we believe, sufficient to prove
to the impartial reader that the fault lies more with
the intolerance of the teacher, than the poems under
his review. Mr. Benjamin tells us that these difficulties

were not only experienced by himself, while a teacher in a Government School, but that they are complained of still, by many of his colleagues. If that be really the case, we are at one with him in advocating the elimination of all such verses from Government text-books, rather than see a false interpretation placed upon them. If no one can be found to enter into the true spirit of the poet's meaning and expound the real significance of his ethical stanzas for the instruction of the students, it is far better for all parties to be without them than to have erroneous ideas inculcated, and impressed upon young minds incapable of forming an independent judgment. The work before us has at the same time its objectionable feature in other poems left unmentioned by the critic. Some are positively indecent; such, for instance, as the description of Damayanti, a conversation between Rama and Sita when meeting alone in a forest, and going over their past days of bliss. Such descriptions of marital relations are not precisely the scenes to be impressed upon plastic and undeveloped minds. No language is too strong to condemn the disgraceful carelessness of the tutors who have permitted for years such reading to be left in the hands of their pupils without a protest. In this instance the *Marathi*-reading community is certainly under a grateful obligation to Mr. Benjamin for initiating this movement and laying a just complaint before the educational authorities. We also concur in his opinion that the poems relating to the struggle between Bheema and Duryodhana ought to be expunged from the school-texts, although my reasons are quite

different from those advanced by the critic. Taking
exception but to the dead-letter sense, he only depre-
cates an exhibition of cruel and brutal feelings between
two cousins. Unfortunately, however, our *Puranas*
are generally abused by "learned" critics without a
proper understanding of the *inner* sense and the morality to be conveyed. If our readers will turn to the back
pages of this Magazine, they will find the real meaning
of the allegory of the war between the *Pandavas and*
the *Kauravas*. If the former represent the higher (or
spiritual) part of man and the latter the earthly
(sensual), and if *Krishna* (the only manifested deity,
the *Logos* in each man's heart) is spoken of as being
the adviser of the former in conquering and killing the
latter, where then, we ask, is the "disgusting brutality"
fathered upon that most sublime of poems, the *Bhaga-
vat Gita?* We are not, however, at present concerned
with metaphysics or philosophy. And, as we are agreed
that the poems complained of should not be taught
to children promiscuously, since on the one hand the
teachers themselves are as yet unable to realize the
profound significance and the philosophical spirit of
some of them, and that, on the other, there are some
really indecent stanzas among them, we conclude our
somewhat lengthy review of Mr. Benjamin's criticism
with a hope that the proper authorities will lend an ear
to his just complaint. We beg at the same time our
learned author's pardon for dwelling at length upon the
points of disagreement between him and ourself, since
the necessities of the case demanded the present action.
On the whole, the book supplies a deficiency which was

long being felt; and every credit is due to Mr. Benjamin for interesting himself in the welfare of a people who are not of his race. We would recommend it to every person who has a real and earnest desire to improve the educational standard of Marathi children. As a Maratha we sincerely thank the erudite author for his advocacy in behalf of our children.

THE WORK OF THE BRANCHES

MEMORANDUM

[Supplement to *The Theosophist*, January, 1884.]

NOTWITHSTANDING the repeated protest of the Parent Theosophical Society, there does yet seem to linger in the minds of individual members and of some Branches, a tendency to look upon the whole movement as a school where *Yoga Vidya* and Occultism may be learnt in a much more expeditious and easy way than heretofore. This arises out of an ignorance of the laws of Occult Institutions and those governing psychological development. Since the commencement, the Theosophical Society has tried to impress the fact that the Laws of Nature are immutable; and no living being, however high and powerful, can ever alter them to suit the convenience of students. The attempt, therefore, which is now being made is not to carry on the vain and profitless task of finding a short cut to *Brahma Vidya*, since this is an impossibility, but to revive once more its knowledge, and thus to stimulate a true aspirant to adapt his life and thoughts to that standard which will better him and lead him gradually to such ways as run their courses to the Divine Wisdom. It will thus be seen that the Theosophical Society promises no Teachers, no Gurus, to take every member, upon joining, under their special charge. Mr. Sinnett was distinctly warned on this point when he asked for the assistance of some adept as the guiding genius of

the Simla Eclectic Theo. Socy., as will be seen on reference to his *Occult World*. No doubt there are individual
members who have been fortunate enough to be
accepted as *Chelas*, but their acceptance was due not
to the fact of their being Fellows, but because they had
been living the life and have voluntarily passed through
the training and tests, enjoined upon aspirants for
occult knowledge of every age and nationality.   In
their case the Theosophical Society was only the means
of giving them the conviction of their intuitive beliefs,
and thus urging them to follow the promptings of their
inner consciousness.   For the comparatively easy mode
they thus had of gaining the conviction, they have to
make up by helping the building up of the Theosophical
Society and putting it on a secure basis. This explanation ought to make it clear that what the Society
expects from all its Branches and individual members,
is co-operation and help in its grand task of uniting
the East and the West, the North and the South, in
a Scientific Brotherhood armed against dissension and
consequent failure by the principle of mutual Toler-
ation and mutual Intellectual Sympathy.   It is an
unthinkable proposition that any man with average
intelligence cannot contribute his quota towards the
realization of this noble scheme. If each man were
but to do his duty to search, to investigate, to study,
to digest, and join with his fellow-men, actuated by
the same noble aspirations, in giving to mankind the
benefits of their labour, the day would not be very
far off when the Masters of Occultism might find the
necessary conditions to enable them to once more

live in the world as openly and freely as did their predecessors of times long, long gone by, and give to such a prepared people the benefits of THEIR knowledge. Until that blessed day comes, a duty is before us: we have to hasten its approach. And this cannot be done by merely joining the Theosophical Society and without preparation, training or qualifications, expecting the Adepts to place within our reach tremendous weapons of Power, FOR KNOWLEDGE IS POWER, which in the hands of the ignorant and the wicked is fraught with dangers to their holders and to Humanity at large. Enough has already been given out to bring home to any one, endowed with ordinary intelligence, fairness, and desire for knowledge — conviction of the truth of this Science and the Powers it confers upon its devotees. When once all this is clearly understood, the only question for solution is how best to promote the Cause, and thus by an unselfish effort for the good of our fellow-men and their regeneration, to fit ourselves for the higher life of a true co-worker with those who have devoted themselves to the amelioration of the moral and spiritual condition of Humanity. There are various ways of accomplishing this result, but as one man's meat is another man's poison, the Parent Theosophical Society has always endeavoured to leave the practical working of its Branches to their members, who are, or should be, the best judges of the circumstances they have to work under, and the material that can be utilized. Psychology is a vast field wherein many workers may employ

themselves with advantage.   The tastes of individuals must differ, but surely there can be found two
or three in every Branch interested in the same subject.   If a Branch divides itself into various Committees for the investigation of various subjects of
Science, and communicates its results at general meetings, much good will ensue.   Various articles in the
Theosophist and other publications of the like nature
might be taken up by different members, and the
Society given the benefit of every individual exer-
tion.   Knotty questions arising out of such studies
might be referred to the Head-quarters in the form
of an article, or in any other shape which may be
found best under the circumstances.   Every legitimate demand for help and assistance has been, and
will always be, granted by the Founders to their co-
workers in this cause of Humanity.   Several other
matters of Reform might be undertaken by other
Committees, without, of course, infringing upon any
individual's or people's religious or social right.   For
those who are capable of an unselfish impulse to work
for the moral and spiritual regeneration of Humanity,
there is plenty to do.   And it is men of this stamp
that are the pillars of such a grand movement, which
must necessarily depend upon their co-operation and
zeal for its success.

These are the lines upon which Branches are expected to be organised and worked.

By order.   DAMODAR K. MAVALANKAR,
Joint Recording Secretary, Theosophical Society.
ADYAR (MADRAS), *15th December* 1883.

THE WORK OF THE BRANCHES

[Supplement to *The Theosophist*, March, 1884]

MY esteemed friend and brother, Pandit Parmeshri Dass, President of the Branch Theosophical Society at Bara-Banki, writes to say that he finds the memo. on the above subject in the last month's *Theosophist,* has been entirely misunderstood. The following passage therein has been the cause of misapprehension:—

Since the commencement, the Theosophical Society has tried to impress the fact that the Laws of Nature are immutable; and no living being, however high or powerful, can ever alter them to suit the convenience of students. . . . It will thus be seen that the Theosophical Society promises no Teachers, no Gurus, to take every member, upon joining, under their special charge. . . . No doubt there are individual members who have been fortunate enough to be accepted as Chelas, but their acceptance was due not to the fact of their being Fellows, but because they have been living the life and have voluntarily passed through the training and tests, enjoined upon aspirants for occult knowledge of every age and nationality.

Upon this it is argued:—

One's own *Karma* is the essence irrespectively of his connection or non-connection with the Theosophical Society — in other words, all depends upon one's living the life enjoined upon aspirants for occult knowledge. The act of joining the Society is immaterial inasmuch as *the life* being an essential thing, fellowship in the Society carries no weight with it. The Society thus confers no benefit as a prerequisite on its members, in addition to the result of their own *Karma.* This being so, a Theosophist and an outsider stand upon the same footing; hence no one should join the Society.

This strange logic passes my comprehension.

"All appears yellow to the jaundiced eye," says the poet. One blinded by selfishness cannot therefore pierce through the thick veil before his eyes, and all his conceptions must therefore be narrow. My friend's reply to the above superb reasoning is:—

It is true that living the life is essential — but the life lived by a Fellow of the Theosophical Society has an advantage over that lived by an outsider. A fellow, by the act of joining, places himself in a position wherein the essential qualification can immediately and directly attract the notice of the MAHATMAS. A Theosophist has to exert less in point of *attractive force* than an outsider, for the latter is not so near the MAHATMAS as the former. Both of them do not therefore stand upon the same footing. All that the passage in the Memo. on the *Work of the Branches* meant to convey was that the Theosophical Society was not an improved sort of Miracle Club or School of Magic wherein for ten rupees (or any sum whatever) a man could become a Mahatma between the morning bath and the evening meal; but that in addition to merely joining the Society, a man should live the requisite life and wait patiently for the results which will come in due time.

The Pandit's reply is correct so far as it goes, but it is incomplete. It does not give the reasons why a Theosophist is nearer to the MASTERS than an outsider. It also omits certain other important considerations. With a view to avoid any further misunderstanding, I shall go a little fuller into the subject, being at the same time as brief and concise as possible. If the critics had read carefully the whole of the memo. and digested it thoroughly, they would probably have not been led into such curious conclusions as they now put forth. It is admitted that the Theosophical Society has been engaged in doing good, with unparalleled success, to Humanity; that, had it not been for its exertions, people would have gone in their own ways as heretofore, would have paid no attention to the writings of the ancient sages and would have remained in entire ignorance of the glorious truths contained therein, not because they could not have been found if properly searched into, but because the earnest spirit of enquiry which has now been raised could never have asserted itself. It is therefore a duty we owe to the Theosophical Society to encourage and support it by all possible means, if we have the least sense of gratitude within us. Moreover, it is within almost every one's mouth that more and more important facts of the Esoteric Philosophy are being gradually given out through the instrumentality of the Theosophical Society. Have the critics reflected to what causes this fact is due? It is because the leaders and promoters of the Association find that their labour is not being thrown entirely upon barren ground, but that their work is being more and more appreciated, as is proved by important additions to its ranks; they thus feel encouraged to continue their arduous task more and more cheerfully. But let it be once proven that the work has created no interest, and that those for whom exertions are being made prefer to stubbornly remain blind to all higher considerations, and the theosophical leaders will be compelled to drop the work in spite of themselves. Is not the fact that the moral if not the active support given by people to the Society by joining it acts as a stimulant for

renewed work — is not this fact a sufficient induce-
ment for right thinking men not to keep aloof from
the movement? Again, the Theosophical Society being a Universal Brotherhood embraces all Humanity:
as such it may very well be recognized as one complete organism. All its doings are *its Karma*. And
just as the different organs derive nourishment from
the joint work of the whole body; so also each member of this huge organism has a part of its nourishment from the accumulated store of the *Karma* of
the Theosophical Society as a whole. And who will
dispute the fact that that Association has been acquiring an immense amount of good *Karma* by its bene-
ficent work of increasing human happiness by promoting knowledge and by uniting together different
people into one bond of an Intellectual Brotherhood?
Still further: it is a well-recognized principle that
Union is Strength; and therefore if any Association
could afford large opportunities for doing good, it
is the Theosophical Society. Selfishness having sealed
the eyes of the critics to the fact that they form but
a part of the INTEGRAL WHOLE, they fail to perceive
that the good of their Fellowmen is their own good.
The cloud of self-benefit darkens their mental horizon, through which their sight cannot pierce to have
a glance at the future results of their attitude. They
see no superior advantage within the narrow range
of their vision, and therefore they conclude no such
advantage exists. They cannot understand that of
all the Associations now existing in the world, the
Theosophical Society is the only one that can be em-

ployed to the best advantage for promoting human
happiness by bringing people to realize the common
foundation of all Religions. And that the *Illumi-
nated* have therefore adopted it as the channel of
communication between themselves and the outer
world. As such, it forms the centre of light, and he
who steps into its sphere from the outer darkness,
comes within the radius of vision of the BLESSED
ONES. To advance further depends upon his *active*
goodness and work. By joining he has got his reward of giving an expression to his sympathy and
thus affording moral support — and that reward is
that he puts himself in a prominent position whence
he can be more easily perceived than those who prefer to remain in the outer darkness.

DAMODAR K. MAVALANKAR,
Joint Recording Secretary, Theosophical Society.
ADYAR (MADRAS),
3rd February 1884.

OXFORD MISSION SHOTS AT OCCULTISM

[Supplement to *The Theosophist*, January, 1884.]

OUT of the clear sky of a correspondent's remarks on the comparative merits of Buddha and Christ, the thunderbolt has been hurled against Occultism by the Indra of the *Epiphany*. The startled Theosophist but meekly enquires how his humble self could be suspected of intrusion in such sublime regions as the arena of discussion of our contemporary's correspondent — "A. B. C." In the meantime, however, as Great Indra threatens to bring his *Meghástra* into play, it is necessary to avert the impending downpour by pointing out its unseasonableness. It is but proper that the mis-conceptions, so unmistakably glaring, should be, if possible, removed. The *Epiphany* thus begins what is meant to be a reply to its correspondent's remarks:—

" I never grumble when Theosophists tell me that in order to experience the power of the invisible worlds vouchsafed to them I must first practice *Yogi*.* It is quite clear to me that there is a power working in them, to be attained only by certain processes. The only questions with me are (1) is the power of a kind worth attaining? (2) what is the nature and source of the power? (3) what is the trustworthiness of its result? To these questions I answer something as follows. 1. The power of supreme wisdom or of working what

---

*The learned Editor of *the Epiphany* probably means *Yoga*. *Yogi* is the person who practises *Yoga*.

men call miracles is to my mind worthless compared
with the power of love. I must learn to love, to labour
for others, to desire their good more than my own,
before I can be fit to be trusted with occult powers,
which at present would only tempt ME to pride, and
be ill-used. . . ."

The erudite critic is manifestly unaware of the fact
that the true *Yogi* does not study Occultism for the
purpose of acquiring powers. In his onward spiritual
progress toward deliverance from the shackles of *Maya*,
the *Siddhis* come to him of themselves. There can be
no psychological perfection so long as the *Ego* is in the
least affected by the trammels of *Avidya*, and these
Siddhis, however high they may be, are yet within the
domain of illusion. Every student, even a tyro, of
occultism knows that the acquisition of *Brahma-Vidya*
is dependent entirely upon the development of a feeling
of universal love in the mind of the aspirant. For his
final goal, the attainment of *Mukti* is the very identification of the *Jivatma* with *Paramatma*, the Universal
Spirit, which manifests itself in ALL — which can never
be accomplished except by one's putting one's-self
en rapport with Nature through a cultivation of the
feeling of unselfish Philanthropy. It will thus become
apparent to a mind free from preconception that the
Yoga Siddhis are only the accessories of *Brahmavidya*,
i. e., Esoteric Theosophy, the acquisition of which is
guided only by unselfish philanthropy and universal
love. The misconception in the above extract is evidently due to the Reverend writer's confounding the
path, pursued by a *real Yogi*, with that of ordinary

jugglers and sorcerers. While the powers of the former
are psychological, those of the latter are physical, pure
and simple. If the writer had carefully studied the important articles in the *Theosophist* on this subject and
various other publications on Rosicrucianism and Esoteric Theosophy, before hastily penning his remarks,
the present controversy would have been saved. He
says that he must "labour for others and desire their
good" more than his own. The *true Yogi* replies:—
"We postulate that the good of others is our own, since
we are a part of the integral whole, and therefore it is
not logical or wise to think of mere relative good to
others." When the student has once realised this
important fact — and until he has, he is not a fit student
— where then is there room left for "pride" from
which the Reverend writer shrinks with such pious
horror? Self-conquest is the first step on the ladder
of *Brahmavidya* leading to *Nirvana* or *Mukti*. If it
is thoroughly comprehended that *Avidy*a in every
shape is to be got rid of, and if the way to achieve
that object is found to be as stated in the preceding
remarks, the basis on which the Reverend gentleman
has raised a structure of fears concerning *Yoga* is
necessarily removed, and the whole edifice thus must
tumble down. One or two more points may also be
noticed, with advantage. He says:—

"The trance consciousness in me may be the gateway to imperfect and distorted visions, the creations
of brain in an unnatural tension, and not free from its
own preconceptions."

Precisely so: this is just what the occultist guards

himself against by first passing through the process
of unlearning before beginning to learn. He rests
neither upon the deductive nor the inductive method
solely, but employs both before accepting any fact.
More than this: he practically and experimentally
demonstrates to himself the truth of the conclusion
he arrives at, before taking them as final. Human will
is merely the manifestation of the *Divine Will* or
rather *Paramatma*. But its action or expression depends upon its associations and the medium through
which it has to act. It is all these disturbances or
the veils of *Maya*, that the occultist guards himself
against in his studies, and it will be admitted that
this mode of procedure is a purer source of knowledge than any other where the counteracting influences are allowed their full sway. In conclusion, the
Reverend gentleman adds:—

". . . . His (Buddha's) noblest merit is that he
never claimed to be God. If Christ did so claim to
be without being so in reality, He must have been one
of the world's least souls, its most deluded Prophets.
Do you believe this?"

Before answering this query, it is essential to enquire
whether Christ's Divinity is to be assumed on blind
faith, or is the reason of the reader appealed to above?
In the former case, silence is gold, but in the latter,
the question becomes serious. In the first place, we
defy the Christians to point out to us one sentence,
one word, in the *Four Gospels* proving in plain and
unambiguous language that Christ ever claimed or
declared himself to be God. On the contrary — "Why

callest thou me good?   There is none good but *one,*
that is, God" (Matt. XIX 6) — is a rebuke showing
plainly that Christ, far from considering himself God,
looked upon any attempt to attribute Divinity to him
as blasphemy; no amount of ecclesiastical sophistry can successfully distort the meaning.   "I and my
Father are one," is entirely weakened by "I ascend to
my Father and your Father, to my God and your
God."   Moreover, the present writer very much doubts
whether Christ, even if he did claim to be God, could
ever have claimed divinity, *as generally understood,* if
he was, as he is represented.   What was there more,
indeed, in Christ, not possessed by Buddha?   Nay,
the *impartial* student, whether Occidental or Oriental,
must admit that in moral grandeur and unselfish
philanthropy, Buddha is unequalled, at all events not
inferior to Jesus.   The whole question of divinity
must, therefore, rest either upon their personal claims
and powers, or those of their later followers, namely
their respective clergy.   Pride is inconsistent with
genuine greatness, and humility is the essential qualification of a true philosopher.   In this respect too,
Buddha shows his superiority in not claiming divinity
which might more appropriately be attributed to him
by his unphilosophical followers than to the Galilean
Prophet by his.   As regards their respective powers,
or (so-called) "supernatural" gifts, the question can
very well be decided by those possessed by their
respective followers at the present day.   The readers
of *Esoteric Buddhism* and the *Occult World* need, of
course, no further dilation on this point.

Before concluding, an instance of the wonderful argumentative powers of the learned writer in the *Epiphany* may as well be noticed. While admitting the philosophical force of the defence of Vedic Pantheism and Idolatry by Babu Ishan Chandra Ghose, he remarks:—

"It may be very true that a mind capable of grasping only one million out of the thirty-three millions of idle personifications would have a very complex idea of God. But we would ask for an honest and candid answer as to whether the uneducated masses do not rather worship one or a few of these personifications. The Rishis made the analysis: what idol-worshipper, except an educated one like yourself, ever makes the corresponding synthesis?". . . .

The fallacy of this argument is self-evident and needs no comment. The Babu may well retort by asking in his turn how many Christians, even of education and culture, understand the teachings of their religion in that high sense, put upon them by the philosophical few? The perversions and misconceptions that a religion suffers at the hands of its ignorant followers are no argument against the religion itself. The vices and superstitions of the lower order of the Hindus do not injure their philosophical faith any more than the following incident degrades the high moral worth of the teachings of Christ. Only the other day the papers published the account of an English Christian husband having *sold his wife for a quart of beer*!! And the parties to the contract, witnesses and all, were so strong in a sense of their innocence, that each and every one acknowledged the fact freely in open court. The excellence of a religion depends upon its intrinsic philosophical value and its moral influence upon its followers. It is only Statistics and History that can show which Faith has acquitted itself most honorably of its task.

REJOINDER*

[Supplement to *The Theosophist*, March, 1884.]

I SHALL briefly reply to the remarks of the *Epiphany*. I am sorry I failed to gather from the words, "the power *of* Supreme wisdom or *of* working what men call miracles," even in the light of the parallel phrase "the power of the invisible worlds," that by "what men call miracles," was not meant "simply physical marvels, but marvels both physical and psychical," as, otherwise some waste of words would have been prevented.

We maintain that the highest ideal of love is to be found only in *Brahmavidya* or Esoteric Theosophy; our ideal of love being a perfect union with the ALL by an utter abnegation of the self and by ardent sleepless

---

*[Rejoinder to an Editorial in the *Epiphany* which discusses Dâmodar's "Oxford Mission Shots at Occultism." This Editorial was republished in the Supplement to *The Theosophist*, March, 1884, page 49, under the title "Theosophy and Love."
— EDS.]

endeavours for the good of all sentient beings — even the brute creation, whose sufferings, and wholesale slaughter, are made entirely subservient to the pleasure of Christians and Mahomedans. If the ideal of the Christians is different,— they are welcome to it; only let them not place it higher than ours, unless they are prepared to support their action by the force of arguments. I am glad to find an attempt has been made in this direction by my friendly critic, and proceed to examine it with the attention it deserves.

"It is in no spirit of pride" says the *Epiphany*, "that we state it as a part of our Creed that, however unloving nominal Christians may be, perfect love is only attainable by man through union with Christ, nay, the very gateway to love for the mass of men must be in Christ's love for us. Such a theory has nothing to do with any estimate of persons, but is a necessary corollary of our belief that God became incarnate for love of us. For, if that be a true doctrine, the recognition of the fact of such tremendous love must be the natural preliminary to being intoxicated and transformed by it, the first step in the true Yoga."

The great incentive to love among Christians is, we are told, the realisation of the fact that Christ, or, in other words, the perfect God, incarnated himself, moved by love, for the redemption of man. Without stopping to question the necessity of such a step in one who, if God, might have avoided it by suppressing the original act of injustice — namely, the "apple incident," — we may here say that there are other doctrines in the Christian faith, and regarded as equally true, which are calculated to weaken if not to completely neutralize the force of this argument. How can we say the Christian "God is love," when he delivers up helpless Humanity, brought into existence without its consent, to the mangling tooth of sin and suffering for a small transgression of its first parents? Even human justice does not hold a son liable for the debts of his father beyond the extent of that father's assets. And how is it that not even the blood of Jesus could restore man to the "blissful seat" from which he had fallen? It may here be urged that the all-Merciful Father has ordained evil but for the ultimate good of man. But the other side may with equal justice contend that an Omnipotent cruel Ahriman has created all apparent good for the ultimate destruction of his creatures, not unlike the Satan of the Middle Ages, granting a short festive season to his servants as a prelude to the eternal damnation of their souls. The real fact is, that our inner self perceives, although the perception in very many cases is clouded by preconceived notions, that love and charity are but the law of our being, and that the violation of the law is always attended with suffering. It is no argument against this proposition that the general mind is not conscious of such being the case, any more than it is necessary for the miser to be aware of the true worth of riches when counting his unsunned hoards with a greedy eye.

Our friendly critic then charges me with a *petitio principii*:—

If you then require "unselfish philanthropy" as a "guide to the acquisition of Brahmavidya," you are from the point of view of the positive experience of millions, indulging in a *petitio principii*.

Nothing of the kind. It is enough if I am supported
by the "positive experience" of one man — and such
a man is always to be found in the person of the
Great Beggar Prince of Kapilavastu. The only logical
misdemeanour committed in the present transaction is
that of hasty generalisation chargeable on the critic
himself, in deriving a general proposition from a particular one, however extensive that particular proposition may absolutely be.

The subordination of love to power, attributed to
Theosophy, is due to the learned critic's misconception
of what is said in *the Elixir of Life*,* which has never
been claimed as a complete exposition of the subject.
The objections now raised clearly show that the article
on "Morality and Pantheism" in the *Theosophist* for
November last,† has not been properly considered.
There it is distinctly said:—

Inactivity of the physical body (*Sthula sarira*) does not indicate a condition of inactivity either on the astral or physical
plane of action. The human spirit is in its highest state of
activity in *Samâdhi*, and not, as is generally supposed, in a dormant quiescent condition. And, moreover, it will be seen by
any one who examines the nature of Occult dynamics, that a
given amount of energy expended on the spiritual or astral plane
is productive of far greater results than the same amount expended on the physical objective plane of existence. When an

*[An article by G..... M..... F.T.S. (Godolphin Mitford),
in *The Theosophist*, March and April, 1882; republished in *Five
Years of Theosophy*, pp. 1-32. See also footnote (*infra*) p. 130.
—Eds.]

†[By Mohini M. Chatterji; republished in *Five Years of
Theosophy*, pp. 212-220.   — Eds.]

adept has placed himself *en rapport* with the Universal Mind, he becomes a real power in nature. Even on the objective plane of existence, the difference between brain and muscular energy, in their capacity of producing wide-spread and far reaching results, can be very easily perceived. The amount of physical energy expended by the discoverer of the steam engine might not have been more than that expended by a hard-working day-labourer. But the practical results of the cooly's work can never be compared with the results achieved by the discovery of the steam engine. Similarly, the ultimate effects of spiritual energy are infinitely greater than those of intellectual energy.

To pass to the concluding remarks of the *Epiphany*. My arguments with reference to Hindu idolatry have been misunderstood by the critic. What I mean is this:— That, as no idolatry is sanctioned by the Hindu Scriptures, it is quite unjust to condemn the symbols of Hindu Religion, which are not without a certain similarity in principles to the Christian Eucharist, simply on the ground that the ignorant masses cannot always perceive the underlying spiritual truth. It would be as reasonable to charge the grotesque eccentricities of the Salvation Army on the purity of the Christian faith.   — D. K. M.

WHITE AND BLACK MAGIC

[Supplement to *The Theosophist*, February, 1884.]

HAVING just had a little leisure I was going over Mirza Moorad Alee's* letter in the *Philosophic Inquirer* of the 6th Instant. Col. Olcott's reply covers the whole ground in essentials, and I would have remained contented with it, especially that I may not be the cause, directly or indirectly, of any more exciting the nervous system of one upon whom I once looked with great respect and affection for his intellectual powers and what seemed to be unflinching devotion to Truth — had it not been for the fact that I apprehend the readers of the *Philosophic Inquirer* will not form correct ideas concerning white and black magic, were not the subject entered into a little deeper than Col. Olcott had the leisure to do.

The first time that Mirza Moorad Alee came to the Headquarters of the Theosophical Society in Bombay to stop with us a few days, the very first thing he told me was:—"If you ever want to progress on the right path, beware of sensual appetites dragging you down, and above all take care of the *Brothers of the Shadow, the Sorcerer*s, with some of whom I have had personal dealings, to which fact I trace all my present suffering, struggle, and misery." These are not his exact words, but this is the idea he con-

---

*[See page 130. — Eds.]

veyed to me, and confirmed in all his subsequent conversations. I therefore stand aghast now at reading:— "The Theosophist leaders never 'discouraged' but rather encouraged me in such practices (of black magic)" —as Mirza Moorad Alee says in his letter under consideration. I cannot believe he is wilfully misrepresenting facts, but will fain attribute his present forgetfulness to mental aberration, caused by nervous exhaustion brought on by his futile struggle to get over the horrors of black magic and rise up to the spiritual glories of an Adept. When he joined us he had already opened the door and was gone too far to be able to shut it against the workings of the sorcerers with whom he had had "personal dealings." I only pity his fall and hope he will not have to share the fate of all black magicians. He is misrepresenting the meaning of *Nirvana* when he uses it as a synonym for *annihilation*. Yes: it *is* annihilation, not of the spiritual Ego, but of the lower principles in man, of the animal Soul, the personality which must perish. The powers of black magic are due to the will-power engendered by a concentrated form of selfishness. This is possible only when the *Manas* — the fifth principle of man, as the occultist calls it — resides very firmly in his lower principles. A careful study of the *Fragments of Occult Truth**

---

*[By "Lay Chela," a series published in *The Theosophist*, October 1881 to May 1883. Republished in *The Complete Works of H. P. Blavatsky*, Vol. III, pp. 98-142. Consult *Index* of *The Mahatma Letters to A. P. Sinnett* for references indicating the source of this material.   — Eds.]

and other literature on Esoteric Theosophy knows*
that these lower principles are destructible and must
therefore be annihilated. Of course, the greater the
powers of a black magician, the greater must be his
selfishness. The energy of cohesion being thus very
powerful, it must take a very long period before annihilation is complete. For aught we know, it (not
his physical body which cannot live so long) may
extend over thousands — nay a million — of years.
The tendency for evil is there; the desire for mischief
is strong: but there are no means for the gratification of sensual appetites: and the miserable being
suffers the throes of dissolution for a very, very long
period until he is totally annihilated. While, on the
other hand, the white magician, by his training as
described in the *Elixir of Life*, gradually kills his
lower principles, without any suffering, thus extend-
ing over a long period their dissolution; and his
Manas identifies itself with his higher — the sixth and
seventh — principles. Every tyro in Occultism knows
that the sixth principle being but the vehicle of the
seventh — which is all-pervading, eternal essence —
must be permanent. From the foregoing remarks it
is evident that it is the black magician whose lot is
annihilation; while the *adept*, the white magician, enjoys the blissful condition of absolute existence where
there is no pain or pleasure, no sorrow or joy, since
these are all relative terms, and the state is one of
supreme bliss; in short the latter enjoys an immor-

---

*[shows? — EDS.]

tality of life. It is therefore amusing to see how Mirza Moorad Alee Beg has endeavoured to represent black as white and *vice versa*. But his sophistry will be plain to every student of the Occult Philosophy.

CONTEMPLATION

[From *The Theosophist*, February, 1884.]

A GENERAL misunderstanding of this term seems to prevail. The popular idea appears to be to confine oneself for half an hour — or at the utmost two hours — in a private room, and passively gaze at one's nose, a spot on the wall, or, perhaps, a crystal. This is supposed to be the true form of contemplation enjoined by *Raj Yoga*. It fails to realize that true occultism requires "physical, mental, moral and spiritual" development to run on parallel lines. Were the narrow conception extended to all these lines, the necessity for the present article would not have been so urgently felt. This paper is specially meant for the benefit of those who seem to have failed to grasp the real meaning of Dhyan, and by their erroneous practices to have brought, and to be bringing, pain and misery upon themselves. A few instances may be mentioned here with advantage, as a warning to our too zealous students.

At Bareilly the writer met a certain Theosophist from Farrukhabad, who narrated his experiences and shed bitter tears of repentance for his past follies — as he termed them. It would appear from his account that the gentleman, having read *Bhagavat-Gita* about fifteen or twenty years ago and not comprehending the esoteric meaning of the contemplation therein enjoined, undertook nevertheless the practice and carried it on for several years. At first he experienced a sense of pleasure, but simultaneously he found he was gradually losing self-control; until after a few years he discovered, to his great bewilderment and sorrow, that *he was no longer his own master*. He felt his heart actually growing heavy, as though a load had been placed on it. He had no control over his sensations; in fact the communication between the brain and the heart had become as though interrupted. As matters grew worse, in disgust he discontinued his "contemplation." This happened as long as seven years ago; and, although since then he has not felt worse, yet he could never regain his original normal and healthy state of mind and body.

Another case came under the writer's observation at Jubbulpore. The gentleman concerned, after reading Patanjali and such other works, began to sit for "contemplation." After a short time he commenced seeing abnormal sights and hearing musical bells, but neither over these phenomena nor over his own sensations could he exercise any control. He could not produce these results at will, nor could he stop them when they were occurring. Numerous such examples may be multiplied. While penning these lines, the writer has on his table two letters upon this subject, one from Moradabad and the other from Trichinopoly. In short, all this mischief is due to a misunderstanding of the significance of contemplation as enjoined upon students by all the schools of Occult Philosophy. With a view to afford a glimpse of the Reality through the dense veil that enshrouds the mysteries of this Science of Sciences, an article, the "Elixir of Life," was written. Unfortunately, in too many instances, the seed seems to have fallen upon barren ground. Some of its readers only catch hold of the following clause in the said paper:—

Reasoning from the known to the unknown meditation must be practised and encouraged.

But, alas! their preconceptions have prevented them from comprehending what is meant by meditation. They forget that it "is the inexpressible yearning of the inner Man to 'go out towards the infinite,' which in the olden time was the real meaning of adoration" — as the next sentence shows. A good deal of light will be thrown upon this subject if the reader were to turn to the preceding portion of the same paper, and peruse attentively the following paras. on page 141 of the *Theosophist* for March, 1882 (Vol. III, No. 6):—

So, then, we have arrived at the point where we have determined,— literally, *not* metaphorically — to crack the outer shell known as the mortal coil, or body, and hatch out of it, clothed in our next. This 'next' is not a spiritual, but only a more ethereal form. Having by a long training and preparation adapted it for a life in this atmosphere, during which time we have gradually made the outward shell to die off through a certain process . . . we have to prepare for this physiological transformation.

How are we to do it? In the first place we have the actual, visible, material body — man, so called, though, in fact, but his outer shell —to deal with. Let us bear in mind that science teaches us that in about every seven years we *change skin* as effectually as any serpent; and this so gradually and imperceptibly that, had not science after years of unremitting study and observation assured us of it, no one would have had the slightest suspicion of the fact. . . . Hence, if a man partially flayed alive, may sometimes survive and be covered with a new skin,— so our astral, vital body . . . may be made to harden its particles to the atmospheric changes. The whole secret is to succeed in evolving it out, and separating it from the visible; and while its generally invisible atoms proceed to concrete themselves into a compact mass, to gradually get rid of the old particles of our visible frame so as to make them die and disappear before the new set has had time to evolve and replace them. . . . We can say no more.

A correct comprehension of the above scientific process will give a clue to the esoteric meaning of meditation or contemplation. Science teaches us that man changes his physical body continually, and this change is so gradual that it is almost imperceptible. Why then should the case be otherwise with the *inner man?* The latter too is constantly developing and changing atoms at every moment. And the attraction of these new sets of atoms depends upon the Law of Affinity — the desires of the man drawing to their bodily tenement only such particles as are *en rapport* with them or rather giving them their own tendency and colouring.

For science shows that thought is dynamic, and the thought-force evolved by nervous action expanding itself outwardly, must affect the molecular relations of the physical man. The *inner men*, however sublimated their organism may be, are still composed of actual, *not hypothetical*, particles, and are still subject to the law that an 'action' has a tendency to repeat itself; a tendency to set up analogous action in the grosser 'shell' they are in contact with and concealed within. (*The Elixir of Life.*)

What is it the aspirant of *Yog Vidya* strives after if not to gain *Mukti* by transferring himself gradually from the grosser to the next more ethereal body, until all the veils of *Maya* being successively removed his *Atma* becomes one with *Paramatma?* Does he suppose that this grand result can be achieved by a two or four hours' contemplation? For the remaining twenty or twenty-two hours that the devotee does not shut himself up in his room for meditation — is the process of the emission of atoms and their replacement by others stopped? If not, then how does he mean to attract all this time,— only those suited to his end? From the above remarks it is evident that just as the physical body requires incessant attention to prevent the entrance of a disease, so also the *inner man* requires an unremitting watch, so that no conscious or unconscious thought may attract atoms unsuited to its progress. This is the real meaning of contemplation. The prime factor in the guidance of the thought is WILL.

Without that, all else is useless. And, to be efficient for the purpose, it must be, not only a passing resolution of the moment, a single fierce desire of short duration, but *a settled and continued strain, as nearly as can be continued and concentrated without one single moment's remission.*

The student would do well to take note of the italicized clause in the above quotation. He should also have it indelibly impressed upon his mind that

It is no use to fast *as long as one requires* food. . . . To get rid of the inward desire is the essential thing, and to mimic the real thing without it is barefaced hypocrisy and useless slavery.

Without realizing the significance of this most im-

portant fact, any one who for a moment finds cause
of disagreement with any one of his family, or has
his vanity wounded, or for a sentimental flash of the
moment, or for a selfish desire to utilize the divine
power for gross purposes — at once rushes in for contemplation and dashes himself to pieces on the rock
dividing the known from the unknown. Wallowing
in the mire of exotericism, he knows not what it is
to live in the world and yet be not of the world; in
other words to guard *self* against *self* is an incompre-
hensible axiom for nearly every profane. The Hindu
ought at least to realize it by remembering the life
of Janaka, who, although a reigning monarch, was
yet styled *Rajarshi* and is said to have attained *Nirvana*. Hearing of his widespread fame, a few sectarian bigots went to his Court to test his *Yoga*-power.
As soon as they entered the court-room, the king
having read their thought — a power which every
chela attains at a certain stage — gave secret instructions to his officials to have a particular street in the
city lined on both sides by dancing girls who were
ordered to sing the most voluptuous songs. He then
had some *gharas* (pots) filled with water up to the
brim so that the least shake would be likely to spill
their contents. The wiseacres, each with a full *ghara*
(pot) on his head, were ordered to pass along the
street, surrounded by soldiers with drawn swords to
be used against them if even so much as a drop of
water were allowed to run over. The poor fellows
having returned to the palace after successfully passing the test, were asked by the King-Adept what they

had met with in the street they were made to go through. With great indignation they replied that the threat of being cut to pieces had so much worked upon their minds that they thought of nothing but the water on their heads, and the intensity of their attention did not permit them to take cognizance of what was going on around them. Then Janaka told them that on the same principle they could easily understand that, although being outwardly engaged in managing the affairs of his state, he could at the same time be an Occultist. He too, while *in* the world, was not *of* the world. In other words, his inward aspirations had been leading him on continually to the goal in which his whole inner self was concentrated.

Raj Yoga encourages no sham, requires no physical postures. It has to deal with the inner man whose sphere lies in the world of thought. To have the highest ideal placed before oneself and strive incessantly to rise up to it, is the only true concentration recognized by Esoteric Philosophy which deals with the inner world of *noumena*, not the outer shell of *phenomena*.

The first requisite for it is thorough purity of heart. Well might the student of Occultism say, with Zoroaster, that purity of thought, purity of word, and purity of deed, — these are the essentials of one who would rise above the ordinary level and join the "gods." A cultivation of the feeling of unselfish philanthropy is the path which has to be traversed for that purpose. For it is that alone which will lead to

Universal Love, the realization of which constitutes the progress towards deliverance from the chains forged by Maya around the Ego. No student will attain this at once, but as our VENERATED MAHATMA says in the *Occult World*:—

> The greater the progress towards deliverance, the less this will be the case, until, to crown all, human and purely individual personal feelings, blood-ties and friendship, patriotism and race predilection, will all give way to become blended into one universal feeling, the only true and holy, the only unselfish and eternal one, Love, an Immense Love for Humanity as a whole.

In short, the individual is blended with the ALL.

Of course, contemplation, as usually understood, is not without its minor advantages. It developes one set of physical faculties as gymnastics does the muscles. For the purposes of physical mesmerism, it is good enough; but it can in no way help the development of the psychological faculties as the thoughtful reader will perceive. At the same time, even for ordinary purposes, the practice can never be too well guarded. If, as some suppose, they have to be entirely passive and lose themselves in the object before them, they should remember that by thus encouraging passivity, they, in fact, allow the development of mediumistic faculties in themselves. As was repeatedly stated — the Adept and the Medium are the two Poles: while the former is intensely active and thus able to control the elemental forces, the latter is intensely passive, and thus incurs the risk of falling a prey to the caprice and malice of mischievous embryos of human beings, and — the Elementaries.

CONTEMPLATION*

[From *The Theosophist*, April, 1884.]

IN the article on the above subject in the February *Theosophist* occurs the following:—

1. Without realizing the significance of this most important fact, any one who for a moment finds cause of disagreement with any one of his family, or has his vanity wounded, or for a sentimental flash of the moment, or for a selfish desire to utilize the divine power for gross purposes — at once rushes in for contemplation and dashes himself to pieces on the rock dividing the known from the unknown.

I cannot understand how an ordinary man, who has, on one hand, the above-mentioned defects in his nature, (which he generally tries to control, though sometimes with questionable success); and who, on the other hand, tries also to practise contemplation as explained in the article, runs the danger of being ruined. What are the dangers? Can they be named, and the particular causes which give rise to them?

2. To have the highest ideal placed before oneself and strive incessantly to rise up to it, is the only true concentration recognized by Esoteric Philosophy.

This passage is too learned for an ordinary man. Can an example of "the highest ideal" be given? How is the ordinary man of the world to strive after it? Suppose an ordinary man of the world rises in the calm hours of the morning after a moderate rest, what is he to do? What kind of ideas should he fill

---

*[Comment by "F. T. S." with Dâmodar's Note appended herewith. —Eds.]

his mind with? How is he to sit? How is he to carry on the contemplation so as to steer clear of all shoals and rocks in the sea of occultism? The greatest aim of the man in question is to spiritualize himself as much as could be done *safely*, so that if he cannot eventually be accepted as a chela, in this life — he may at least have the *assurance* to lead the life of an ascetic in the next birth.

An F. T. S.

———

Note. — I regret the whole article is totally misunderstood. All I meant to say was that temporary estrangement, from family or friends, does not constitute an essential qualification for advancement in occultism. This ought to be plain to one who weighs carefully my illustration of Janaka. Although *in* the world, to be not *of* it. Failing to realise the meaning of this important teaching, many a people rush in from a sentimental disgust of worldliness, arising probably out of some worldly disappointment — and begin practising what they consider to be a true form of *contemplation.* The very fact that the *motive* which leads them to go in for this practice, is as is described in the quotation given by my correspondent — this fact itself is a sufficient indication that the candidate does not know the "contemplation" of a *Raja Yogi.* It is thus impossible in the nature of things that he can follow the right method; and the physical practice, which he necessarily undertakes, leads him to the disastrous results adverted to in the article.

Any reader, who has intuition enough to be a practical student of occultism, will at once see that to work up to perfection is the highest ideal that a man can have before him. That is not the work of a day nor of a few years. "The Adept *becomes;* he is NOT MADE" — is a teaching which the student must first realise. The aspirant works up to his goal through a series of lives. Col. Olcott says in his *Buddhist Catechism:* —

". . . Countless generations are required to develope man into a Buddha, and *the iron will to become one runs throughout all the successive births.*"

That *"iron will"* to become *perfect* must be *incessantly* operating, without a single moment's relaxation, as will be apparent to one who reads *carefully the article as a whole.* When it is distinctly said that during the time that this contemplation is not practised, *i.e.,* the iron will is not exerting, the process of the emission and attraction of atoms is not stopped, and that the desires, instinctive or otherwise, must be so regulated as to attract only such atoms as may be suited to his progress — I cannot understand my correspondent when he asks me what he should do at a particular hour in the morning. He should cultivate only such thoughts as would not be incompatible with the highest ideal he has to work up to. By perfection, which should be his highest ideal, (I must add) I mean that *divine* manhood which the Occult Philosophy contemplates the seventh race of the seventh Round will attain to. This, as every tyro knows, depends largely upon a cultivation of the feeling of

Universal Love, and hence an earnest desire to do some practical philanthropic work is the first requisite. Even this state, I admit, is not *absolute perfection:* but that maximum limit of ultimate Spiritual perfection is beyond our comprehension at present. That condition can only be intellectually realized as a practical ideal by those *divine men* — Dhyan-Chohans. To be identified with THE ALL, we must live in and feel through it. How can this be done without the realisation of the feeling of Universal Love? Of course Adeptship is not within the easy reach of all. On the other hand, occultism does not fix any unpleasant place or locality for those who do not accept its dogmas. It only recognises higher and higher evolution according to the chain of causation working under the impulse of Nature's immutable law. The article on "Occult Study"* in the last number gives the necessary explanation on this point.

It is painful for me to find that the very thing I attempted to point out in that article to be mischievous in its results, is again put forward as a desirable attribute or adjunct of true contemplation. I would ask my correspondent to read again the same article, with these additional remarks, before thinking of the necessity of any peculiar or particular posture for the purpose of *contemplation.* I, at any rate, am unable to prescribe any specific posture for the kind of *incessant cotemplation* that I recommend.

— D. K. M.

*[Republished in *Five Years of Theosophy*, pp. 221-9. — Eds.]

CONTEMPLATION — II

[From *The Theosophist*, August, 1884.]

NOTWITHSTANDING the article on the above subject in the February *Theosophist*, many of its readers still seem to imagine that "contemplation" is a particular form of gazing or staring at something, which process, when undergone a set number of hours every day, will give psychological powers. This misunderstanding is apparently due to the fact that the main point discussed has been lost sight of. Instead of realising that there is but one chief idea meant to be conveyed by that article by arguing it through many of its phases, it seems to be imagined that almost every sentence expresses quite a distinct idea. It may not therefore be uninteresting or unprofitable to revert to the subject and put forward the same idea from another stand-point and, if possible, in a clearer light. It must first be borne in mind that the writer of the article did not at all mean to imply the act of gazing by the word "contemplation." The former word would have been made use of, were that the idea. "The Imperial Dictionary of the English Language," (1883) — defines the word contemplation thus:—

(1) The act of the mind in considering with attention; meditation; study; continued attention of the mind to a particular subject. Specifically — (2) Holy meditation; attention to sacred things.

Webster's Dictionary thoroughly revised — also gives the same meaning.

Thus we find that contemplation is the "con-

tinued attention of the mind to a particular subject," and, religiously, it is the "attention to sacred
things." It is therefore difficult to imagine how the
idea of gazing or staring came to be associated with
the word contemplation, unless it be due to the fact
that generally it so happens that when any one is
deeply absorbed in thought, he apparently seems to
be gazing or staring at something in blank space. But
this gazing is the effect of the act of contemplation. And, as usually happens, here too the effect
seems to be confounded with the cause. Because the
gazing attitude follows the act of contemplation, it
is at once assumed that gazing is the cause which
produces contemplation! Bearing this well in mind,
let us now see what kind of contemplation (or meditation) the *Elixir of Life* recommends for the aspirants
after occult knowledge. It says:—

> Reasoning from the known to the unknown meditation must
> be practised and encouraged.

That is to say, a *chela's* meditation should constitute the "reasoning from the known to the unknown."
The "known" is the phenomenal world, cognisable by
our five senses. And all that we see in this manifested
world are the effects, the causes of which are to be
sought after in the noumenal, the unmanifested, the
"unknown world": this is to be accomplished by meditation, *i.e.*, continued attention to the subject. Occultism does not depend upon one method, but employs
both the deductive and the inductive. The student
must first learn the general axioms. For the time
being, he will of course have to take them as assump-

tions, if he prefers to call them so. Or as the *Elixir of Life* puts it:—

All we have to say is that if you are anxious to drink of the *Elixir of Life* and live a thousand years or so, you must take our word for the matter, at present, and proceed on the assumption. For esoteric science does not give the faintest possible hope that the desired end will ever be attained by any other way; while modern, or the so-called exact science laughs at it.

These axioms have sufficiently been laid out in the articles on the *Elixir of Life* and various others treating on occultism, in the different numbers of the *Theosophist*. What the student has first to do is to *comprehend* these axioms and, by employing the deductive method, to proceed from universals to particulars. He has then to reason from the "known to the unknown," and see if the inductive method of proceeding from particulars to universals supports those axioms. This process forms the primary stage of true contemplation. The student must first grasp the subject intellectually before he can hope to realise his aspirations. When this is accomplished, then comes the next stage of meditation which is "the inexpressible yearning of the inner man to 'go out towards the infinite.' " Before any such yearning can be properly directed, the goal, to which it is to be its aim to run, must be determined by the preliminary stages. The higher stage, in fact, consists in realising practically what the first steps have placed within one's comprehension. In short, contemplation, in its true sense, is to recognise the truth of Eliphas Levi's saying:—

To believe without knowing is weakness; to believe, because one knows, is power.

Or, in other words, to see that "KNOWLEDGE IS POWER." The *Elixir of Life* not only gives the preliminary steps in the ladder of *contemplation* but also tells the reader how to *realise* the higher conceptions. It traces, by the process of contemplation as it were, the relation of man, "the known," the manifested, the phenomenon, to "the unknown," the unmanifested, the noumenon. It shows to the student what ideal he should contemplate and how to rise up to it. It places before him the nature of the inner capacities of man and how to develope them. To a superficial reader, this may, perhaps, appear as the acme of selfishness. Reflection or contemplation will, however, show the contrary to be the case. For it teaches the student that to comprehend the noumenal, he must identify himself with Nature. Instead of looking upon himself as an isolated being, he must learn to look upon himself as a part of the INTEGRAL WHOLE. For, in the unmanifested world, it can be clearly perceived that all is controlled by the "Law of Affinity," the attraction of one to the other. There, all is Infinite Love, understood in its true sense.

It may now be not out of place to recapitulate what has already been said. The first thing to be done is to study the axioms of Occultism and work upon them by the deductive and inductive methods, which is real contemplation. To turn this to a useful purpose, what is theoretically comprehended must be practically realised. It is to be hoped that this explanation may make the meaning of the former article on this subject clearer.

THE PHILOSOPHY AND SCIENCE OF
VEDANTIC RAJA YOGA*

[From *The Theosophist*, March, 1884.]

I FEEL really obliged to my friend and brother, Babu Siris Chandra Vasu, B. A., for the presentation of a copy of a Treatise on "The Philosophy and Science of Vedantic Raja Yoga," edited by him. It is the reprint of a book which was first published about four years ago, and a notice of which will be found on page 147 of Vol. 1 of the *Theosophist*. At the time the curious autobiography of the author was published in these columns, his book was passing through the press; and although the account of the Swami's (the author's) life looked rather odd, and a trifle too fantastic, the Editor of the *Theosophist* naturally enough abstained from hazarding an opinion upon the merits of a work as yet unpublished. The neutral attitude has since been unfortunately mis-understood, one way or another; therefore, a few re-marks on the book in its present form will not be uncalled for.

A careful and attentive perusal of the Treatise forces the earnest student of Philosophy to the con-clusion that a large portion of it is either allegorical or that it is a mystification. But the latter is an un-tenable supposition. Would, it is asked, the highly

---

*Edited by Babu Siris Chandra Vasu, B. A., F. T. S.

educated Editor have undertaken the publication of a work, apparently so full of impossibilities — nay absurdities, had it no hidden merits? The alternative, therefore, to which one is reduced is, that the work is a parable, that it is purposely veiled, like so many other treatises on Occultism — in short an allegory. It is needless here to repeat the impracticability of certain occurrences given out by the author as his personal experiences; and it must be said that the Editor has, to some extent, in a special foot-note hastened to extricate his hero and himself out of a really perilous situation. Turning, however, to the philosophical portion of the work, two or three important points must not be omitted to be noticed. The author begins by taking Paramatma as the Guru, and Jivatma the disciple. The latter at the same time is defined to be "the reflected light or ray" of the former, *i. e.*, the *Jivatma* referred to in the work under notice is identical with the seventh principle of the Occultist. And yet a passage on page 2, reads:—

The *Jivatma* having reached the sublimest height of knowledge, both theoretical and practical, by perfectly understanding all the principles of righteousness and virtue in all the religions of this as well as of the world above, and having enjoyed all the worldly pleasures with great avidity, the pleasures of a kingly life for a short space of time in a corner of this vast universe of the Almighty, at whose call the royal heads even lie prostrate, the pleasures resulting from the voluptuous beauty of the fair sex and all other sensual pleasures, and strived hard for the accumulation of wealth, and giving himself to all kinds of whims and caprices of his unsteady and changeful mind, in short, after enjoying all the pleasures, both intellectual and sensual, of this

world, and finding them worthless and vain, comes to the conclusion that no worldly pleasure is lasting and eternal. Being
thus disgusted with all worldly enjoyments, the Jivatma feels
deep remorse and begins to repent sincerely.

An occultist who will have the patience to master
this interminable sentence, need not be long in finding
out that the author has used the word *Jivatma* in
three different senses, namely, the animal soul, the
human soul and the spiritual soul, or, the fourth, the
fifth and the sixth (which is the vehicle of the seventh)
principle. Atma — the seventh principle — is *alipta*,
and can neither enjoy nor suffer. It is the fourth
principle which generates the desire for material enjoyment and the human soul which takes delight in
sensual pleasures, but at the same time its upper
strata, in which is reflected the light of the sixth, try
through its own inherent powers to bring the lower
principles under subjection. Otherwise, it is incon-
ceivable how a principle, or substance, which has been
immersed in one sort of enjoyment or suffering, can of
itself turn its course into another channel. It may
be argued that, after all, these principles are but different manifestations of the same *Paramatma*, and hence
might be all included under the heading of *Jivatma*.
A little reflection will, however, show that position to
be indefensible. For the variety in the manifestation
of the same essence must be due to the difference in
the vehicles of manifestation. If these *vehicles* be
different, how can they be called by one common
name? Nor does it require a very deep thinking to
find out that it is the *vehicles* of manifestation that

are named, for *the manifested* being one, is absolute existence and shows no different attributes. It is therefore a matter of great regret that all throughout the book the word *Jivatma* is used to denote so many different principles, and thus is sure to mislead the unwary reader. The second important point to be noticed is the fact that *Asans,** &c., are enjoined for the practice of *Vedantic Raj Yoga.* To an occultist it is of course evident that the author has adopted the technical terms of *Hatha Yoga,* which will disclose the real *Raj Yoga* system, only when esoterically interpreted. In one place a process is described for subjugating the twelve kingdoms, beginning with the lowest one, which is situate in the *Kundalee.* A student of psychology knows that the method refers to the imperfections of the flesh which are to be conquered one by one, beginning with the grossest. It is a matter, however, of great concern as to how many of the readers will feel disposed to give that attention to the work, which alone may, under favourable circumstances, lead them to a correct understanding of the underlying esoteric meaning — (I still persist in giving the author the benefit of the doubt, and feel ready to admit such a meaning in his work). Thirdly, the language put into the mouth of the Guroo is such as to confuse the reader greatly before he can find out whether by "preceptor" the Paramatma is meant, or — the author himself. These are among the chief peculiarities that permeate almost

---

*[Bodily postures adopted in Hatha-Yoga. — Eds.]

the whole of the Treatise; and hence it is very doubtful whether its perusal will do any good to the general public. For only those can understand it who have studied esoteric philosophy up to a certain point; and for them the work contains very little they do not know: while the ordinary reader will be misled by the exoteric phraseology adopted, and consequently find the Treatise positively misleading and harmful. However, the motives of the author and the editor being no doubt perfectly benevolent, it is hoped that these remarks may help to remove all grounds of apprehension in the future. The editorial notes and appendices added to the second edition are of a certain importance, and if properly understood, are calculated to throw light upon some of the most obscure passages in the text. They also help to a clearer understanding of the Adwaita Doctrine as propounded by Srimat Sankaracharya, which, unfortunately, the author puts in a very misleading form. The Editor is deserving of all praise and thanks for having, by his notes, attempted to rescue his reader, who, otherwise, would have been left hopelessly floundering in a sea of misconceptions. We would recommend the little Treatise to our students on account of its Appendix. We hope that they will carefully peruse it, for it does an infinite credit to the Editor.

Since the above Review was in type, Mr. R. C. Bary, the publisher of the Treatise, has kindly sent a copy of the same to the *Theosophist* office. In the absence of the Editors from Madras, I beg to thank Mr. Bary on their behalf, for the pamphlet.

SELF-MESMERISATION

[Supplement to *The Theosophist*, April, 1884.]

A BROTHER Theosophist, writing from Midnapore, mentions wonderful cures by the process of self-mesmerisation. During an attack of choleric diarrhoea he perceived a nerve current rising up to the stomach in front and then descending along the spinal chord. By concentrating his attention on the current, he tried to change its direction. In an hour he was much relieved and fell asleep. After getting up, however, he found he had another attack. He took a dose of an opiate and then meditated as he did before. Although he did not go to sleep in the latter case, he got perfectly cured. He feels, he says, quite sure that a single dose of three grains of opium could never have cured a disease which the doctors had pronounced to be of a serious nature. On another occasion he had an attack of lumbago. The pain was so intense that he could not walk erect. He concentrated his attention on the part affected and imagined that the affected portion of the spinal chord had become curved, although in reality there was no such curvature. He then concluded that there must be some displacement of the spinal chord of the *Pranamaya* body. Efforts were made to restore that particular portion of the *Pran*. The effect of the imagination was to produce "a state of strain" on the affected part. This was done for some length of time before sleeping. The next morning the patient was all right. Our brother thinks these two instances of self-cure may prove interesting and instructive to his Fellow-Theosophsts who can employ with advantage the same process, should they suffer from the same or similar complaints.

[The "Brother-Theosophist" may *possibly* have received enough training from some hatha-yogin to preserve himself from the dangerous reactions arising from interference with the delicate balance of the prânic currents in the body, but it is more likely that he was acting like a blind man walking on the edge of a precipice, unknowing of his peril. Being well aware of what mental and physical dangers *prânâyâma* attempts lead to, Theosophy strongly discountenances it and it is practically certain that H. P. Blavatsky would not have allowed this article to appear, but she was traveling in Europe at this time with Col. Olcott. Its publication seems to be one of the errors of judgment into which Dâmodar occasionally fell and for which he had to suffer, as explained elsewhere. — EDS.]

THE METAPHYSICAL BASIS OF "ESOTERIC BUDDHISM"

[From *The Theosophist*, May, 1884.]

THE pamphlet of Mr. C. C. Massey, an F. T. S., of the London Lodge of the Theosophical Society, is a valuable contribution to the discussion now being raised by the publication of Mr. Sinnett's *Esoteric Buddhism*. It is a trite axiom that truth exists independent of human error, and he who would know the truth, must rise up to its level and not try the ridiculous task of dragging it down to his own standard. Every metaphysician knows that Absolute Truth is the eternal Reality which survives all the transient phenomena. The preface to the *Isis Unveiled* expresses the idea very clearly when it says:— "Men and parties, sects and creeds, are the mere ephemera of the world's day, while Truth, high seated on its rock of Adamant, is alone eternal and supreme." Language belongs to the world of relativity, while Truth is the Absolute Reality. It is therefore vain to suppose that any language, however ancient or sublime, can express Abstract Truth. The latter exists in the world of ideas, and the ideal can be perceived by the sense belonging to that world. Words can merely clothe the ideas, but no number of words can convey an idea to one who is incapable of perceiving it. Every one of us has within him the latent capacity or a sense dormant in us which can take cognisance of Abstract

Truth, although the development of that sense or, more correctly speaking, the assimilation of our intellect with that higher sense, may vary in different persons, according to circumstances, education and discipline. That higher sense which is the potential capacity of every human being is in eternal contact with Reality, and every one of us has experienced moments when, being for the time *en rapport* with that higher sense, we realise the eternal verities. The sole question is how to focalise ourselves entirely in that higher sense. Directly we realise this truth, we are brought face to face with occultism. Occultism teaches its votaries what sort of training will bring on such a development. It never dogmatises, but only recommends certain methods which the experience of ages has proved to be the best suited to the purpose. But just as the harmony of nature consists in symphonious discord, so also the harmony of occult training (in other words, individual human progress) consists in discord of details. The scope of Occultism being a study of Nature, both in its phenomenal and noumenal aspects, its organisation is in exact harmony with the plan of Nature. Different constitutions require different details in training, and different men can better grasp the idea clothed in different expressions. This necessity has given rise to different schools of Occultism, whose scope and ideal is the same, but whose modes of expression and methods of procedure differ. Nay, even the students of the same school have not necessarily a uniformity of training. This will show why it is that until a certain stage is reached, the *Chela* is generally left to himself, and why he is never given verbal or written instructions regarding the truths of Nature. It will also suggest the meaning of the neophyte being made to undergo a particular kind of sleep for a certain period before each initiation. And his success or failure depends upon his capacity for the assimilation of the Abstract Truth his higher sense perceives. However, just as unity is the ultimate possibility of Nature, so there is a certain school of Occultism which deals only with the synthetic process, and to which all the other schools, dealing with analytical methods wherein alone can diversity exist, owe their allegiance. A careful reader will thus perceive the absurdity of a dogmatism which claims for its methods a universal application. What is therefore meant by the Adwaitee Philosophy being identical with the Arhat Doctrine, is that the final goal or the ultimate possibility of both is the same. The synthetical process is one, for it deals only with eternal verities, the Abstract Truth, the noumenal. And these two philosophies are put forth together, for in their analytical methods they proceed on parallel lines, one proceeding from the subjective and the other from the objective stand-point, to meet ultimately or rather converge together in one point or centre. As such, each is the complement of the other and neither can be said to be complete in itself. It should be distinctly remembered here that the Adwaitee Doctrine does not date from Sankaracharya, nor does the Arhat Philosophy owe its origin to Gautama Buddha. They were but the latest expounders of these two systems which have

existed from time immemorial as they must. Some
natures can better comprehend the truth from a subjective stand-point, while others must proceed from
the objective. These two systems are therefore as
old as Occultism itself, while the later phases of the
Esoteric Doctrine are but another aspect of either of
these two, the details being modified according to the
comprehensive faculties of the people addressed, as
also the other surrounding circumstances. Attempts
at a revival of the knowledge of this Truth have
been numberless, and therefore to suggest that the
present is the first attempt in the world's history, is
an error which those whose sense has just been awakened to the glorious Reality are apt to commit. It
has already been stated that the diffusion of knowledge is not limited to one process. The possessors of
it have never jealously guarded it from any personal
or selfish motives. In fact such a frame of mind pre-
cludes the possibility of the attainment of knowledge.
They have at every opportunity tried all available
means to give its benefit to humanity. Times there
were undoubtedly when they had to rest content with
giving it only to a few chosen pupils, who, it should be
remembered, differ from ordinary humanity only in
one essential particular, and that is, that by abnormal
training they bring on a process of self-evolution in
a comparatively very short period, which ordinary
humanity may require numberless ages to reach during the ordinary course of evolution. Those who are
acquainted with the history of Count St. Germain and
the works of the late Lord Lytton, need not be told

that even during the past hundred years constant efforts have been made to awaken the present races to a sense of the knowledge which will assist their progress and ensure future happiness. It should not be, moreover, forgotten that to spread a knowledge of philosophical truths forms but a small fraction of the important work the occultists are engaged in. Whenever circumstances compel them to be shut out from the world's view, they are most actively engaged in so arranging and guiding the current of events, sometimes by influencing people's minds, at others by bringing about, as far as practicable, such combinations of forces as would give rise to a higher form of evolution and such other important work on a spiritual plane. They have to do and are doing that work now. Little therefore do the public know what in reality it is that they ask for when they apply for *Chelaship*. They have to thus pledge themselves to assist the MAHATMAS in that spiritual work by the process of self-evolution, for, the energy expended by them in the act of self-purification, has a dynamic effect and produces grand results on a spiritual plane. Moreover, they gradually fit themselves to take an active share in the grand work. It may perhaps be now apparent why "THE ADEPT BECOMES; HE IS NOT MADE," and why he is the "rare efflorescence of the age." The foregoing considerations should never be lost sight of by the reader of *Esoteric Buddhism*.

The great difficulty which an ordinarily philosophic mind has to contend against, is the idea that consciousness and intelligence proceed out of non-consciousness and non-intelligence. Although an abstruse metaphysical intellect can comprehend or rather perceive the point subjectively, the present undeveloped state of humanity, at any rate, can conceive the higher truths only from an objective stand-point. Just as, therefore, we are obliged to talk of the setting of the sun, in common parlance, although we know that it is not the movement of the sun that we really refer to, and just as in geocentric system we have to speak as though the earth were a fixed point in the centre of the universe so that the unripe mind of the student may understand our teachings, so in the same manner the Abstract Truth has to be presented from an objective point of view, so that it may be more easily comprehended by minds with not a very keen metaphysical intellect. Thus one may say that Buddhism is rational Vedantism, while Vedantism is transcendental Buddhism. Keeping this difference in view, an explanation of the difficulty above put forth may be given from the Buddhist stand-point. If the reader will here recall the answer of the MAHATMAS to Question V of "An English F. T. S.," published in the *Theosophist* for September 1883,* he will remember

---

*[In *The Theosophist* of September, 1883, "An English F. T. S." (Frederic Myers) asks a series of ten questions suggested by the reading of Sinnett's *Esoteric Buddhism*. Answers I to V contain some of the most important teaching found in *The Theosophist*, being written by the Mahâtmans themselves. (See *The Mahatma Letters to A. P. Sinnett*, p. 396.) The rest of the questions are answered by T. Subba Row. The pertinent passage from Answer V about the mineral-monad can be found in *The Secret Doctrine*, I, 178-9. See also footnote p. 125. — EDS.]

the explanation concerning "the mineral monad." The one Life permeates ALL. Here it may be added that consciousness and intelligence also permeate ALL. These three are inherent potentially everywhere. But we do not talk of the life of a mineral, nor of its consciousness or intelligence. These exist in it only potentially. The differentiation which results in individualisation is not yet complete. A piece of gold, silver, copper or any other metal, or a piece of rock, &c., has no sense of separate existence, because the mineral monad is not individualised. It is only in the animal kingdom that a sense of personality begins to be formed. But for all that, an occultist will not say that life, consciousness or intelligence, do not potentially exist in the minerals. Thus it will be seen that although consciousness and intelligence exist everywhere, all objects are not conscious or intelligent. The latent potentiality when developed to the stage of individualisation by the Law of Cosmic Evolution, separates the subject from the object, or rather the subject falls into *Upadhi*,* and a state of personal consciousness or intelligence is realized. But the absolute consciousness and intelligence which has no *Upadhi* cannot be conscious or intelligent, for there is no duality, nothing to wake intelligence or to be conscious of. Hence the *Upanishads* say that *Parabrahm* has no consciousness, no intelligence, for these states can be cognised by us only on account of our individualisation, while we can have, from our differentiated and personal state, no conception of the un-

---

*[Objective or vehicular form. — EDS.]

differentiated, non-dualistic consciousness or intelligence. If there were no consciousness or intelligence in Nature, it were absurd to talk of the Law of Karma or every cause producing its corresponding effect. The MAHATMA, in one of the letters published in the *Occult World*, says that matter is indestructible, but enquires whether the modern Scientist can tell why it is that Nature *consciously* prefers that matter should remain indestructible under organic rather than inorganic form. This is a very suggestive idea in regard to the subject under notice. At the beginning of our studies we are apt to be misled by the supposition that our earth, or the planetary chain, or the solar system, constitutes infinity and that eternity can be measured by numbers. Often and often have the MAHATMAS warned us against this error, and yet we do, now and then, try to limit the infinity to our standard instead of endeavouring to expand ourselves to its conception. This has led some naturally to a sense of isolation, and to forget that the same Law of Cosmic Evolution which has brought us to our present stage of individual differentiation, is tending to lead us gradually to the original undifferentiated condition. Such allow themselves to be imbued so much with a sense of personality that they try to rebel against the idea of Absolute Unity. Forcing themselves thus in a state of isolation, they endeavour to ride the Cosmic Law which must have its course: and the natural result is annihilation through the throes of disintegration. This it is which constitutes the bridge, the dangerous point in evolution referred to by Mr. Sinnett in his *Esoteric Buddhism*. And this is why selfishness, which is the result of a strong sense of personality, is detrimental to spiritual progress. This it is that constitutes the difference between white and black magic. And it is this tendency to which reference is made when talking of the end of a Race. At this period, the whole humanity splits up into two classes, the Adepts of the good Law and the Sorcerers (or *Dugpas*). To that period we are fast rushing; and to save humanity from a cataclysm which must overtake those who go against the purposes of Nature, the MAHATMAS, who are working with her, are endeavouring to spread knowledge in a manner to prevent its abuse as far as possible. We should therefore constantly remember that the present is not the apex of evolution, and that if we would not be annihilated, we must not allow ourselves to be influenced by a sense of personal isolation and consequent worldly vanities and shows. This world does not constitute infinity, nor does our solar system, nor does the immeasurable expanse our physical senses can take cognisance of. All these and more are but an infinitesimal atom of the Absolute Infinity. The idea of personality is limited to our physical senses which, belonging as they do to the *Rupa Loka* (world of forms), must perish, since we see no permanent form anywhere. All is liable to change, and the more we live in transient personality, the more we incur the danger of final death, or total annihilation. It is only the seventh principle, the *Adi Buddha*, that is the Absolute Reality. The objective stand-point, how-

ever, adds further that *Dharma,* the vehicle of the
seventh principle or its Upadhi, is co-existent with its
Lord and Master, the *Adi Buddha;* because it says
nothing can come out of nothing. A more correct
form of expressing the idea would be that in the state
of *Pralaya* the sixth principle exists in the seventh
as an eternal potentiality to be manifested during
the period of cosmic activity. Viewed in this light
both the seventh and the sixth principles are Eternal
Realities, although it would be more correct to say
that the seventh principle is the only Reality, since
it remains immutable both during cosmic activity as
also during cosmic rest, while the sixth principle, the
Upadhi, although absorbed into the seventh during
Pralaya, is changing during Manvantara, first differ-
entiating to return to its undifferentiated condition as
the time for *Pralaya* approaches. It was from this
standpoint that Mr. Subba Row was arguing in his
article on "A Personal and an Impersonal God,"*
which was meant as a reply to Mr. Hume, who was
then talking of the Arhat Philosophy.

Now the Vedantin doctrine says that *Parabrahm*
is the *Absolute Reality* which never changes and is
thus identical with the *Adi Buddha* of the Arhats.
While *Mulaprakriti* is that aspect of Parabrahm,

*[This article appeared in *The Theosophist,* Feb. and March,
1883, as a Reply to an article by H. X. (A. O. Hume), *The
Theosophist,* Dec., 1882. Both the original article and Subba
Row's answer were republished in "A Collection of the Esoteric
Writings of T. Subba Row, F. T. S., B. A., B. L." published by
Tookaram Tatya.   — EDS.]

which at the time of *Manvantara* emanates from itself *Purush* and *Prakriti,* and which thus undergoes change during the period of cosmic activity. As *Purush* is force, which remains immutable throughout, it is that aspect of *Mulaprakriti* which is identical with *Parabrahm.* Hence it is that *Purush* is said to be the same as *Parabrahm,* or the *Absolute Reality.* While *Prakriti,* the differentiated cosmic matter, constantly undergoes change, and is thus unpermanent, forming the basis of phenomenal evolution. This is a purely subjective stand-point from which Mr. Subba Row was arguing with the late Swami of Almora who professed to be an Adwaitee. A careful reader will thus perceive that there is no contradiction involved in Mr. Subba Row's statements, when he says from the objective standpoint that *Mulaprakriti and Purush* are eternal, and when again from a subjective standpoint he says that *Purush* is the only eternal Reality. His critic has unconsciously mixed up the two stand-points by culling extracts from two different articles written from two different points of view and imagines that Mr. Subba Row has made an error.

Attention must now be turned to the idea of the *Dhyan Chohans.* It has been already stated above that the sixth and the seventh principles are the same in all, and this idea will be clear to every one who reads carefully the foregoing remarks. It has also been added that the sixth principle, being a differentiation of *Mulaprakriti,* is personal, however exalted and ubiquitous that personality may be. In the Adwaitee Philosophy the *Dhyan Chohans* correspond to

Iswara, the Demiurgus. There is no *conscious Iswara
outside* of the 7th principle of Menu [Manu?] as
vulgarly understood. This was the idea Mr. Subba
Row meant to convey when he said:— "expressions
implying the existence of a conscious Iswar which are
to be found here and there in the *Upanishads,* are not
to be literally construed." Mr. Subba Row's statement is therefore neither "perfectly inexplicable," nor
"audacious," as it is consistent with the teaching of
Sankaracharya. The *Dhyan Chohans,* who represent
the aggregate cosmic intelligence, are the immediate
artificers of the worlds, and are thus identical with
Iswara or the Demiurgic Mind. But their consciousness and intelligence, pertaining as they do to the
sixth and the seventh states of matter, are such as
we cannot cognise, so long as we prefer to remain in
our isolation and do not transfer our individuality to
the sixth and the seventh principles. As artificers of
the worlds, they are the primary principle of the Universe, although they are at the same time the *result*
of Cosmic Evolution. It is an incorrect understanding of the consciousness of *Dhyan Chohans* that has
given rise to the current vulgar notion of God. Little
do the dogmatic theists realise that it is within their
power to become *Dhyan Chohans* or *Iswara,* or at
least they have the latent potentiality in them to rise
to that spiritual eminence if they will but work *with*
Nature. They know not themselves, and thus allow
themselves to be carried away and buried under a sense
of personal isolation, looking upon Nature as something apart from themselves. They thus isolate them-

selves from the *spirit* of Nature, which is the only eternal Absolute Reality and hurry towards their own disintegration.

The reader will now perceive that *Esoteric Buddhism* is not a system of materialism. It is, as Mr. Sinnett calls it, "transcendental Materialism" which is non-materialism just as the absolute consciousness is non-consciousness and the absolute personality, of which Mr. Massey talks, is non-personality.

Mr. Massey's description of evolution from the idealist stand-point, with which his pamphlet closes, no occultist will disagree with. The book shows such various phases of thought that different portions must evidently have been written at different times. It is undoubtedly a valuable addition to the existing literature on the subject and will be read with extreme interest by the students of "The metaphysical basis of *Esoteric Buddhism.*"

––––––

POSTCRIPT

After the above was in type, a copy of the "Reply to the 'Observations' of Mr. T. Subba Row, F. T. S.," by Mrs. Kingsford and Mr. Maitland of the *London Lodge of the Theosophical Society,* came to hand. Most of the questions raised therein having been discussed in the foregoing article, attention must now be confined to three or four important points put forth in the present pamphlet.

It has been authoritatively declared, more than once, in the *Theosophist* that the eighth sphere must

not be confounded with the *visible* moon. The authors
of the pamphlet are therefore undoubtedly right in
this respect.

Speaking from a subjective stand-point, to talk of
locality and time is absurd, since the latter are mere
relative terms and as such restricted only to the phenomenal. Abstract space and eternity are indivisible;
and therefore to try to fix time and place, as though
they were absolute realities, is neither metaphysical nor
philosophical. However, objective stand-point is essential, as has been already pointed out. In the econo-
my of Nature, every thing is right in its place, and
to ignore a certain plane is just as illogical as to over-
estimate it. True knowledge consists in a right sense
of discrimination: to be able to perceive what phenomenon performs what function, and how to utilize
it for human progress and happiness. Both the objective and subjective stand-points, as much as the
inductive and deductive methods, are therefore essential for the attainment of *true* knowledge which is
true power. In doing so, it is human habit and nature
to associate certain phenomena with certain abstract
ideas, having of course determined beforehand the exact relation between these two. With these remarks,
it may be left to the intuition of the readers to find
out the relation between the phases of the moon and
the states of being known to occultists as the eighth
sphere.

Next we come to the question of the *Dhyan Chohans*. What they are conceived to be has already
been stated in the foregoing article. It may however

be remarked here that the learned and gifted authors of the pamphlet under consideration seem to mix up both the subjective and the objective stand-points when they say:—

"We confess that the difficulty propounded by us respecting the alleged part taken by the Dhyan Chohans in the production of the Cosmos is not removed by the statement that 'as there can be no beginning of Eternity, so there can be no first *Dhyan Chohans*,' — *if we are to regard these as human, and not Emanations, but products of Evolution.* For, both logically and chronologically, the producer must precede the product, the manifester the manifestation. Unless, indeed, it be that we are called on to believe that prior to, and independently of, *manifestation* is no — *Being;* a belief which would involve the doctrine that the manifest *exhausts* Being; in other words, that the Cosmos *is* God."

Perhaps the difficulty may be removed when it is remembered that the *Dhyan Chohans* represent the cosmic intelligence and consciousness, and that our conception of chronology is inconsistent with the idea of Eternity, and when the subjective and objective stand-points are realized in their distinct aspects. The *Dhyan Chohans* may be considered as the *Elohim* of the *Kabala,* while the "Seven spirits of God" of the Cabalists are represented in the Oriental teaching by the primary *seven Centres of Energy* which subsist "indefeasibly in the Divine Nature, as the seven rays of the prism in light."

We may assure the erudite authors that, according
to the Oriental occult teaching, "When a race has
reached the Zenith of its physical intellectuality and
developed its highest civilization, its progress towards
absolute evil" is arrested by the destruction, as far as
possible, "of its false and pernicious *system* of thought
and conduct . . . by means of such further interior
unfoldment of man's spiritual consciousness as will
supplement and correct mere intellect and pure intuition, and thus enable man to realise his higher po-
tentialities."   The formation and the growth of the
Theosophical Society is one of the indications of the
fact, as has already been pointed out. Moreover, from
a proper understanding of the doctrine of Karma and
of what has already been said in the *Fragments,** &c.,
concerning the after-states of suicides and those who
die premature deaths, it will be obvious that the influence of the results of the evil actions of *Dugpas*
is likely to be worse, under certain conditions and
circumstances, when they are destroyed than when
alive. In the first place, their *elementaries* are likely
to affect a number of sensitives who may thus be
dragged, unconsciously to themselves, towards evil.
Then, the premature death of one evil personality is
likely to influence innumerable other evilly inclined
personalities by the Law of Affinity, as in life the
former has not had full opportunities of working out
the effects of its bad *Karma*. As they are all, more
or less, actuated by merely selfish and personal con-

*["Fragments of Occult Truth." — EDS.]

siderations, there can be no complete unity among them, and their "powers" are generally exercised and sometimes exhausted in matters of dissensions among parties and sects. The conditions being such as above indicated, it will be seen that the physical destruction of a race would tend to increase rather the evil effects than otherwise. At the same time, it should not be forgotten that those entities who have as it were reached the grandeur and the eminence of a Prince of Black magicians, ultimately tend to so group themselves as to make it impossible for them to have their influence spread beyond a very limited area. This opportunity may be taken advantage of; and none will deny that it *is* a certain kind of physical destruction by which they are all focalised together, as it were, in a spot, until a total annihilation results. It is to this destruction that Mr. Subba Row refers in his "Observations."* The phrase "Absolute evil" has been made use of in the same sense as a mathematician sometimes uses the terms "Zero" and "Infinity" — to indicate a theoretical limit.

A few words may now be said in connection with

---

*[These "Observations" of T. Subba Row were republished in the collection of his Esoteric Writings published by Tookaram Tatya. In this article, p. 353, Subba Row, referring to the series of Answers to ten Questions by "An English F. T. S." (see footnote p. 114) says: "The 'Replies' — as every one in our Society is aware of — were written by three 'adepts' . . . none of whom is known to the London Lodge, with the exception of one — to Mr. Sinnett. The sentence quoted and fathered upon Madame Blavatsky is found in the MSS sent by a Mahatma who resides in Southern India [Narayana]. . . ." — EDs.]

the idea of *Buddha*. When Mr. Subba Row talks of
the historical aspect of Buddha, he probably refers to
Gautama Buddha, who was a historical personage.
It must, of course, at the same time be remembered
that every entity that identifies itself with that ray
of the Divine Wisdom which is represented by Gautama, is a Buddha; and thus it will be evident that
there can be but one Buddha at a time, the highest
type of that particular ray of Adeptship.

As the purpose of this writing has been elucida-
tion of truth by means of discussion — spirit which
should animate every true philosophical disquisition—
we hope we have succeeded in leaving entirely out of
consideration every personal question — which so often
mars the force of metaphysical arguments. The chief
aim of the Theosophical Society is human enlightenment and true progress, which can be gained only by
impersonal intelligent discussions, thus promoting a
Brotherhood formed upon the basis of mutual intellectual sympathy.

III

Comments and Answers to Questions

[This chapter contains some of the most important material from the pen of Dâmodar, consisting of comments and notes by him to articles written by other students, and also answers to questions from inquirers. Wherever possible the articles or questions which Dâmodar comments upon, have been summarized.

In each case Dâmodar's signature, as it appears in *The Theosophist,* has been appended to his contributions in order that there may be no confusion as to authorship. — EDS.]

THE "OCCULT WORLD" AND THE "SPIRITUALIST"

[From *The Theosophist*, August, 1881.]

HAVING just read in the London *Spiritualist* a review of Mr. Sinnett's book "The Occult World," I find in it more than a doubt expressed as to the reality of the "Brothers," that body of mystics to which the personage known as "Koot Hoomi Lal Singh" belongs. The Editor of that paper would have his readers believe that the said person is a creation of Madame Blavatsky's fancy. "Mr. Sinnett" he says "has never seen Koot Hoomi, nor does he mention that any other Theosophist in India has had that privilege."

As some other persons may express the same doubts, and also some, while admitting their genuine character, may attribute them to agency other than that to which Madame Blavatsky refers them (the so-called "Brothers" &c.,) I hereby declare that not only have I within the last few days *seen* one of the persons so designated at the Headquarters of the Society at Bombay, but that I have very good reasons (which I cannot go into more fully now) to know that the said persons are *not* "spirits" but real human beings exercising powers out of the ordinary. Both *before* and *after* my connection with the Theosophical Society I have known and conversed with them *person-*

ally and witnessed the most wonderful results (which would ordinarily be described as miraculous), but I must emphasise my declaration that I *do not* regard them as *supernatural* and am altogether materialistic (or rather *naturalistic*) in my conceptions of the agency producing them. Further I testify that I have the strongest conviction based on reasons which, though authoritative, are purely natural and physical, that the said "Brothers" are a mysterious fraternity the ordinary location of which is the regions north of the Himalayas.

Mirza Moorad Alee Beg, F. T. S.,*
*Acting President of the "Saorashtr Theosophical
Society" at Bhaunagar.*

———

The criticisms upon Mr. Sinnett's book *"The Occult World"* force upon me the duty of testifying from *personal* experience and knowledge to the fact that those whom we call our "Brothers of the First Section" of whom "Koot Hoomi Lal Singh" is one, and who possess the so-called "miraculous" powers, are real and living beings and not disembodied spirits as the Editor of the *Spiritualist* would have his readers think. It is but by a long course of study and training that such can be attained. It is *not belief* with me but *knowledge*, for, if I have seen one of them, I have at least seen about half a dozen on various occasions, in broad daylight, in open places, and have talked to

*[Real name Godolphin Mitford, an English Occult student.
— EDS].

them, not only when Madame Blavatsky was in Bombay but even when she was far away and I here. I have also seen them at times when I was travelling. I was taken to the residences of some of them and once when Col. Olcott and Mme. Blavatsky were with me. Further than that I cannot say, and shall not give any more information either about them or the places they reside in, for I am under a solemn obligation of secrecy and the subject is too sacred for me to be trifled with. I may, however, mention that I know "Koot Hoomi Lal Singh" personally and have seen and conversed with him when Mme. Blavatsky was here as also when she was far away. But under what circumstances I am not at liberty to disclose.

We Hindus who know the "Brothers" think it equally absurd and ridiculous to insinuate that either Madame Blavatsky is a lunatic or an impostor, or that persons like Mr. Sinnett could have ever become her dupes. Neither is she a medium, nor are the "Brothers" "disembodied Spirits."

DAMODAR K. MAVALANKAR, F. T. S.

PERT QUESTIONS AND PLAIN ANSWERS

[Supplement to *The Theosophist*, May, 1882.]

HOW little the "beliefs and creeds" of the Theosophical Society — which has *no* belief or creed — are understood by the average public in India after three years of constant explanations, may be inferred by the letter that follows. Crude and childish as it is, yet, finding in it the echo of the public bigotry and blindness to facts and practical proofs, we give it room in our *Supplement*. Unless we are greatly mistaken, it was written under a direct inspiration than which there is not a more bigoted or more intolerant one the world over — we mean that of a Protestant missionary. [Editorial Note in *The Theosophist*. —Eds.]

TO THE EDITOR OF THE "THEOSOPHIST"

9th March, 1882.

MADAME, — With reference to a leading article that appeared in the *Bombay Gazette* of the 4th instant, (from the pen of a correspondent, signing himself "Senex,") and also to an extract from Bishop Sargent's Journal, dated October the 24th, which also appeared in the *Bombay Gazette* of the same date (Saturday, March 4th, 1882), allow me to make the following conclusions:—

"Senex" speaks of "Theosophy" to be a new religion imported into Bombay. Is "Theosophy" a religion, or a belief? Does the Theosophical Society propagate any kind of belief (directly or indirectly)?* The Theosophical Society comprises three sections, and each section comprises three classes. I ask whether there is a single member recognized of the first or second section who is permitted (according to the rules of those sections) to retain his orthodox religious views.† I presume to answer the question in the negative. *Multum in parvo,* "Theosophy" tends to a Buddhistic philosophical and religious belief. Though the rules of the Theosophical Society do not directly compel one to renounce his orthodox religious views, yet indirectly they do so, for one has to renounce his religious orthodoxy if he desires (to be recognized) to be initiated into the higher sections. The "neophytes" receive instruction in what is called "the occult sciences" unknown to the scientists of this day, which sciences treat of "the spirits," and certain fluids and forces in nature. Furthermore "Occultism" teaches man how he can hold direct communication with these forces (by the so-called Occult Psychological Telegraphy), and how he can have a certain amount of control over them, so as to direct these forces, and make them the means of accomplishing certain wonderful phenomena. If such be the case, "Occultism"

---

*Useless to repeat that which was asserted over and over again — namely, that the Theosophical Society, *as a body,* has no religion. — ED. [of *The Theosophist*]

†Most undoubtedly every one of them is allowed to do so if he likes; but whether, after learning *the* truth, he will do so and persist in his dogmatic views, is another question.

— ED. [of *The Theosophist*]

disproves the truth of miracles (superhuman powers).*
"Occultism," then, affects all the popular faiths of
this planet, which claim to be of Divine origin (*i. e.,*
revealed by God to man miraculously through some
prophet).† In short, "Occultism" teaches that Paul,
Moses, Confucius, Mahomet, Zoroaster, and Buddha
were liars and deceivers when they said that they
received Divine inspirations.‡ Thus "the Occult Sciences" as professed by Koot-Hoomi and his brother
(and sister) Theosophists do indirectly affect the religions of this world. Mr. Sinnett, in his work entitled
"The Occult World," informs us that the Corresponding
Secretary of the Theosophical Society "is an adept
to the extent of possessing this magnificent power of
psychological telegraphy with her Occult friends."

"Senex" goes on to say that "Theosophy" is a specu-
lation of certain visionaries who pretend to be able to

---

*Most undoubtedly it does. It rejects the very idea of there
being anything *supernatural* (*i. e.,* above, below, or outside of
nature) in this infinite Universe — as a stupendous fallacy.
— Ed. [of *The Theosophist*]

†To "claim," is one thing, and "to be" — and to prove it —
is quite another. — Ed. [of *The Theosophist*]

‡We would advise our young friend to study a subject before he presumes to speak of it. Buddha never claimed to have
received "Divine Inspiration," since Buddha rejected the very
idea of a god, whether *personal* or *impersonal.* Therefore,
Occultism does *not teach* that he was a "liar," nor does it give
that abusive epithet — so generously bestowed by the Christian
padris on all and every other prophet but their own — any more
to Moses, than to Mahomet, or Zoroaster, least of all to Confucius, since, no more than Gautama Buddha, has that great
sage ever claimed "divine" inspiration. — Ed. [of *The Theos.*]

hold direct communication with the Deity and to direct and combat the influence of the Deity ("the Supreme Light") by the medium of Genii, (spirits), or demons, or by the agency of stars or fluids (as electricity).* It must not be forgotten that Spiritualists are already wrangling on points of spiritualistic dogma. "Senex" (referring to the spirits of the dead) is of opinion that the theory of the "Theosophists" (that the raiment is fashioned "out of the cosmic matter of the universe") is a trifle less absurd than that of the Spiritualists. I see no difference between "Occultism" of the Theosophists and "Spiritualism" as professed by Zöllner, Mrs. Hauffe, Eglinton, Slade† and a score of other mediums in the United States, except that the Spiritualists perform their phenomena through spirits pneumatic, (?) while the adepts of theosophy do theirs by nature's laws *without the aid of spirits* (*apneumatic*). Bishop Sargent informs us "that the king-cocoanut, planted by Col. Olcott and the Tinnevelly Brothers in the temple-yard of the Great Pagoda of Tinnevelly, was soon after removed, and that the whole temple-yard had to be ceremonially purified of the contamination it had thus contracted by the intrusion of the foreign-

---

*If our correspondent is unable to appreciate journalistic humour and wit, and takes the definition copied out by "Senex" from Webster's Dictionary as a Gospel Truth, we cannot help him to more intuitive perceptions than he is endowed with.
— Ed. [of *The Theosophist*]

†This is to be deplored, but so long as our correspondent will rush into print to discuss upon subjects he knows nothing about, he is sure to commit such ridiculous blunders.
— Ed. [of *The Theosophist*]

er."* Yet Colonel Olcott makes no mention of this in his address at the Framjee Cowasjee Institute of the 12th January.†

Either the Theosophical Society has its inconsistencies or the Bombay public have not been correctly informed concerning these matters.

Would you kindly satisfy me (by letter) on the following points:—

(1) Whether an adept of "theosophy" like Koot-Hoomi and others can "foretell future events"; whether they have such powers?

(2) Whether "adepts" have the power of curing diseases?

(3) And, lastly, whether "adepts" have the power of temporarily raising the dead as "Senex" gives me to understand.   I remain yours &c.,

                                        *   *   *

---

*Which only proves that Bishop Sargent also speaks of what he knows nothing about, or gladly repeats unproved missionary calumnies. (See the remarks under the heading "Milk for Babes and Strong Meat for Men" on page 5 of the Supplement to the last issue). — ED. [of *The Theosophist*]

†Pleading "guilty" to never reading or paying attention to missionary and other pious organs, and not being endowed with omniscient clairvoyance to help him following the constant intrigues of their editors and their inventions against our Society and its Founders, Colonel Olcott could not "mention" that which he was not aware of: namely that, after the calumny had been well spread by our meek and humble missionaries and as effectively shown to be false, no less a personage than a "Bishop" would take it up, and circulate what he knew was a malicious falsehood. — ED. [of *The Theosophist*]

ANSWER TO * * * 'S MISCONCEPTIONS

SECRETARY'S OFFICE OF THE THEOSOPHICAL SOCIETY,
BREACH CANDY, BOMBAY, INDIA, 10th March, 1882.

SIR, — The Editor of the "THEOSOPHIST" having no leisure to answer letters, but turning that work over to the Secretaries, I have the pleasure to reply to your letter of 9th March. You seem to rest all your arguments upon the two letters in the *Bombay Gazette* of the 4th instant. One of these is from a correspondent, while the other one is an extract from Bishop Sargent's Journal, dated 24th October, 1881. When reading "Senex's" letter, we were the first to laugh over it heartily, as it is very witty and quite free from any malicious innuendoes, such as some of the hard-headed bigots have been wont to use against us.

At any rate, it is easy to perceive that the writer's intention was far from conveying any such absurd conclusions as you seem to have arrived at — such as "temporarily raising the dead!" Some people seem entirely impermeable to literary wit. They have no sense of true humour, and seem incapable of appreciating it. Hence — their perversion of the meaning.

"Theosophy" and the "Theosophical Society" are two quite different things, since the latter, embracing the former, includes still a few other things. Permit me to remind you that, in our *Rules,* our objects are defined as follows:—

(1) To form the nucleus of an Universal Brotherhood of Humanity, without distinction of race, creed or colour.

(2) To promote the study of Aryan and other Eastern literature, religions and sciences, and vindicate its importance.

(3) To investigate the hidden mysteries of Nature and the Psychical Powers latent in man.

Of these, the first is the most important for us. It is urged that this Idea is Utopian. But whether it is or is not, is quite beside the question. What people want to know is, whether it is conducive to the happiness and well-being of humanity, and so, worthy of being given a trial — or not. And if it is, that is all we care for. How far we have succeeded in our endeavours, can be seen from the practical results of our work. If we have succeeded so far, it is because we ever kept in mind that we could admit only those who were capable of understanding what that term of Universal Brotherhood meant, and of appreciating the honour of having been accepted within its ranks. Therefore, we extended the Brotherhood only to those who could comprehend and hoped to conquer the immense difficulties encountered between Intellectual Solitude and Intellectual Companionship. This is a position difficult to master; but once mastered, the Theosophical Society has found many recruits capable of forming and leading companies of their own. Thus has the Idea spread, thus have numerous Branches been formed, and thus have our operations extended almost all over the world. And the practical benefits, accruing from such an organisation, each of our members can testify to, any day. Composed, as we are, of various nationalities and divers religious creeds, it was essentially necessary that we should have certain stringent rules to enforce harmony. And how could we do that except by allowing no one to enter before he pledged himself to abide by the principle of mutual religious Tolerance and Sympathy? There is a great deal of difference between orthodoxy and bigotry. A person may be very orthodox and not at all a bigot. An orthodox will cling tenaciously to his views, whatever they may be, while a bigot will try his best to *enforce* his ideas upon others, whether they be willing or not. We, therefore, have to admit only such persons who will not interfere with the views of their Fellow Members, but will try to promote mutual Intellectual Sympathy. Between calm and philosophical discussion and bigoted compulsion, there is a world of difference; and a person, who desires to arrive at Truth, must accept it from whatsoever quarter and wheresoever it may be found. Most of us, Asiatics, believe that we can find it in ancient religions, and, therefore, encourage their study. And here comes in Theosophy. But it is a term which is not properly understood, I fancy, by the majority of our critics: hence — there have been many misconceptions about our Society. Ordinary people say that Theosophy, derived from "*Theos* — God" and "*Sophia* — wisdom," means the wisdom of God. Hence they rashly jump to the conclusion that we are all believers in a *Personal* Deity. No graver mistake could ever be committed. "Theosophy" with us (and it did so with Plato and other ancient Theosophists) means "divine wisdom," or rather the knowledge of that which is yet a mystery to the ordinary run of mankind. In this sense, even a Materialist is a Theosophist, because he is ever trying to find the operation of such laws of nature as have not yet been discovered; a Buddhist, — who recognizes no God, — is also one, for he strives to attain to a knowledge of that which he terms "Motion" and with its help to attain "Nirvana"; so also is a Vedantist, as he is in pursuit of the knowledge of that which he calls "Parabrahm," and thus reach "Moksha"; similarly is a Zoroastrian, for he is striving after that course which will enable him to perceive, with his inner eye, the God Zoroaster saw; and so on and on. But, if we take the religious history of the founders of all these different faiths, we find that they proceeded by the same path and arrived at the same conclusions. It might be said: "How is it then that there should be so many antagonistic passages in different religious books?" Here then comes in true Theosophy, which is the only key to unlock the mysteries of all these noble, ancient philosophies. Secure this key, and all these inconsistencies will fade away. At least those, who have tried it and have succeeded, assert this to be a fact. For a student of occultism, these externals have no charm. He tries to penetrate into the spirit of everything. For him, all exotericism is a mere wrangling of terms.

Most certainly, our superior sections are meant only for occultists. Therefore, very few people are in any of those sections. Occultism is not meant for all. Just as, although surgery is open for all, yet not every one can be a skillful surgeon, so also, not every one can be a good occultist. In that line, as in every other, it is better not to touch it at all than to prove a failure. As occultism is not meant for the public, very few can appreciate it or understand its true significance and they, therefore, invent one of their own. Nevertheless, it does seem absurd to find such misconceptions about occultism. Certainly, the students are taught by its proficients to believe there is no such thing as a "miracle." That the idea of something taking place outside of the Laws of Nature is absurd; and, therefore, we reject it most emphatically. To us, however *apparently* miraculous a thing may appear, yet, we are sure that it always happens in obedience to the impulse of forces of Nature, not of any supernatural cause. This is the position assumed by the occultist. Therefore, he has never said that the miraculous phenomena attributed to the world's sages were not genuine; but only that they were *not* "miracles," in the sense of the supernatural, and were performed through their knowledge of the operations of the hidden or occult forces of Nature. Anyone can produce them; any one — who is possessed with the purity of Buddha, undergoes the same training and obtains the same knowledge, — may become a Boddhisatwa. Gautama "Buddha" never claimed, to the knowledge of men, any *divine* inspiration — that is, any influence *external* to himself, since he rejected the very idea of the existence of God. He obtained his Buddhahood by developing his *latent* psychological faculties, which every man more or less possesses. The occultists, therefore, never called him or any one of the personages enumerated by you — *"liars."* From

the above you will also realize, it is to be hoped, that
no Eastern occultist ever "pretended" or claimed to
"hold *direct* communication with the Deity;" since
he believes in and invokes no other Deity but the one
enthroned within his own being. Having thoroughly
realised that man is the microcosm within the macro-
cosm, he does not go to seek that in the external universe, which he fails to find within himself.

If you see no difference between occultism and
vulgar Spiritualism, it is to be regretted, but it is
not our fault. We cannot read books and understand
things for you. Instead of seizing one or two humour-
ous remarks made by witty correspondents and *interested* enemies, if you had carefully, and, *with an impartial spirit,* read our various books and publications,
you would have been spared the trouble of writing
your letter.

If you take Bishop Sargent's words as Gospel-
Truth, we do not. Here, again, if you had read the
other side of the case, you would not have committed
such a mistake, as the Editor's *note* above will perhaps convince you of having made. I again refer you
to the *Subodha Patrika* of 4th December, 1881, as we
cannot waste our time with persons, who will take up
ex parte statements, to establish their own *preconceived*
theories. You will find in the *Subodha Patrika* above
referred to, the two trustees themselves, of the temple
where Colonel Olcott planted the cocoanut, stating
that the worshippers of the place, of their own accord,
formally purified the place, *according to their usual
custom,* and that no disrespect, as no exception, was

meant to Colonel Olcott. According to custom, they would have purified the place just in the same way, if any other European or even *a Hindu of a lower caste* had entered the place.

The cocoanut plant was never "rooted out," nor was it ever removed from its original place. On the contrary, it is well taken care of, and surrounded by a fence, within the enclosures of which it flourishes and thrives, as if defying the calumnies and malicious lies of our detractors.

No "inconsistencies" in the Theosophical Society, therefore, exist in the mind of any *evenly* disposed person; but they do, and in a very high degree, in those of *partisans,* as none are as blind as they who WILL NOT SEE.

I am not at liberty to mention anything about the adepts. For myself, I would never even utter their names to the *profane* ears of persons bent only upon picking holes in other people's coats. Enough and too much has already been said by Mr. Sinnett in his *"Occult World,"* and any one, who reads that book carefully, has no need to put such childish questions as you have. Upon one more subject I can enlighten you, however, and that is that no living adept has ever set up the ridiculous claim of being able to "raise the dead," once that a person is really dead. To do so, would be a "miracle" indeed — never yet performed in *history* by any living man — but in *Fables* — by many.

Yours obediently,

DAMODAR K. MAVALANKAR,

Recording Secretary.

SEEING BRIGHT LIGHT WITH CLOSED EYES

[Supplement to *The Theosophist*, September, 1883.]

OUR Brother P. T. Srinivasaingar of Negapatam, writes to ask:—

"Can you please explain the following phenomenon?

"If a man closes his eyes, lets two fingers pass over them, presses the lower eyelids tightly with these fingers (meanwhile the eye being closed) and tries to see, then before 2′ are over, a bright light begins to develop itself before his (is it mind's?) eye."

———

Note.— Our Brother Mr. Srinivasaingar does not seem to have read any works on Mesmerism. If he had, and if, moreover, he had witnessed personally Col. Olcott benumbing the limbs of his patients and incapacitating them, by his will-power, from opening their eyes, once that he had passed his hand over them, our Negapatam friend would have seen the *rationale* of the phenomenon he describes. The effect, he witnesses, is due to Auto-Magnetisation, pure and simple. Once that the eyes are closed and the mind, drawn away from all external objects of sense, is concentrated, what may appropriately be called the sixth sense, or "Siva's eye" — clairvoyant sight — is opened and the Astral Light, one of the correlations of *Akasa,* becomes perceptible. Those who are mediumistic can achieve this quicker than others and in some instances, on certain occasions, without any effort. But these effects will not be under the control of these peculiarly constituted people who become but passive agents of the elementals and the elementaries. He who desires to develop his psychological capacities has to practise self-Magnetisation and, becoming an active operator, has to subject the nature-forces to his WILL. It was with that view that the ancient *Aryans* enjoined the performance of the *Sandhya**** Ceremony now so much neglected and misunderstood!   D. K. M.

---

*[Religious ceremonies performed in India at sunrise, noon, and sunset.   — EDS.]

CAN FEMALES BECOME ADEPTS?

[From *The Theosophist*, October, 1883.]

WILL you kindly let me know whether females can attain to adeptship, and whether female adepts exist at all?   "AN INQUIRER."

Note.— It is difficult to see any good reason why females should not become Adepts. None of us, Chelas, are aware of any physical or other defect which might entirely incapacitate them from undertaking the dreary ordeal. It may be more difficult, more dangerous for them than it is for men, still not impossible. The Hindu sacred books and traditions mention such cases, and since the laws of Nature are immutable, what was possible some thousand years ago must be possible now. If our correspondent had referred to the Editorial Notes, page 148, Vol. III, (Article, *Re-Incarnations in Thibet*),* he would have found the existence of a female Adept hinted at — the pious Chinese Princess who, after living for ten years a married life, renounced it with her husband's consent and became a *Gelung-ma*, or Ani, *i. e.*, a nun. She is believed to be still re-incarnating herself *"in a succession of female Lamas."* The late Tde-shoo Lama's sister is said to be one of such re-incarnations. From this

---

*[See *The Complete Works of H. P. Blavatsky*, Vol. III, footnote, p. 272.   — EDS.]

lady-Adept, the Superior of the Nunnery on the Palte-Lake — a Tibetan pedlar of Darjeeling acknowledged to some Bengal Theosophists, who visited that place last year, to have received a talisman. That pedlar is now supposed to be dead; but those Theosophists who heard repeatedly his statement can testify to the fact. In Nepaul, we all know, there is a high female Adept. And in Southern India, flourished at a recent date, another great female Initiate named Ouvaiyar. Her mysterious work in Tamil on Occultism is still extant. It is styled *Kural,* and is said to be very enigmatically written, and consequently inexplicable. In Benares too lives a certain lady, unsuspected and unknown but to the very few to whom reference has been made in the *Theosophist* in the article "Swami Dayanand's Views about *Yoga*" (page 47, Vol. II).* Further information about these few already mentioned or any other female Adepts we may know of, we do not feel

---

*[This article is the report of a series of questions put to Swâmi Dâyanand by Colonel Olcott, during several interviews at which notes were taken. The passage in question is:

"Q. Can a Yogi thus pass from his own body into that of a woman?

"A. With as much ease as a man can, if he chooses, put on himself the dress of a woman, so he can put over his own *átmá* her physical form. Externally, he would then be in every physical aspect and relation a woman; internally, himself.

"Q. I have met two such; that is to say, two persons who appeared women, but who were entirely masculine in everything but the body. One of them, you remember, we visited together at Benares, in a temple on the bank of the Ganges.

"A. Yes, 'Majji.' "   — EDS.]

at liberty to give. If our numerous correspondents would carefully go over the back Numbers of this journal, they would find many of their questions already anticipated and answered; and thus, they would save us an unnecessary travelling over the same line.

D. K. M.

TO THE EDITOR OF THE THEOSOPHIST

[Supplement to *The Theosophist*, December, 1883.]

MADAME,— Will you, with your usual kindness, enlighten me on the following points, some of them being not satisfactorily understood, even by the perusal of "Fragments of Occult Truth" and "Elixir of Life." The questions are raised, as they occurred to me while reading the said articles in your valuable journal. They are asked in the spirit of an inquirer after truth and not in the spirit of a biassed sceptic. I hope, therefore, you will kindly publish the following questions with replies thereto, in one of your ensuing numbers, of course, as soon as it may please you.

1. It is usually affirmed, what is a fact, that the adepts live very much longer than ordinary mortals. What is the maximum number of years for which they live or can live before they die their physical death like men in general, who live or can live for not more than 200 years at the most?

2. Do all adepts of any particular age, live the same or almost the same number of years? Do adepts of all ages live for about the same number of years?

3. In the article "Elixir of Life" (Vol. III, No. 7, p. 171), we read "By or about the time when the Death-limit of his race is passed, he is actually dead . . . gone to join the gods." What is the exact state of an adept by or about the time, when the Death-limit of his race is passed? If he die a physical death

at such a time, though without the agonies of dying, where is the difference with respect to longevity between him and an ordinary man who dies at about 100 or 150 or 200 at the most?

4. An adept, after he is dead in the sense in which it is used in the said article, is not reborn, having no will to live or *Tanha* as they call it. Where is he not reborn? On this earth as well as on any other sphere? What then becomes of his body, the seven principles of which he is formed?

5. When can it be said that an adept has attained Nirvana or Moksha as the Hindus call it? What is the exact state of his body, *i. e.*, the seven principles of which he is composed, when he attains Nirvana?

6. The ancient Rishis of India, such as Vasistha, Valmiki, Viswamitra, Agastya, and other historical adepts do not exist in flesh and blood. Then, how, *i. e.*, in what form do they exist, if they still exist at all in any other form? What has then become of the septenary men of which they were formed?

7. "A very high adept, undertaking to reform the world, would necessarily have to once more submit to Incarnation." (Vol. III, page 171, No. 7)* How, where, and when does he submit to Incarnation? Does he become incarnate in the sense in which Vishnu is said to have been incarnate by the Hindus?

8. Patanjali, in his Yoga Sutras, says that a perfect Yogi, becomes perfectly strong. Does he mean,

*[Quoted from "The Elixir of Life." — EDS.]

by that, that he becomes physically stronger than the strongest athlete or gymnast, who is generally physically stronger than an ordinary man not taking exercise? And, if so, what makes him so very strong, since he eats very scanty or no food at all? Who is physically stronger — a vegetarian or a flesh eating man, not to say of the psychic powers he, the vegetarian, acquires?

9. Where is a man, an ordinary man, having *Tanha*, reborn immediately after his physical death, is it on this terrestrial globe or on any other planet of our system?

10. What becomes of an Elementary in the long run? Does or can it again become a human being? If it does, or can again become a human being, when is it and where, on this earth again or on any other planet of our system?

By throwing some light on the above questions, in an intelligible manner, you would highly oblige

Yours faithfully,
DINANATH PANDURANG DHUMME

BOMBAY,
21st September, 1883.

Note.— It is to be regretted that the correspondents to this Journal do not seem to realize fully the importance of the following four considerations in putting forth their questions and difficulties.—

(*1st*) The *Fragments* are but mere crumbs, and necessarily incomplete. Moreover, not being intended for serial publication, as they subsequently were, they

cannot but be unsystematic in their arrangement. They
were meant rather as food for thought for such as had
the capacity to develop the crude ideas presented therein, than as a complete exposition of the Esoteric Doctrine.

(*2nd*) Most of these crude ideas have been sufficiently expatiated upon in works like the *Occult
World, Esoteric Buddhism* and other subsequent articles in this magazine. These subsequent expositions
must be carefully studied before framing any questions.

(*3rd*) There are certain facts which can be di-
vulged only to such of the Fellows of the Theosophical
Society as have proved their worthiness to receive them;
others can be taught only to *chelas* as they progress;
while the rest unfold themselves to INITIATES in their
onward march towards BUDDHAHOOD.

(*4th*) For a comprehension of many of these truths
the development of the "sixth sense" to which reference
has already been made in the replies to "An English
F. T. S." — is an essential qualification.

If these four facts could but be realised by the
well-meaning and earnest correspondents of the *Theosophist*, much unnecessary writing would be saved.
Being bounded by these lines, the questions of Mr.
D. P. D. may now be answered to a certain extent.

Esoteric Buddhism sufficiently deals with the first
question. The physical life of the ADEPT is determined
more or less by the conditions of the race in which
he is born, by the energy of his Will and by various
other circumstances. It will be admitted that each
subsequent race after the middle point is once passed,

must be more and more spiritual. So one ADEPT having to contend with a lesser amount of materiality than his predecessors, has his way much smoother. The exact number of years which an ADEPT of a particular race may live is a perfectly immaterial question and can be set down more to unscientific curiosity than to any philosophical enquiry. It must be at the same time remembered that when a certain stage is reached, the conditions which surround the ADEPTS of different races being nearly identical, their periods of existence must be almost the same. In this answer, question number 2 is anticipated. For a further explanation *Esoteric Buddhism* may be studied with advantage.

Question three would never have been put by one who had properly *studied* the article on *Elixir of Life* and understood the spirit it conveys. Suffice it to say that the passage in that article which tells us that the higher bodies become accustomed to the atmospheric conditions of the earth before the grossest ones are cast off, is a broad hint for a student of occultism who has begun to live the life. Question four is partly answered in the above reply and partly in *Esoteric Buddhism*.

The ADEPT attains *Nirvana* or *Moksha* when he identifies himself wih the ONE LIFE or rather puts himself *en rapport* with it. His state then is something like that of the *Dhyan Chohans* of the Buddhists or the *Prajapatis* of the Hindus. D. P. D. would do well to study the *Upanishads*.

The four *Rishis* mentioned in the article live now as

Dhyan Chohans. This of course does not mean that all the ancient sages have reached that stage.

The incarnation of *Adepts* is to be understood in the same sense in which Occultists interpret the incarnations of *Vishnu.*

What *Patanjali* means is that the *Yogi* becomes strong owing to the development of his Will Power to an enormous extent. Upon what he lives, is sufficiently answered in the article on the *Elixir of Life.* *Akasa* is the mother of all phenomena and the source of nourishment of him who knows how to use it. Vegetables have properties which are not fully known, and if certain undiscovered (to the general world) vegetables were prepared and eaten in a certain way, there is no reason why they should not give even more strength than animal food. Meat-eating is full of dangers, not only psychological but even physical; and the law which teaches the spread of contagion ought to have made this fact evident. How many diseases are inherent in an organised body and yet remain unsuspected? Vegetable diet is not attended with so many dangerous results.

The question of rebirth is extensively treated upon in the *Fragments* and in *Esoteric Buddhism* and it would be mere waste of space to go over the same ground. The tenth question also is pretty fully discussed there.   — D. K. M.

(Chela)

ON PRAYER

[From *The Theosophist*, March, 1884.]

[The following is a reply to a letter from "K. C. M." who asks what is the real meaning of prayer, and if there is any harm in the various forms or methods of approaching the "Great-self" in prayer. He says: ". . . I find that prayer is allowed in all the known religions of the world. There must have been some strong grounds for enjoining the practice. Was it because the Teachers thought it advisable not to meddle with the natural feelings of their followers? . . ." — EDS.]

WE act upon the principle that what is meat for one is death for another. While, therefore, some people may not be able to develop their latent psychic capacities without prayer, there are others who can. We set no value upon the words uttered. For, if the words had any effect, how is it that different religionists, although using different forms of expression, obtain the same result? Again, those who pray silently and intensely gain their object, while those who merely mumble some formula without understanding the meaning, get no answers to their prayers. As has been said in *Isis Unveiled,* we believe prayer is the giving of expression to the desire, which generates Will. And this WILL is all-powerful; its effect depending, of course, upon all the surrounding conditions. Philosophers can be but few. They need no external ceremony or object for the purpose of concentrating their Will-force. We cannot expect the ordinary mortals, whose sensuous perceptions and avocations do not permit them to penetrate behind the mask, to do without the help of some external process. What we regret is the degeneration of this real prayer — the outward expression of the inward feeling — into a meaningless jumble of words. The prayer of the philosopher is his contemplation, an article on which subject will be found in the last number of the *Theosophist*.*   — D. K. M.

---

*[This refers to Dâmodar's own article on Contemplation, which appears in Chapter II of the present volume. — Eds.]

"PHENOMENA"

[Supplement to *The Theosophist*, April, 1884.]

IN the Supplement to the February issue, I find registered two occurrences under the head "Phenomenal,"* which are remarkable,— remarkable, not in the hackneyed unmeaning sense of the newspapers, but remarkable in the literal sense of the word — worthy of remark.

My first observation is that the record of these occurrences says either too much or too little for the reading public, among whom are members of the Theosophical Society and the uninitiated as well. It says too much, because while publishing a lot of details connected with the phenomena, it excites a hope well warranted under the circumstances in the breast of every one, that members of the Theosophical Society, in addition to the mental and moral progress they secure, are constantly under the guidance of their "Masters," who interfere (pardon the word) in almost every trifling affair of this world, even to the extent of compensating in hard cash for the pecuniary losses which the members may "unjustly" be subjected to — a hope which I need hardly say is thoroughly out of

---

*[The article in question is too long and detailed to summarize, and, though interesting in itself, is not needed for an appreciation of Dâmodar's illuminating remarks upon the use of phenomena made by the Mahâtmans in the early days of the Theosophical Society.   — EDS.]

place and almost inconsistent with the high moral
tone of the eloquent and impressive admonition which
the President addresses to the candidates at the initiation time.

The record again says too little, because while the
writers honestly believe that they have given to the
public all that is necessary for them to know that the
occurrences registered are free from jugglery, there is
an amount of omission, very important omission indeed,
which leaves a very unpleasant impression that the
statements published are only those elicited in the
"Examination-in-chief" of a witness by a partial advocate; that much of the cross-examination and re-exam-
ination have been most unwisely omitted, and that
fuller statements were deemed either ruinous to the
cause and purposely suppressed or omitted from an
inadequate appreciation of their great importance. I
believe it is the latter.

The object of the first phenomenon was to check
Mr. S. Ramaswami Iyer's vehement talk. He was
doing this in the presence of a venerable lady, which
fact alone should have curbed the ribald license of
the tongue. And *what was* this "rather warm" and
"vehement" tone, which a single look from any ordinary lady, much more of Madame Blavatsky could
not chasten and tone down? Was the interference
from the spiritual world a necessity in the case? I
find the substance of all this big talk omitted in the
record, and that purposely — an omission which I do
not regret; and knowing, as I do, some particulars connected with it, it would be a breach of ordinary

propriety were I to mention them in spite of the intentional silence of Mr. Cooppooswami Iyer: but I must say that to *my* mind at least the cause that excited the vehement tone was most trivial compared with the grand machine that was used for its removal: a quiet snub from Madame Blavatsky would have done all the good the young man required, and Master S. Ramaswami Iyer in his teens would have richly deserved a few cuts on the back from the strong hand of the President.   As it is, there has been a waste of energy and force, which is one of the sins against Laws of nature and (pardon me) an abuse of power. Suppose an officer, who is a Theosophist as well, is ordered to lead a forlorn hope, would you not think him fit for the lunatic Asylum if he talked "vehemently" and "rather warmly" against the orders and waited for a Mahatma to give him an encouraging word?   And why should he not wait in hope inasmuch as the Mahatma had condescended to do so in one case, comparatively a trivial case, and could not in fairness be justified in withholding his aid in another and more serious case?

Now the next case.   Does the Mahatma undertake to indemnify every Theosophist who bears "an unjust expense?"   The absurdities of the question are on its very face, and yet one would be justified in raising it.   The "unjust" nature of the expense Mr. Subrammanya Iyer has not explained: that explanation would have shewn how far the Theosophist who bore the expense was not himself to blame for it, how far he was not a careless victim of his own credulity and deserved the indemnity.　There are fools and villains in this world, and the latter are constantly living at the expense of the former, and a great deal of the consequent misery is due to ignorance, to wipe off which is the grand object of the Mahatmas, not in the direct way, which has been most singularly adopted in the present instance, but by teachings.

"But who are you to lay the law down for the Mahatmas?　They act as they will, your duty is to believe and admire," will probably be the remark of the Editor of the *Theosophist*.　A similar reprimand has been addressed in the "Occult World."　I shall bear this reprimand and, aye, a great deal more.　God knows I am not a critic for the sake of criticism. Knowledge is my thirst, and the publications of such phenomena push me back a considerable distance in my way onwards.　Would it be difficult for the Mahatmas to exhibit a phenomenon at each initiation? Would not the Theosophical Society be simply mobbed for initiation under such circumstances? and yet how long would such a state of things last? and how long would the initiated remain content after the first experience?　The craving is the most unhealthy ever known and is never satiated.　Miracles, using the word in its ordinary sense, have never done much good. On the grandest occasions — I cannot even conceive of such occasions — a miracle may be justifiable: but man's fate in this world is to struggle on, is to study, is to see through the hollowness of this material world by observation and contemplation, and not to be waiting for money compensations for "unjust" losses or for words of encouragement from the Mahatmas at every petty annoyance that he must suffer by thousands as long as he is in this world.

Theosophy has a deep foundation of its own; if its sublime principles were not found sufficient enough to convert the world, such phenomenal occurrences as these would prove simply impotent. They may for a time excite curiosity, wonder, and be the talk of a few for a month: then they lose their effect and there is a craving for more: you *must* satisfy it: you try to repress it, it is at your peril. K. H.'s letters in the "Occult World" are explicit on this point: his *theory* is sublime: his participation, however, in the two recorded phenomena has staggered me. Will you teach me to reconcile the theory with the practice?

"A Student."

Note.— I must state at the outset that I have the greatest respect for the writer, for he is one of the very, very few enlightened natives of India who have joined our Society for the sake of the Philosophy and its high aims and objects and not for the sake of "phenomena." In fact what kept him so long from us was the latter. If the percentage of such exceptional men were to steadily increase, that would indeed be a very hopeful sign of the intellectual and philosophical progress of humanity. In the present case, our brother's remarks are directed against the two articles appearing under the heading of "Phenomenal" in the February Number. I shall, however, show that his criticisms, although well meant, are to some extent misdirected.

In the first place, he seems to think that the interference of Mr. Ramaswamier's GURU, in what he calls a trivial matter, was a waste of power. This observation betrays an ignorance of the mode of communication between the Adepts and their *Chelas* or fellow-initiates. A careful consideration of the article on PRECIPITATION* will show that the *Adept* and the *Chela* or another Adept are like the two signallers at the two ends of a Telegraphic line. It is only when the batteries are out of order, or moisture or some such cause prevents the free working of the wires — that expense has to be undergone to restore or keep the communication intact. In the same way the Adepts have to use *no power* in communicating with one another or with their *Chelas of a certain degree*, unless either of them is ill or exhausted by fatigue, &c., or unless some antagonistic influence interferes with the Astral Wires, if I may use the expression. In the case under notice, Mme. Blavatsky, who is in constant communication with the Adepts, was there. The presence of all the *Chelas* helped to keep the Astral Telegraph free from any disturbance, and little or no power had to be used to send the letter in question to Mr. Ramaswamier. Mme. Blavatsky could no doubt have checked the vehemence of the language used by Mr. R., but at the same time Mr. Coopooswami Iyer's description indicates that the check exer-

---

*[Unsigned article in *The Theosophist*, Dec.-Jan., 1883-84; republished in *Five Years of Theosophy*, pp. 518-521. — EDS.]

cised by the *Mahatma* was only *one* of the purposes of the letter in question. Advantage was probably taken of the opportunity, while communicating serious matters, to also add a few words of reprimand in regard to the subject then vehemently discussed. This latter fact, however, was "phenomenal" for those who have no idea of the possibilities of Occult powers, and naturally enough Mr. Coopooswami Iyer gave prominence to the same. My brother should remember that what is "phenomenal" for an outsider, is not necessarily so for a *Chela*. If others were to see my MASTER as I see Him, they would consider it a "phenomenon": I do not, for I know that as the usual mode of communication between an Adept and his *Chela*. The same remarks more or less apply to the second phenomenon mentioned by Mr. Subramania Iyer. There was no *intention* of exhibiting "occult powers." The absence of Mme. Blavatsky and other *Chelas* would have prevented the occurrence; for in that case an appreciable amount of "power" would have to be used to lay the Astral Telegraphic Line. The two gentlemen in question only took advantage of the opportunity of their presence on those occasions to mention what they saw, for the benefit of those who were then absent. Surely our philosophic brother does not mean to deny that the overwhelming testimony of eye-witnesses to facts, influences people in favour of the same, and that there are many, who now "despise phenomena" as *tamasha*, but were led to a study of the philosophy by the force of unrebuttable evidence poured forth before them through the "Occult" literature. Happy would be that day indeed when the *noumenal* will supersede the phenomenal; but till then we have a duty to perform, and that is to hasten its approach, though not by any radical means. If these occurrences then, in which no special power had to be exercised, can stimulate not a few to enquire into the philosophy, why should they be lost, without turning them to some advantage, however slight that advantage may be? I would also refer those interested in the matter to the article on "Occult Phenomena" in the current number of the *Theosophist*.*

D. K. M.

---

*[Article signed AN AMERICAN BUDDHIST. The writer shows that there is nothing 'magic' in the work of the Mahâtmans, but that they use what for them are simple and natural means to carry on their work among the Theosophists. The sooner, says the author, ignorant critics "accustom themselves to look upon our revered Masters as teachers and friends and wise men, instead of looking at them with the same feeling of awe and superstition and fear with which the Fiji-islander looks upon his Deity; the sooner will they find that the so-called 'Occult Phenomena' are neither intended to convert incredulous sceptics, nor are they produced for the purpose of astonishing the public; but are principally methods of communication or instruction. To appreciate a thing properly and according to its true value, we must neither depreciate its importance, nor over-estimate the same." — EDS.]

THE BEST FOOD FOR MAN

[From *The Theosophist*, April, 1884.]

[The following is a comment by Dâmodar on an article by Purmeshri Dass, F. T. S., in its turn commenting on an article in *The Theosophist* (Dec., 1883, March, 1884) by Mrs. Anna Kingsford, M. D., F. T. S., entitled "The Best Food For Man." Purmeshri Dass's article takes an even stricter stand than does Mrs. Kingsford herself for the cause of vegetarianism, and criticises her for advising that cheese, milk, butter, and eggs may be properly used to fill out a vegetarian diet. — EDS.]

NOTE.— I beg to remind my brother that Theosophy admits of no dogmatic assertion of the fitness of things; therefore no particular kind of food is ordered imperatively, neither is there any that is "forbidden" or "prohibited" in the strict sense of the terms. The Occultist, after careful investigation of all the facts and circumstances of the *whole* case and their impartial consideration with a broad and enlightened vision, *recommends* a certain course of action as the best. He always takes his stand in the middle, and, surveying the lines pointing to the extremities, comes to a decision. There are people who argue that destruction is the order of the universe, that everywhere we see one creature preying upon another, itself being the food of a third, and that it is therefore perfectly natural for people to kill animals for food. There are others who say that everywhere is to be seen in nature a feeling of love, an affection — the

mother taking care of the children and so on. Therefore no life should be destroyed. There are not a few
who say that they use animal food merely because
they find animals already dead or killed, but that on
no account would they allow slaughter intended solely
for themselves. A dispassionate consideration of these
three arguments is now necessary. The first class show
that they have not risen above their animal nature.
Otherwise they would see that this beastly tendency,
this desire for the assimilation of animal food with
their physical frames, has the effect of chaining them
down to a physical plane from the meshes of which
no rising is possible unless a more human feeling begins to assert itself. The latent spark of this noble
feeling is inherent in animals too, for if they did not
have it, they would not feel that tenderness towards
their young which they manifest. This class, therefore, we must leave out of consideration for the present. The sophistry of the third class is self-evident.
Our answer to them is that they must remember that
an appreciable decrease in the number of flesh eaters
must have the effect of lessening the number of slaught-
ered animals. If they use the flesh of dead animals,
they may just as well be asked to follow the example
of the Chinese who do not spare the flesh of dead persons. We must now divert our attention to the second
class. If the theory that no life should be destroyed
be carried to its legitimate extent, the very existence
of man would become impossible, for even the air he
breathes is full of animalculae, which he must inhale
when the respiratory process is in operation. Nay —

we can go still further: the ONE LIFE permeates *all;* each and every atom has latent life in it, and therefore every atom we displace in our movements is an injury to life. The great problem is how to get out of this difficulty. The Occultist recognises the important fact that everything in nature progresses gradually and nothing is achieved by starts or jumps. At the same time he realises that destruction and creation are relative and interchangeable terms, since destruction relates only to form — the substance remaining always permanent — and that the destruction of one form is the creation of another. These relative ideas therefore cease, when the phenomenal and the noumenal are blended together into THE ONE SUBSTANCE. The aim of the Occult Student is therefore to gradually progress on the path of perfection, so that he may get out of this world of forms and be merged into the ARUPI TOTALITY. This is not the work of a day, nor of a few years, but of *ages.* He therefore gradually by a special training induces in himself such conditions as would enable him to rise higher and higher on the path of perfection. He does nothing violently: he only anticipates, by his knowledge, the usually slow processes of Nature, and he conforms his mode of living to the then conditions of his existence, bearing also in mind that it is but temporary since a higher state of existence requires a better mode. The neophyte gradually leaves off eating until he reaches a stage where no food is necessary. And the ultimate stage is that where all relativity ceases and he identifies himself with the ABSOLUTE EXISTENCE. So long, therefore,

as we are in the phenomenal world, we cannot but
guide our actions by the law of relativity and have
always to make a choice between two evils. A true
philosopher, one who has put himself *en-rapport* with
his *Buddhi,* makes the right choice. It is for this
reason that Occult Science is useful. It gives its votaries a right sense of discrimination and enables them
to adopt only that course which would not come in
the way of progress, while ordinary humanity, engulfed
in the trammels of *Avidya,* gropes in the dark and
many a time does exactly the opposite of what may
be conducive to progress. This should not be assumed
to mean an occultist is infallible; but by his superior
knowledge he is in a better position to do what is right
than one whose perceptions are clouded by *Maya.*
This explanation, I believe, is sufficient to show that
*no hard and fast rules can be laid down for general
guidance.* There is an infinite gradation of progress
towards the ABSOLUTE, where alone all difference can
come to an end. As regards the use of animal food,
the answer to the first class of men under consideration covers the point.   D. K. M.

EXPLANATION WANTED

[From *The Theosophist*, May, 1884.]

A FEW years ago I was visiting some relatives in Z. . . . Switzerland, one evening there was a social gathering at our house, and it was proposed to try to hold a circle. The Protestant minister who was present objected, but his objection was overruled, and the table began to tip. The spirit (?), on being asked its name, gave that of a seamstress, who had died only shortly before. On hearing this name every one began to laugh, because the said seamstress had been a very queer and eccentric person; but soon this hilarity was followed by a more serious mood, because on being asked where she was, she (the spirit) said that she was in hell. She then related that she had poisoned her mother, gave the name of the poison, the name of the place where it was bought, and other detailed circumstances. She also gave the particulars of her own burial and the text of the funeral sermon; but this part of the communication can be explained by the presence of the identical minister who preached it.

However there was no suspicion about her mother's death having been an unnatural one; but public opinion, being aroused by this spirit communication, it provoked enquiry and investigation. The body was exhumed and examined, the poison was found, the purchase of the same traced to the indicated chemist shop, and the story corroborated in every detail.

A. v. H. . . .

Note.— The corroboration of the facts concerning
the murder of the communicating spirit's mother will
perhaps be taken by some as a proof that it was a
"genuine *spirit*" communication. Let us see, however,
if any other explanation, more reasonable and scientific,
can be given. It has been stated on the authority of
our occult doctrines that in the case of ordinary humanity, the *shell* (composed of the fourth, and the grossest
portion of the fifth, principles) survives the death of
the physical body for a certain period. This period
largely depends upon the *Karma* of the individual,
whether in mental desires or physical acts. Thus it is
not difficult to conceive the possibility that the feeling
of repentance for the horrible act of *matricide* may
have so strongly impressed the dying thought of the
seamstress as to effect for the time being the union
between the fourth and the lower portions of the fifth
principle, wherein reside memory and physical consciousness. The presence of the minister — one of a
class whose whole bent of mind, owing to professional
proclivities, is generally directed towards penitent sin-
ners — and the further fact of his being the very priest
who officiated at her funeral are sufficient to give the
shell a stimulus, if any were needed (since the seamstress had died but a very short time previous to the
seance and consequently hardly needed any) to give
vent to a thought of so oppressive a nature. The con-
fession of the "shell" of the seamstress that she "was
in hell," is enough to show to any thinking mind that
the communicating principle could not have been a
"spirit," and spoke of hell simply because it found the

ready picture of one in the priest's brain.   It is needless to mention here that occultism admits of no orthodox Hell, although evil personalities have their various degrees of mental suffering in the state of *Avitchi*.

D. K. [M. ?]*

---

*[Signed "D. K." but possibly by Djual Khool. — Eds.]

ESOTERIC BUDDHISM AND HINDUISM

[From *The Theosophist,* June, 1884.]

[Note by Dâmodar to an article signed "A Brahman Theosophist" discussing A. P. Sinnett's book *Esoteric Buddhism* in connexion with Hindûism. — EDS.]

NOTE.— We print the above letter as it expresses in courteous language and in an able manner the views of a large number of our Hindu brothers. At the same time it must be stated that the name of *Esoteric Buddhism* was given to Mr. Sinnett's latest publication, not because the doctrine propounded therein is meant to be specially identified with any particular form of Faith, but because *Buddhism* means the doctrine of the *Buddhas,* the Wise, *i. e., the* WISDOM-RELIGION. At least that was the understanding on which the name was permitted to be used. We have now only to make one remark in regard to what our correspondent says concerning *Exoteric Hinduism.* The Hindus have devoted ages to a study of religious problems. Hence all possible phases of thought are propounded by different schools. Extreme materialists, positivists, theists, dualists, non-dualists, &c. &c., can, one and all, quote some ancient authority or other in their favour. Hence it is extremely difficult to say whether exoteric Hinduism is nearer the Esoteric Doctrine than any other Faith. One can say that a *particular form* of Hinduism approaches the Occult Doctrine much nearer than any other; and that is all. We must say a few words more. Although the book of Mr. Sinnett employs a Buddhistic phraseology, our correspondent must have noticed that the *Theosophist* almost invariably uses the Vedantic form of expression. Thus readers of the Theosophic literature will see that, although the two Faiths may use different phraseology, the ideas underlying the same are identical.

D. K. M.

THE ASTRAL BODY

[From *The Theosophist*, January, 1885.]

[The following is appended as a footnote to a statement made in an open letter, under the above title, to the Editor of the *Statesman*, and signed "L. S." The statement commented upon by Dâmodar is as follows: ". . . For, let it be understood, the fundamental doctrine of all Theosophic teaching is this,— that there are truths which cannot be reached by our ordinary mental processes; and that there have been, at all times, men, who, by an extraordinary process, which, for the want of a better designation, we shall call psychic, did succeed in grasping, more or less clearly, a portion of those hidden truths. This you have now come to acknowledge in one of your articles of your impression of the 30th instant; but you just behave in this respect, as one of those *who ought to have known long before,* and you tell us now 'that the doctrine is a travesty of a very solemn doctrine taught by the Christian Scriptures, &c.' " —EDS.]

THE correspondent of the *Statesman* might well have retorted by saying that if Theosophy is *supposed* to be "a travesty of a very solemn doctrine taught by the Christian Scriptures," the latter themselves are, not unoften, a very ridiculous caricature of some of the most "solemn" teachings and doctrines inculcated in "Heathen" scriptures of remote antiquity; and that, while the Theosophical Society does not claim to teach any nothing [anything] new but, on the contrary, proclaims its intention of a revival of ancient learning and wisdom, *popular* Christianity, at any rate, pretends to have received a "Revelation" only 1884 years ago, implying thereby that, before that time, there was no such thing as "divine wisdom," or civilization, or learning. The aim of the Theosophical Society is to try to remove such "travesties" from all popular theologies by uniting together their intellectual representatives in the search after "Truth," and thus helping to make religion scientific and science religious. If some of the prominent members of the Theosophical Society had now and then to speak in uncomplimentary terms of exoteric Christianity, it is because the "travesties" of "solemn doctrines" by the latter now and then assume a most offensive form and also because its intolerant spirit manifests itself in a dangerous aspect.   — D. K. M.

IV

Historical

[The material in this chapter is of a varied character, being composed of articles, official reports, editorial notes, letters, etc., either written by or about Dâmodar. They are grouped together solely because of their historical interest. Though arranged chronologically they are not intended to form any particular sequence of events, each item merely giving an interesting glimpse of some aspect of Dâmodar's activities and character. — EDS.]

MADAME BLAVATSKY and COLONEL OLCOTT

[Supplement to *The Theosophist*, December, 1881.]

[The letter to which the following note was appended by Dâmodar was written by Col. Olcott to the Editor of the *Ceylon Times* and is dated October 31, 1881. Olcott replies to the false charges made by the *Bombay Gazette* that he was an impostor, and presents his credentials and testimonials from the United States War, Navy, Treasury, and State Departments, and various other responsible authorities in Washington and New York by whom he had been employed. He had just returned from Tinnevelly where he had addressed large and enthusiastic meetings. Alarm had been aroused by the enemies of Theosophy who published outrageous slanders in the effort to destroy it by vilifying its representatives. Full particulars are given in *The Theosophist* for December, 1881, January, 1882, and in Olcott's semi-autobiographical *Old Diary Leaves.* — EDS.]

A T the same time that our President —who, for a period of nearly three years had abstained from answering his calumniators, wisely treating the anonymous, cowardly slanders with the contempt they merit — was penning the above; and while numerous letters of congratulations from Hindu correspondents and messages full of enthusiasm and gratitude from our Tinnevelly Theosophists were pouring into our office, there appeared a new proof of the insatiable malice of our opponents. That malice and the bitterness of their hatred of the Theosophists have finally reached that degree of blind fury that vitiates the most ordinary perceptions. To lie openly and in the most impudent, shameless manner has become their last expediency. When our readers will have noticed the Official Report of Tinnevelly Branch which follows the present, and a few articles from other correspondents, they will be able to judge for themselves. In a letter from an unknown Tinnevelly correspondent of the *Madras Standard* the following *truthful* statement is given:—"The natives of this place" writes the informer, "are very sorry for all the hubbub and commotion caused by the arrival of Colonel Olcott, the Theosophist, among them. *The Branch Society — the members of which invited him here — were very disappointed in their expectations. They now call him 'IMPOSTOR AND PRETENDER' —* to use their own words" . . . !!

By this time our "Branch Society" will have read the above statement. We all sincerely hope our Tinnevelly Brothers will not refuse themselves the satisfaction of pointing out publicly to the "Tinnevelly correspondent of the *Madras Standard*" that the greatest "impostor" is that man who, taking advantage of the voice of the press, imposes upon the public barefaced LIES under the guise of news; "that the term 'pretender,'" is to be applied only to individuals of his stamp, who *pretending* to the name of a "correspondent" have a right but to that of a "penny-a-line" slanderer, whose lies would disgrace any respectable paper. A very reliable organ — as a source of information — is the *Madras Standard* — we see!

DAMODAR K. MAVALANKAR,
Joint Recording Secretary,
Parent Theosophical Society.

LETTER No. XXXVII*

[Received at Allahabad, January, 1882.]

. . . In conclusion Master sends you His best wishes and praying you may not forget Him, orders me to sign myself, your obedient servant,

THE "DISINHERITED."

P.S. Should you desire to write to Him though unable to answer Himself Master will receive your letters with pleasure; you can do so through D. K. Mavalankar.   "DD."

THE WORK OF THE THEOSOPHICAL SOCIETY

THE BOMBAY THEOSOPHICAL SOCIETY

[Supplement to *The Theosophist*, March, 1882.]

SINCE the President-Founder's return from Ceylon, there has been a sudden increase of interest among the members, and an unusual number of fresh initiations. The meeting-hall at the Head-quarters has twice been decorated with flowers, palms, and flags: the first time when some of our Australian brothers were received, and the second, on the evening of January 11, when H. H. Daji Raja, Thakore Sahib of Wadhwan, his Dewan Ganpatrao Laud, Esq., and Rawal Shree

---

*[From *The Mahatma Letters to A. P. Sinnett.* — EDS.]

Hurreesingjee Roopsingjee, of Sihore, cousin of H. H. the Thakore Sahib of Bhavnagar — all members of our Society — attended. His Highness of Wadhwan is President of the Saorashtr Theosophical Society, and his companions are members. All take a deep interest in our work, especially that part which is connected with the study of arcane science. The two young nobles have, by their affability and lack of all pretentiousness, won the sincere regard of their Bombay brothers. The floral and other decorations on both occasions reflected great credit upon the taste of Fellows, Monsieur and Madame Coulomb, who kindly took entire charge of the affair.

The preliminary business of the meeting having been transacted, nine candidates for fellowship were then ushered in by their respective sponsors. In a short and impressive speech delivered by the President-Founder, Colonel Olcott, he explained, to the audience, the noble aims of the Society, dwelt at length upon the grandeur of the idea of Universal Brotherhood, the importance of the culture of Oriental Science and Philosophy, and lastly upon the necessity of the diligence, zeal and co-operation of the members.

He then conducted the initiation ceremony. All this occupied about an hour and a half. At the request of the President-Founder, Mr. K. M. Shroff, the Councillor of the Parent body, one of the most energetic fellows of the Society, addressed the meeting, explaining to the members to their entire satisfaction, certain phenomenal occurrences that had recently come under his personal observation and had also been witnessed by His Highness Daji Raja Chandrasingji, the Raja's Dewan and by Rawal Shree Harreesinghji of Sihore, and a few others.

His Highness the Raja of Wadhwan was then introduced to the meeting by Dr. D. E. Dudley, President of the Bombay Branch, and a formal reception was given by the Society to His Highness. After all the members present, had been introduced to His Highness by Messrs. Shroff and Banàji, the Secretary of the Bombay Branch, the Thakore Sahib made a short speech in English and then addressed the Brethren in Gujarathi.

H. H., our distinguished visitor, who is the Vice-President of the Parent Theosophical Society, is also President of the Saorashtr Branch.

The meeting was then adjourned. Still more applications having been received, another meeting was held on the 16th of February.

DÂMODAR K. MÂVALANKAR,
Joint Recording Secretary,
Parent Theosophical Society.

PERSONAL ITEMS

[Supplement to *The Theosophist*, August, 1882.]

MR. DAMODAR K. MAVALANKAR, F. T. S., the Manager of the THEOSOPHIST and the Recording Secretary of the Parent Theosophical Society, has gone to Poona for a month or two, to take some needed rest. The health of our self-sacrificing young Brother had become very delicate of late, owing to bigoted persecutions and an injudicious overwork undertaken out of pure devotion to the cause of theosophy, than which there is nothing dearer to him in this world. Very happily he has been prevailed upon to change for the monsoon season the damp killing atmosphere of Bombay for the drier and far cooler climate of Poona. Mr. A. D. Ezekiel, F. T. S., has kindly offered the invalid a brotherly hospitality in his house, and volunteered to take every care of him during his stay at that city. We hope a month of quiet rest and the sympathetic circle of his friends and Brother-Fellows will do him a deal of good. Theosophy reckons few such unselfish — and none more ardent — workers for her cause than Mr. Damodar K. Mavalankar, our Recording Secretary. . . .

[An unsigned editorial note. — EDS.]

A PROTEST

[From *The Theosophist*, September, 1882]

[This 'Protest' is in answer to an article signed "H. X." and entitled "C. C. M." AND "ISIS UNVEILED," being a letter by Mr. A. O. Hume addressed to H. P. Blavatsky in which he frankly and bluntly declares his real attitude towards Theosophy and the Mahâtmans. His haughty and cynical language roused the Hindû chelas to furious indignation. In an editorial note H. P. Blavatsky mentions that she publishes the letter at the request of the Masters themselves. The subject is treated at length in *The Mahatma Letters to A. P. Sinnett*, pages 292-3.
— EDS.]

WE, the undersigned, the "Accepted" and "Probationary" Hindu *Chelas* of the HIMALAYAN BROTHERS, their disciples in India, and Northern Cashmere, respectfully claim our right to protest against the tone used in the above article, and the bold criticisms of H. X. — a *lay* Chela. No one who has once offered himself as a pupil has any right to openly criticise and blame our MASTERS simply upon his own unverified hypotheses, and thus to prejudge the situation. And, we respectfully maintain that it befits ill one, to whom positively *exceptional* favours were shown, to drag their personalities as unceremoniously before the public as he would any other class of men.

Belonging, as we do, to the so-called "inferior" Asiatic race, we cannot help having for our Masters that boundless devotion which the European condemns as *slavish*. The Western races would however do well to remember that if some of the poor Asiatics arrived at such a height of knowledge regarding the mysteries of nature, it was only due to the fact that the Chelas have always blindly followed the dictates of their Masters and have never set themselves higher than, or even as high as, their Gurus. The result was that sooner or later they were rewarded for their devotion, according to their respective capacities and merits by those who, owing to years of self-sacrifice and devotion to *their* Gurus, had in their turn become ADEPTS. We think that our blessed MASTERS ought to be the best judges how to impart instruction. Most of us have seen and know them personally, while two of the undersigned live with the venerated MAHATMAS, and therefore know how much of their powers is used for the good and well-being of Humanity. And if, for reasons of their own, which we know must be good and wise, our Gurus abstain from communicating "to the world all the knowledge they possess" it is no reason why "lay Chelas" who know yet so little about them should call it "a sin" and assume upon themselves the right of remonstrating with, and teaching them publicly what they imagine to be their duty. Nor does that fact that they are "educated European gentlemen" — alter the case. Moreover our learned Brother, who complains of receiving so little from our MASTERS, seems to lose sight of the, to him unimportant, fact that Europeans, no less than natives, ought to feel thankful for even such "crumbs of knowledge" as they may get, since it is not our MASTERS who have first offered their instruction, but we ourselves who, craving, repeatedly beg for it. Therefore, however indisputably clever and highly able, from a literary and intellectual stand-point, H. X.'s letter, its writer must not feel surprised to find that, overlooking all its cleverness, we natives discern in it, foremost and above all, an imperious spirit of domineering — utterly foreign to our natures — a spirit that would dictate its own laws even to those who can never come under *any one's* sway. No less painfully are we impressed by the utter absence in the letter, we are now protesting against, of any grateful acknowledgment even for the little that has confessedly been done.

In consequence of the above given reasons, we, the undersigned, pray our Brothers of the THEOSOPHIST to give room in their Journal to our PROTEST.

DEVA MUNI . · . · .

PARAMAHANSA SHUB-TUNG . · . · . · .

T. SUBBA ROW, B. A. B. L., F. T. S.. · . · . · .

DARBHAGIRI NATH, F. T. S.

S. RAMASWAMIER, B. A., F. T. S.

GUALA K. DEB, F. T. S.

NOBIN K. BANERJRE, F. T. S.

T. T. GURUDAS, F. T. S.

BHOLA DEVA SARMA, F. T. S.

S. T. K. . . . . CHARY, F. T. S.

GARGYA DEVA, F. T. S.

DAMODAR K. MAVALANKAR, F. T. S.

HOW A "CHELA" FOUND HIS "GURU"*

(Being Extracts from a private letter to Damodar
K. Mavalankar, Joint-Recording Secretary of the
Theosophical Society.)

[From *The Theosophist*, December, 1882.]

. . . WHEN we met last at Bombay I told you
what had happened to me at Tinnevelly.
My health having been disturbed by official work and
worry, I applied for leave on medical certificate and
it was duly granted. One day in September last, while
I was reading in my room, I was ordered by the audible
voice of my blessed Guru, M——— Maharsi, to leave
all and proceed immediately to Bombay, whence I had
to go in search of Madame Blavatsky wherever I
could find her and follow her wherever she went. Without losing a moment, I closed up all my affairs and left
the station. For the tones of that voice are to me the
divinest sound in nature; its commands imperative
I travelled in my ascetic robes. Arrived at Bombay,
I found Madame Blavatsky gone, and learned through
you that she had left a few days before; that she was
very ill; and that, beyond the fact that she had left
the place very suddenly with a *Chela*, you knew nothing
of her whereabouts. And now, I must tell you what
happened to me after I had left you.

Really not knowing whither I had best go, I took

---

*Published by permission. [ED. of *The Theosophist*.]

a through ticket to Calcutta; but, on reaching Allahabad, I heard the same well-known voice directing me to go to Berhampore. At Azimgunge, in the train, I met, most *providentially* I may say, with some Babus (I did not then know they were also Theosophists since I had never seen any of them), who were also in search of Madame Blavatsky. Some had traced her to Dinapore, but lost her track and went back to Berhampore. They knew, they said, she was going to Tibet and wanted to throw themselves at the feet of the Mahatmas to permit them to accompany her. At last, as I was told, they received from her a note, informing them to come if they so desired it, but that she herself was prohibited from going to Tibet just now. She was to remain, she said, in the vicinity of Darjeeling and would see the BROTHERS on the Sikkhim Territory, where they would not be allowed to follow her. . . . Brother Nobin, the President of the Adhi Bhoutic Bhratru Theosophical Society, would not tell me where Madame Blavatsky was, or perhaps did not then know it himself. Yet he and others had risked all in the hope of seeing the Mahatmas. On the 23rd at last, I was brought by Nobin Babu from Calcutta to Chandernagore where I found Madame Blavatsky, ready to start, five minutes after, with the train. A tall, dark-looking hairy *Chela* (not Chunder Cusho), but a Tibetan I suppose by his dress, whom I met after I had crossed the river with her in a boat, told me that I had come too late, that Madame Blavatsky had already seen the Mahatmas and that he had brought her back. He would not listen to my supplications

to take me with him, saying he had no other orders
than what he had already executed, namely — to take
her about 25 miles, beyond a certain place he named
to me and that he was now going to see her safe to the
station, and return. The Bengalee brother-Theoso-
phists had also traced and followed her, arriving at
the station half an hour later. They crossed the river
from Chandernagore to a small railway station on the
opposite side. When the train arrived, she got into
the carriage, upon entering which I found the *Chela!*
And, before even her own things could be placed in
the van, the train, against all regulations and before the
bell was rung — started off, leaving Nobin Babu, the
Bengalees and her servant, behind. Only one Babu
and the wife and daughter of another — all Theosophists and candidates for *Chelaship* — had time to get
in. I myself had barely the time to jump in, into the
last carriage. All her things — with the exception of
her box containing the Theosophical correspondence —
were left behind together with her servant. Yet, even
the persons that went by the same train with her, did
not reach Darjeeling. Babu Nobin Banerjee, with
the servant, arrived five days later; and they who had
time to take their seats, were left five or six stations
behind, owing to another unforseen accident (?) at
another further place, reaching Darjeeling also a few
days later! It requires no great stretch of imagination
to know that Madame Blavatsky had been or was,
perhaps, being again taken to the BROTHERS, who, for
some good reasons best known to them, did not want
us to be following and watching her. Two of the Ma-

hatmas, I had learned for a certainty, were in the neighbourhood of British territory; and one of them was seen and recognised — by a person I need not name here — as a high *Chutuktu* of Tibet.

The first days of her arrival Madame Blavatsky was living at the house of a Bengalee gentleman, a Theosophist; was refusing to see any one; and preparing, as I thought, to go again somewhere on the borders of Tibet. To all our importunities we could get only this answer from her: that we had no business *to stick to and follow her,* that she did not want us, and that she had no right to disturb the Mahatmas, with all sorts of questions that concerned only the questioners, for they knew their own business best. In despair, *I determined, come what might,** to cross the frontier which is about a dozen miles from here, and find the Mahatmas, or — Die. I never stopped to think that what I was going to undertake would be

---

*I call the especial attention of certain of my anxious correspondents to this expression, and in fact to Mr. Ramaswamier's whole adventure. It will show the many grumblers and sceptics who have been complaining to me so bitterly that the Brothers have given them no sign of their existence, what sort of spirit it is which draws the Adepts to an aspirant. The too common notions, that the mere joining of our Society gives any *right* to occult instruction, and that an inert sentimental desire for light should be rewarded, arise from the lamentable ignorance which now prevails with respect to the laws of mystical training. Gurus there are now, as there have always been in the past; and now as heretofore, the true Chela can find among them one who will take him under his care, if like our Tinnevelly Brother he has determined "to find the Mahatmas or — die!"
— D. K. Mavalankar

regarded as the rash act of a lunatic. I neither spoke nor did I understand one word of either Bengalee, Urdu, or Nepaulese, nor of the Bhootan, or Tibetan languages. I had no permission, no "pass" from the Sikkhim Rajah, and yet was decided to penetrate into the heart of an independent State where, if anything happened, the Anglo-Indian officials would not — if even they could — protect me, since I would have crossed over without their permission. But I never even gave that a thought, but was bent upon one engrossing *idea* — to find and see my Guru. Without breathing a word of my intentions to any one, one morning, namely, October 5, I set out in search of the Mahatma. I had an umbrella, and a pilgrim's staff for sole weapons, with a few rupees in my purse. I wore the yellow garb and cap. Whenever I was tired on the road, my costume easily procured for me for a small sum a pony to ride. The same afternoon I reached the banks of the Rungit River, which forms the boundary between the British and Sikkhim territories. I tried to cross it by the aërial suspension bridge constructed of canes, but it swayed to and fro to such an extent that I, who have never known in my life, what hardship was could not stand it. I crossed the river by the ferry-boat and this even not without much danger and difficulty. That whole afternoon I travelled on foot, penetrating further and further into the heart of the Sikkhim territory, along a narrow footpath. I cannot now say how many miles I travelled before dusk, but I am sure it was not less than twenty or twenty-five miles. Throughout, I saw nothing but

impenetrable jungles and forests on all sides of me, relieved at very long intervals by solitary huts belonging to the mountain population. At dusk I began to
search around me for a place to rest in at night. I
met on the road, in the afternoon, a leopard and a wild
cat; and I am astonished now to think how I should
have felt no fear then nor tried to run away. Throughout, some secret influence supported me. Fear or
anxiety never once entered my mind. Perhaps in my
heart there was room for no other feeling but an intense anxiety to find my *Guru*. When it was just
getting dark, I espied a solitary hut a few yards from
the roadside. To it I directed my steps in the hope of
finding a lodging. The rude door was locked. The
cabin was untenanted at the time. I examined it on
all sides and found an aperture on the western side.
It was small indeed, but sufficient for me to jump
through. It had a small shutter and a wooden bolt.
By a strange coincidence of circumstances the hill-
man had forgotten to fasten it on the inside when he
locked the door! Of course, after what has subsequently transpired I now, through the eye of faith, see
the protecting hand of my *Guru* everywhere around
me. Upon getting inside I found the room communicated, by a small doorway, with another apartment,
the two occupying the whole space of this sylvan mansion. I lay down, concentrating my every thought upon
my *Guru* as usual, and soon fell into a profound sleep.
Before I went to rest, I had secured the door of the
other room and the single window. It may have been
between ten and eleven, or perhaps a little later, that I

awoke and heard sounds of footsteps in the adjoining
room. I could plainly distinguish two or three people
talking together in a dialect that to me was no better
than gibberish. Now, I cannot recall the same without a shudder. At any moment they might have entered from the other room and murdered me for my
money. Had they mistaken me for a burglar the same
fate awaited me. These and similar thoughts crowded
into my brain in an inconceivably short period. But
my heart did not palpitate with fear, nor did I for one
moment think of the possibly tragical chances of the
thing! I know not what secret influence held me fast,
but nothing could put me out or make me fear; I was
perfectly calm. Although I lay awake and staring
into darkness for upwards of two hours, and even
paced the room softly and slowly, without making
any noise, to see if I could make my escape, in case
of need, back to the forest, by the same way I had
effected my entrance into the hut — no fear, I repeat,
or any such feeling ever entered my heart. I recom-
posed myself to rest. After a sound sleep, undisturbed
by any dream, I woke and found it was just dawning.
Then I hastily put on my boots, and cautiously got
out of the hut through the same window. I could hear
the snoring of the owners of the hut in the other room.
But I lost no time and gained the path to Sikkhim
(the city) and held on my way with unflagged zeal.
From the inmost recesses of my heart I thanked my
revered *Guru* for the protection he had vouchsafed me
during the night. What prevented the owners of the
hut from penetrating to the second room? What kept

me in the same serene and calm spirit, as if I were in
a room of my own house? What could possibly make
me sleep so soundly under such circumstances,— enormous, dark forests on all sides abounding in wild
beasts, and a party of cut-throats — as most of the
Sikkhimese are said to be — in the next room with an
easy and rude door between them and me?

When it became quite light, I wended my way on
through hills and dales. Riding or walking, the paths
I followed are not a pleasant journey for any man,
unless he be, I suppose, as deeply engrossed in thought
as I was then myself, and quite oblivious to anything
affecting the body. I have cultivated the power of
mental concentration to such a degree of late that, on
many an occasion, I have been able to make myself
quite oblivious of anything around me when my mind
was wholly bent upon the one object of my life, as
several of my friends will testify; but never to such
an extent as in this instance.

It was, I think, between eight and nine A. M. and I
was following the road to the town of Sikkhim whence,
I was assured by the people I met on the road, I could
cross over to Tibet easily in my pilgrim's garb, when
I suddenly saw a solitary horseman galloping towards
me from the opposite direction. From his tall stature
and the expert way he managed the animal, I thought
he was some military officer of the Sikkhim Rajah.
Now, I thought, am I caught! He will ask me for
my pass and what business I have on the independent
territory of Sikkhim, and, perhaps, have me arrested
and — sent back, if not worse. But — as he ap-

proached me, he reined the steed. I looked at and recognised him instantly . . . I was in the awful presence of him, of the same Mahatma, my own revered *Guru* whom I had seen before in his astral body, on the balcony of the Theosophical Headquarters!* It was he, the "Himalayan BROTHER" of the ever memorable night of December last, who had so kindly dropped a letter in answer to one I had given in a sealed envelope to Madame Blavatsky — whom I had never for one moment during the interval lost sight of — but an hour or so before! The very same instant saw me prostrated on the ground at his feet. I arose at his command and, leisurely looking into his face, I forgot myself entirely in the contemplation of the image I knew so well, having seen his portrait (the one in Colonel Olcott's possession) a number of times. I knew not what to say: joy and reverence tied my tongue. The majesty of his countenance, which seemed to me to be the *impersonation* of power and thought, held me rapt in awe. I was at last face to face with "the Mahatma of the Himavat" and he was no myth, no "creation of the imagination of a *medium*," as some sceptics suggested. It was no night dream; it is between nine and ten o'clock of the forenoon. There is the sun shining and silently witnessing the scene from above. I see HIM before me in flesh and blood; and he speaks to me in accents of kindness and gentleness. What more do I want? My excess of happiness made me

*I refer the reader to Mr. Ramaswamier's letter in *Hints on Esoteric Theosophy*, pp. 72 and 73, for a clearer comprehension of the highly important circumstance he refers to. — D. K. M.

dumb. Nor was it until a few moments later that I was drawn to utter a few words, encouraged by his gentle tone and speech. His complexion is not as fair as that of Mahatma Koot Hoomi; but never have I seen a countenance so handsome, a stature so tall and so majestic. As in his portrait, he wears a short black beard, and long black hair hanging down to his breast; only his dress was different. Instead of a white, loose robe he wore a yellow mantle lined with fur, and, on his head, instead of a *pagri*, a yellow Tibetan felt cap, as I have seen some Bhootanese wear in this country. When the first moments of rapture and surprise were over and I calmly comprehended the situation, I had a long talk with him. He told me to go no further, for I would come to grief. He said I should wait patiently if I wanted to become an accepted *Chela;* that many were those who offered themselves as candidates, but that only a very few were found worthy; none were rejected — but all of them tried, and most found to fail signally, especially — and —. Some, instead of being accepted and pledged this year, were now thrown off for a year. . . . The Mahatma, I found, speaks very little English — or at least it so seemed to me — and *spoke to me in my mother-tongue — Tamil.* He told me that if the *Chohan* permitted Mdme. B. to go to Pari-jong next year, then I could come with her. . . . The Bengalee Theosophists who followed the "Upasika" (Madame Blavatsky) would see that she was right in trying to dissuade them from following her now. I asked the blessed Mahatma whether I could tell what I saw and heard to others.

He replied in the affirmative, and that moreover I would do well to write to you and describe all. . . . .

I must impress upon your mind the whole situation and ask you to keep well in view that what I *saw* was not the mere "appearance" only, the astral body of the Mahatma, as we saw him at Bombay, but the *living man, in his own physical body.* He was pleased to say when I offered my farewell *namaskarams* (prostration) that he approached the British Territory to see the Upasika. . . Before he left me, two more men came on horseback, his attendants I suppose, probably *Chelas,* for they were dressed like *lama-gylongs,* and both, like himself, with long hair streaming down their backs. They followed the Mahatma, as he left, at a gentle trot. For over an hour I stood gazing at the place that he had just quitted, and then, I slowly retraced my steps. Now it was that I found for the first time that my long boots had pinched me in my leg in several places, that I had eaten nothing since the day before, and that I was too weak to walk further. My whole body was aching in every limb. At a little distance I saw petty traders with country ponies, taking burden. I hired one of these animals. In the afternoon I came to the Rungit River and crossed it. A bath in its cool waters renovated me. I purchased some fruits in the only bazar there and ate them heartily. I took another horse immediately and reached Darjeeling late in the evening. I could neither eat, nor sit, nor stand. Every part of my body was aching. My absence had seemingly alarmed Madame Blavatsky. She scolded me for my rash and mad attempt

to try to go to Tibet after this fashion. When I
entered the house I found with Madame Blavatsky,
Babu Parbati Churn Roy, Deputy Collector of Settlements and Superintendent of Dearah Survey, and his
Assistant, Babu Kanty Bhushan Sen, both members
of our Society. At their prayer and Madame Blavatsky's command, I recounted all that had happened to
me, reserving of course my private conversation with
the Mahatma. . . . They were all, to say the least,
astounded! . . . After all, she will not go this year
to Tibet; for which I am sure she does not care,
since she saw our Masters, thus effecting her only
object. But we, unfortunate people! We lose our
only chance of going and offering our worship to the
"Himalayan Brothers" who — I *know* — will not soon
cross over to British Territory, if ever again.

I write to you this letter, my dearest Brother, in
order to show how right we were in protesting against
"H. X.'s" letter in the THEOSOPHIST. The ways of
the Mahatmas may appear, to our limited vision,
strange and unjust, even cruel — as in the case of our
Brothers here, the Bengalee Babus, some of whom are
now laid up with cold and fever and perhaps murmur-
ing against the BROTHERS, forgetting that they never
asked or personally permitted them to come, but that
they had themselves acted very rashly. . . .

And now that I have seen the Mahatma in the
flesh, and heard his living voice, let no one dare say
to me that the BROTHERS *do not* exist. Come now
whatever will, death has no fear for me, nor the ven-
geance of enemies; for what I know, I KNOW!

You will please show this to Colonel Olcott who first opened my eyes to the *Gnana Marga*, and who will be happy to hear of the success (more than I deserve) that has attended me. I shall give him details in person.

S. RAMASWAMIER, F. T. S.

Darjeeling, October 7, 1882.

[See *The Mahatma Letters to A. P. Sinnett*, Letter CIX, page 444. — EDS.]

A MEETING AT ADYAR

FOR THE PRESENTATION OF A SILVER CUP AND TRAY
TO THE FOUNDERS OF THE THEOSOPHICAL SOCIETY
BY THE MEMBERS OF ITS BOMBAY BRANCH

[Supplement to *The Theosophist*, April, 1883.]

THE address of our Brothers at Bombay to the Founders on the eve of the latter's departure from that place to Madras, published on page 8 of the *Supplement* to the *Theosophist* for January last, must have been read with interest by our members.

The sentiments in the address, expressive of the loyalty of our Bombay Branch to the cause of Theosophy and their determination to assist its furtherance are no doubt very gratifying. The expressions therein made use of, are but the indicators of the feelings which our friends at Bombay entertain for the Founders who, whatever their shortcomings, are yet zealously and earnestly working for the IDEA, the promotion and propagation of which has been the chief end and aim of their life. It is but natural, therefore, that the temporary separation, caused by the removal of our Head-Quarters to this place, should evoke an outburst of those feelings in the shape of an address and some other token of fraternal regard and esteem felt for the Founders by their Bombay friends. The latter, therefore, proposed in the "Address" to offer for the acceptance of the Founders, "an article of Indian

make, with a suitable inscription," as a token of their
"sense of appreciation of your labour of love, and as
a keepsake from us." As the article was not then ready,
its presentation had to be deferred. It is, therefore,
after we arrived here, that the Madras Theosophical Society was specially requested by their Bombay
Brothers to present on behalf of their Branch, to the
Founders, a silver cup and tray of Indian make,
specially designed for the purpose. A meeting was accordingly convened on the evening of the 15th February, when M. R. Ry. P. Sreenevas Row Pantulu Garu,
Judge of the Small Cause Court, and one of the Vice-
Presidents of the Madras Branch, made a short speech,
on behalf of our Brothers at Bombay, and presented,
in the name of the latter, the articles to the Founders.
The President-Founder, Col. Olcott, on behalf of Madame Blavatsky and himself, made a suitable reply.
His speech was very impressive and infused vigour and
spirit into the audience. He gave a short sketch of
the working of the Theosophical Society and thanked
the Bombay brothers for the kind and fraternal feelings
which had actuated them. M. R. Ry. T. Subba Row
Garu, Secretary of the Madras Branch, then made a
few remarks upon the subject of Occultism, which were
very interesting and instructive. M. R. Ry. G. Muttu-
swamy Chettyar Garu, Judge of the Small Cause
Court, and one of the Vice-Presidents of the Branch,
also addressed the meeting. After a few more desul-
tory speeches, the meeting was dissolved.

The Founders beg to take this opportunity of
expressing again their deep and sincere feeling of

gratitude for this new token of the fraternal regard entertained for them by their Parsi and Marathi Brothers of Bombay. The article is of exquisite make and bears the following inscription:—

PRESENTED

to

COL. OLCOTT

and

MADAME BLAVATSKY

by the

Bombay Branch

THEOSOPHICAL SOCIETY.

It will ever remain in the Head-Quarters Hall as a token of the appreciation of the humble efforts of the Founders for the good of India, alongside with the beautiful Silver Plate presented to them by the Rohil-khand Theosophical Society — the Bareilly Branch.

(By Order)

DAMODAR K. MAVALANKAR,

Recording Secretary of the

Parent Theosophical Society.

A PSYCHOLOGICAL PHENOMENON*

[From *The Theosophist*, December, 1883.]

WE have much pleasure to be able to lay before the public a remarkable psychological phenomenon, as interesting as it is well authenticated. On November 10th, a European gentleman attached to the Theosophical Head Quarters was engaged in some work in a room adjoining that of Madame Blavatsky, when he heard a voice, which he believed was that of Mr. D — K — M, an officer of the Parent Society, speaking to Madame Blavatsky in her room. As this young man had, to that gentleman's knowledge, left the Head Quarters some weeks previously to join Col. Olcott at Poona, he naturally thought at the time that he had come back and so entered Madame Blavatsky's room to greet the officer in question on his return. But fancy his surprise when on entering the room he found that D — K — M was nowhere to be seen; and his surprise positively grew up to amazement when on enquiring he found that, though this young Brahman was at the moment at Moradabad, N. W. P., yet Madame Blavatsky who was then standing looking very much perplexed, before the shrine setting it in order, had also not only heard that chela's voice, but assured the gentleman that she had a message from

---

*[An unsigned article. — Eds.]

D — K — M, which was of great importance — the words of which *she* was asked to repeat by telegram. She immediately proceeded to have them wired to Moradabad and the message was sent. In the evening, General and Mrs. Morgan from Ooty, Miss Flynn from Bombay, Mr. Mohini Mohan Chatterji from Calcutta, and others then on a visit at Adyar, talked the matter over a good deal, all expressing surprise and intense curiosity as to how far the phenomenon would be verified.

With these prefatory remarks we may safely leave the following documents to speak for themselves and invite our Spiritualistic friends to explain away the occurrence on their orthodox theories. These documents were received from Moradabad five days later:—

"On the evening of November 10, Mr. D — K — M — having at the request of Mr. Shankar Sing of Moradabad promised to ask the Mahatmas whether Col. Olcott would be permitted to treat mesmerically two children, in whom Shankar Sing was interested, and having at his request gone to the Adyar Head-quarters in the *Shukshma sarira* (astral body) told us that he had received a message at the Adyar "Shrine"; at the same time he also said that he had asked Madame Blavatsky to give Col. Olcott a confirmation of his visit as well as of the order received through the shrine from Col. Olcott's *guru* by sending a telegram to him, D — K — M. or Shankar Sing; after which he reported (4-50 P. M.,) its substance in these words:—
"*Henry can try the parties once, leaving strongly*

mesmerised Cajaputti *oil to rub three times daily to relieve sufferers.* Karma *cannot be interfered.*"

(Signed) Shankar Sing.	(Signed) Narottam Dass.
(") Pundit B. Sankar.	(") L. Venkata Varada-rajulu Naidu.
(") W. T. Brown.	(") Toke Narainasamy Naidu.
(") Purmeshri Dass.	(") Chiranjee Lall.
(") Parshotham Dass.	(") H. S. Olcott.
(") Ishri Prasad.	(") Pran Nath Pandit.

The telegram mentioned by D — K — M. has just been received (8-45 A. M., November 11th) as a deferred or night message of 34 words, in which the above exact words are repeated. Madame Blavatsky says a "voice from the Shrine" spoke the words, and adds that D — K — M. heard the voice, and the telegram is sent at his request.

Copy of the telegram received from Madame H. P. Blavatsky by Mr. D — K — M.

(Class D)

To Moradabad   From Adyar (Madras)

Words.	Days.	Hours.	Minutes.
49	10	17	15

"To D — K — M.   From
care of Col. Olcott, President   H. P. Blavatsky.
Theosophical Society,

"Voice from Shrine says Henry can try parties once, leaving strongly mesmerized Cajaputti *oil, rub three times daily to relieve suffering.* Karma *cannot be interfered with.* D— *heard voice; telegram sent at his*

request." Noted that the telegram is dated Adyar, 5-15 P. M., or but 25 minutes later than the time when D—K—M.'s psychic message was reported at Moradabad. The two places are 2,281 miles apart.

(Signed)	Ishri Prasad.	(Signed)	Purashotham Dass.
"	W. T. Brown.	"	Chendra Sekhara.
"	H. S. Olcott.	"	Toke Narainasamy Naidu.
"	Pundit Sankar.	"	L. Venkata Varadarajulu Naidu."

Editor's [of *The Theosophist*] *Note.* — Mr. D — K — M. is a chela of hardly 4 years' standing, his remarkable psychic powers having received their development but lately. He is of a very delicate health and lives the life of a regular ascetic. Whenever the phenomenon of the separation of the astral from the physical body takes place, we are told, he falls invariably asleep or into a trance a few minutes before.

[Col. Olcott describes this incident, which happened during his tour in Northern India in 1883. See p. 12 of this volume. — EDS.]

TESTIMONY TO PHENOMENA

[Supplement to *The Theosophist*, December, 1883.]

IN the month of August last having occasion to come to Madras in the absence of Col. Olcott and Madame Blavatsky, I visited the Head Quarters of the Theosophical Society to see a wonderful painting of the Mahatma K. H. kept there in a shrine and daily attended to by the chelas. On arrival at the house I was told that the lady, Madame C—, who had charge of the keys of the shrine, was absent, so I awaited her return. She came home in about an hour, and we proceeded upstairs to open the shrine and inspect the picture. Madame C— advanced quickly to unlock the double doors of the hanging cupboard, and hurriedly threw them open. In so doing she had failed to observe that a china tray inside was on the edge of the shrine and leaning against one of the doors, and when they were opened, down fell the China tray, smashed to pieces on the hard chunam floor. Whilst Madame C— was wringing her hands and lamenting this unfortunate accident to a valuable article of Madame B—'s, and her husband was on his knees collecting the *debris,* I remarked it would be necessary to obtain some China cement and thus try to restore the fragments. Thereupon Monsieur C. was despatched for the same. The broken pieces were carefully collected and placed, tied in a cloth, within the shrine, and the doors locked. Mr. Damodar K.

Mavalankar, the Joint Recording Secretary of the Society, was opposite the shrine, seated on a chair, about ten feet away from it, when after some conversation an idea occurred to me to which I immediately gave expression. I remarked that if the Brothers considered it of sufficient importance, they would easily restore the broken article, if not, they would leave it to the culprits to do so, the best way they could. Five minutes had scarcely elapsed after this remark when Damodar, who during this time seemed wrapped in a reverie — exclaimed, "I think there is an answer." The doors were opened, and sure enough, a small note was found on the shelf of the shrine — on opening which we read "To the small audience present. Madame C— has occasion to assure herself that the Devil is neither so black nor so wicked as he is generally represented; the mischief is easily repaired."—

On opening the cloth the China tray was found to be whole and perfect; not a trace of the breakage to be found on it! I at once wrote across the note, stating that I was present when the tray was broken and immediately restored, dated and signed it, so there should be no mistake in the matter. It may be here observed that Madame C— believes that the many things of a wonderful nature that occur at the Head-Quarters, may be the work of the Devil — hence the playful remark of the Mahatma who came to her rescue. The matter took place in the middle of the day in the presence of four people. I may here remark that a few days before I came into the room in my house just as Madame B— had duplicated a ring of

a lady in a high position, in the presence of my wife
and daughter in broad day-light. The ring was a
sapphire and a valuable one — and the lady has preserved it. On another occasion a note came from the
above lady to my wife and was handed into the draw-
ing-room in the presence of several people. On opening it a message was found written across the note in
the well known characters of the Adept. The question
is how the message got into the note? The lady who
wrote it was perfectly astounded when she saw it —
and could only imagine it was done at her own table
with her own blue pencil.

Whilst on the subject of the shrine I may mention
that it is a small cabinet attached to the wall with
shelves and double doors. The picture of the Mahatma that I came to see, lately given to the Founders
of the Society, is a most marvellous work of art. Not
all the R. A.'s put together could equal such a production. The coloring is simply indescribable. Whether
it has been produced by a brush or photographed,
entirely passes my comprehension. It is simply superb.

H. R. MORGAN, F. T. S.,

OOTACAMUND,   *Major-General.*
2nd November 1883.

A GREAT RIDDLE SOLVED

[From *The Theosophist,* December—January, 1883-4.]

ON my return to the Head-quarters from the North, where I had accompanied Col. Olcott on his Presidential Tour, I learnt with regret and sorrow of further and still more malignant strictures by certain Spiritualists on the claims of the Founders of the Theosophical Society to be in personal relations with the Mahatmas of the sacred Himavat. For me, personally, the problem is of course *now* solved. It being impossible, I shall not even undertake to prove my case to those who, owing to prejudice and misconception, have determined to shut their eyes before the most glaring facts, for none are so blind as those who will not see, as the saying has it. I should at the same time [be] considered to have ill performed my duty were I not to put my facts before those earnest seekers after truth, who by sincere aspiration and devoted study, have been bringing themselves closer and closer to the Occult World. The best way, I believe, to carry conviction to an intelligent mind is to narrate the facts in as plain and simple a way as possible, leaving speculations entirely out of consideration.

At the outset I must state what is known to many of my friends and brothers of the Theosophical Society, viz., that for the last four years I have been the

CHELA of Mr. Sinnett's correspondent.* Now and
then I have had occasion to refer publicly to this fact,
and to the other one of my having seen some of the
other VENERATED MAHATMAS OF THE HIMALAYAS, both
in their astral and *physical* bodies. However all that
I could urge in favour of my point, viz., that these
GREAT MASTERS are not disembodied spirits but living
men — would fail to carry conviction to a Spiritualistic mind blinded by its prejudices and preconceptions.
It has been suggested that either or both of the Founders may be mediums in whose presence forms could be
seen, which are by them mistaken for real living entities. And when I asserted that I had these appearances
even when alone, it was argued that I too was developing into a medium.

In this connection a certain remark by Mr. C. C.
Massey in a letter to *Light* of November 17, is very
suggestive, inasmuch as that gentleman is not only
far from being inimical to us but is a Theosophist of
long standing, bent solely on discovering truth and —
nothing but the truth. The following extract from the
said letter will show how great are the misconceptions
even of some of our own fellow-members:—

"Nevertheless, were it an open question, free from authoritative statement, so that such a suggestion could be made without
offence by one who would, if possible, avoid offence, I should
avow the opinion that these letters, whether they are or are
not the *ipsissima verba* of any adept, were at all events penned
by Madame Blavatsky, or by other accepted *chelas*. At least
I should think that she was a medium for their production, and

---

*[The Mahâtman Koot Hoomi. — EDS.]

not merely for their transmission. The fact that through the kindness of Mr. Sinnett I have been made familiar with the handwriting of the letters, and that it bears not the remotest resemblance to Madame Blavatsky's, would not influence me against that opinion, for reasons which every one acquainted with the phenomena of writing under psychical conditions will appreciate. But *I am bound to admit that there are circumstances connected with the receipt by Mr. Sinnett of other letters signed, 'K. H.' which are as regards those, apparently inconsistent with any instrumentality of Madame Blavatsky herself, whether as medium or otherwise and the handwriting is in both cases the same.*"

Bearing well in mind the italicized portion in the above quotation, I would respectfully invite the Spiritualists to explain the fact of not only myself, but Col. Olcott, Mr. Brown, and other gentlemen having on this tour received severally and on various occasions letters in reply to conversations and questions on the same day or the same hour, sometimes when alone and sometimes in company with others, when Mme. Blavatsky was thousands of miles away; the handwriting in all cases being the same and identical with that of the communications in Mr. Sinnett's possession.

While on my tour with Col. Olcott, several phenomena occurred, — in his presence as well as in his absence — such as immediate answers to questions in my Master's handwriting and over his signature, put by a number of our Fellows, and some of which are referred to in the last number of the *Theosophist,* while others need not be mentioned in a document going into the hands of the profane reader. These occurrences took place before we reached Lahore, where we expected to meet in body my much doubted MAS-TER. *There I was visited by him in body, for three nights consecutively for about three hours every time while I myself retained full consciousness,* and in one case, even went to meet him outside the house. To my knowledge there is no case on the Spiritualistic records of a medium remaining perfectly conscious, and meeting, by previous arrangement, his Spirit-visitor in the compound, re-entering the house with him, offering him a seat and then holding a long converse with the "disembodied spirit" in a way to give him the impression that he is in personal contact with an embodied entity! Moreover HIM whom I saw in person at Lahore was the same I had seen in astral form at the Headquarters of the Theosophical Society, and the same again whom I, in my visions and trances, had seen at His house, thousands of miles off, to reach which in my astral Ego I was permitted, owing, of course, to His direct help and protection. In those instances with my psychic powers hardly developed yet, I had always seen Him as a rather hazy form, although His features were perfectly distinct and their remembrance was profoundly graven on my soul's eye and memory; while now at Lahore, Jummoo, and elsewhere, the impression was utterly different. In former cases, when making *Pranâm* (salutation) my hands passed through his form, while on the latter occasions they met solid garments and flesh. Here I saw *a living man* before me, the same in features, though far more imposing in His general appearance and bearing than Him I had so often looked upon in the portrait in Mme. Blavatsky's

possession and in the one with Mr. Sinnett. I shall
not here dwell upon the fact of His having been cor-
poreally seen by both Col. Olcott and Mr. Brown
separately, for two nights at Lahore, as they can do so
better, each for himself, if they so choose. At Jummoo
again, where we proceeded from Lahore, Mr. Brown
saw Him on the evening of the third day of our arrival
there, and from Him received a letter in His familiar
handwriting, not to speak of His visits to me almost
every day. And what happened the next morning almost every one in Jummoo is aware of. The fact is,
that I had the good fortune of being sent for, and permitted to visit a Sacred *Ashrum* where I remained for
a few days in the blessed company of several of the
much doubted MAHATMAS of Himavat and Their disciples. There I met not only my beloved Gurudeva
and Col. Olcott's Master,* but several others of the
Fraternity, including One of the Highest. I regret the
extremely personal nature of my visit to those thrice
blessed regions prevents my saying more of it. Suffice
it that the place I was permitted to visit is in the
HIMALAYAS, not in any fanciful Summer Land and that
I saw Him in my own *sthula sarira* (physical body)
and found my Master identical with the form I had
seen in the earlier days of my Chelaship. Thus, I saw
my beloved Guru not only as a *living* man, but actually
as a young one in comparison with some other Sadhus
of the blessed company, only far kinder, and not above
a merry remark and conversation at times. Thus on

---

*[The Mahâtman Morya. — EDS.]

the second day of my arrival, after the meal hour I
was permitted to hold an intercourse for over an hour
with my Master. Asked by Him smilingly, what it was
that made me look at Him so perplexed, I asked in my
turn:—"How is it MASTER that some of the members
of our Society have taken into their heads a notion that
you were 'an elderly man,' and that they have even
seen you clairvoyantly looking an old man passed
sixty?" To which he pleasantly smiled and said, that
this latest misconception was due to the reports of a
certain Brahmachari, a pupil of a Vedantic Swami in
the N. W. P.*—who had met last year in Tibet the
chief of a sect, an elderly Lama, who was his (my
Master's) travelling companion at that time. The said
Brahmachari having spoken of the encounter in India,
had led several persons to mistake the Lama for himself. As to his being perceived clairvoyantly as an
"elderly man," that could never be, he added, as *real*
clairvoyance could lead no one into such mistaken
notions; and then he kindly reprimanded me for giving
any importance to the age of a Guru, adding that
appearances were often false, &c. and explaining other
points.

    These are all stern facts and no third course is open
to the reader. What I assert is either true or false. In
the former case, no Spiritualistic hypothesis can hold
good, and it will have to be admitted that the Himalayan Brothers are living men and neither disembodied

---

    *The narrative of this Brahmachari is given and repeated
twice over in our last number. See pp. 83-6, and 98-9 *Theosophist* for Dec.-Jany. [It should be *December*, 1883. — EDS.]

spirits nor the creatures of the over-heated imagination of fanatics. Of course I am fully aware that many will discredit my account, but I write only for the benefit of those few who know me well enough to see in me neither a hallucinated medium nor attribute to me any bad motive, and who have ever been true and loyal to their convictions and to the cause they have so nobly espoused. As for the majority who laugh at, and ridicule, what they have neither the inclination nor the capacity to understand. I hold them in very small account. If these few lines will help to stimulate even one of my brother-Fellows in the Society or one right thinking man outside of it to promote the cause the GREAT MASTERS have imposed upon the devoted heads of the Founders of the Theosophical Society, I shall consider that I have properly performed my duty.

Adyar (Madras) }
7th December, 1883. }

A GREAT RIDDLE SOLVED

[From *The Theosophist*, April, 1884.]

R EFERRING to the article of D. K. M. in the last
issue of the *Theosophist*, headed "A great riddle
solved," in which he says the misconception regarding his Master's appearance "was due to the reports of
a certain Brahmachari, the pupil of the Vedanti Swami
in the N. W. P. who had met last year in Thibet the
chief of a sect, an elderly Lama," who was his Master's
travelling companion at the time "the said Brahmachari having spoken of the encounter, in India, had
led several persons to mistake the Lama for himself."
Now I know of a case in which a certain gentleman
of this station saw clairvoyantly the appearance of
D. K. M.'s Guru long before the Brahmachari came
here and spoke of his encounter with the Kuthumba
Lama as he called him. The gentleman in question
saw his (D. K. M.'s) Master's portrait mentioned in
the last edition of the *Occult World*, and was at first
puzzled with the difference of appearance he saw in
the portrait and that he perceived clairvoyantly. But
he remembered the Master's modest remarks that the
figure in the portrait was very much flattered. The
Brahmachari only came some months after the incident, and although he narrated to the gentleman his
interview with the alleged K. H., the gentleman thought
that there must have been some mistake as the Master
could not have been likely to read the *Vedas* in the
manner he was represented as doing.

Another incident happened here about a month ago. A certain initiated *Grihasta* Brahman who had no connection with our Society — but who had nevertheless heard of the Master from his Theosophist friends, resolved one day to see K. H. in his (the latter's) *suksma sariram.* He sat in his room with his door closed, but was disturbed by the noise outside. In the night, or rather in the early part of the morning, he fancied that some one touched his right shoulder lightly, and the appearance of the figure that he described tallied, as far as I could judge, with that which I had heard attributed to D. K. M.'s Master. But as soon as he was conscious of his presence, he was again disturbed by some other noise. He says he was fast asleep, but the touch of the figure roused him. He had not even heard of the portrait with Mr. Sinnett, nor had any acquaintance with the other people who fancied that they had seen the Master.

There are many other instances which came to my knowledge in which D. K. M.'s Master favoured many individuals. But despite his belief and that of the large numbers of the Theosophists that I know of, I confess I am at a loss to reason with those who think that the real K. H. *is* an "elderly" man. These persons do not pretend to say who D. K. M.'s Master is. They say that he may be like the portrait of which I have heard Colonel Gordon, Mr. Sinnett and others speak, but if so, they question whether he is the K. H. well known in Thibet. K.

SIMLA. 31*st Jan.* 1884.

Note.— We know of only one MAHATMA bearing the name of my venerated GURU DEVA who holds a well-known public office in Thibet, under the TESHU LAMA. For aught we know there may be another bearing the same name; but at any rate he is not known to us, nor have any of those, we are acquainted with in Thibet, heard of him. And this personage, my BELOVED MASTER, is, as I have described Him, resembling the portrait in Mr. Sinnett's possession, and *does not look old.* Perhaps the *clairvoyants* are confounding the sect of *Khadampas* with the *Kauthumpas?* The former, although not regular *Dougpas,* are great magicians and indulge in practices an Adept of the good Law would feel disgusted with — such as the well known phenomenon of ripping open the abdomen, exposing the intestines, and then restoring them to their normal place and condition, &c. &c. The latter, the Kauthumpas, are the disciples of my MASTER.

My friend and brother of Simla should not lose sight of the fact that while others claim to have seen my Master clairvoyantly, I say that I saw Him in the North personally, in his living, not his astral body. Col. Olcott and Mr. Brown were also as fortunate as myself in that respect. It is now for the impartial reader to judge whether the testimony of three unimpeachable eye witnesses is more reliable or not than that of one or two clairvoyants (untrained we may add) in matters connected with the *physical* appearance of an individual. Imagination and expectancy are, with various other things, apt to mislead beginners in the Science of Clairvoyance.   D. K. M.

COLONEL OLCOTT AT THE COURT OF
KASHMIR

[Supplement to *The Theosophist*, January, 1884.]

A T Lahore, Col. Olcott was met by a Councillor of
His Highness the Maha Raja Saheb of Kashmir
and Jammu, who had been specially deputed for the
purpose of escorting the President and his party to
Jammu. His Highness had sent a special request that
before proceeding from Lahore to Jammu, Col. Olcott should consent to accept the *khilat** which it is
customary for the Court to offer to its most honoured
guests, as a refusal would be derogatory to his dignity.
The President accepted the kind offer on the distinct
understanding that the presents would be received not
for his personal benefit, but on behalf of, and for the
benefit of the Society. The necessary preliminaries
having been arranged, the party, accompanied by Pandit Gopi Nath, F. T. S., Editor of the *Mittra Vilasa,*
the organ of the orthodox Pandits of Lahore, and by
His Highness' Councillor, left Lahore by the evening
mail of the 21st November, and proceeded from the
Wazirabad Railway station in carriages direct to Sialkot, where they rested for the night. The Maharajah
had sent his State carriages to that place to take the

Khilat is a royal gift peculiar to Asiatic Courts: its richness
and value being proportionate to the munificence of the Sovereign and the rank of the visitor. — ED. [of *The Theosophist*]

party to Jammu which, after about four hours' drive, they reached in the evening of the 22nd. On this side of the Ravi river, two State elephants were in waiting to take the party to the city. One of these was fitted up with a silver *Howdah* in Kashmiri *repoussée* work, with dragon supporters and velvet cushions for the President. An hour's ride brought the party to the barracks, where the bungalow set apart for the British Resident and other distinguished European guests had been fitted up for their accommodation. The next morning, elephants were sent with an officer and a guard of honor, and upon arrival at the Palace, the whole guard presented arms, and His Highness gave audience in full Court. The Maha Rajah Saheb was very well pleased with Col. Olcott's exposition of Theosophy, and expressed great sympathy with the objects of the Theosophical Society, especially its efforts for the revival of the ancient intellectual and spiritual glories of India. Their Royal Highnesses Prince Rama Singh, Commander-in-Chief, and Prince Amara Singh, the junior Prince, also seemed very much interested in the subject. The same evening, Col. Olcott received the Royal presents. According to the ancient custom of the Court, first-class guests receive twenty-one pots of sweetmeats, those of the second class, fourteen, the third-class seven, while the fourth-class are given none. The President was treated as a first-class guest — a distinction shown to Princes and to the British Resident and other high Europeans, and was thus presented with twenty-one pots of sweet-meats and a purse of five hundred rupees as *Dawat,* for which he imme-

diately receipted in his official capacity and on behalf
of the Society. Every day the Maha Rajah Saheb
accorded him an interview of about two hours, and on
some days even two. On each occasion, at the Palace,
a guard of honour old [all] turned out who presented
arms, both at the time of his entering and leaving
the Royal mansion. Two elephants and four saddled
horses were all the time at the disposal of the party
at the barracks — besides armed *chuprasis* and other
servants. Col. Olcott had long discussions on matters
of Aryan Philosophy and Religion with His Highness,
who manifested a most thorough knowledge of the subjects, and seemed extremely gratified to find that the
American *Chela* had derived his knowledge from the
same school to which his own GURU apparently belonged. The Maha Rajah Saheb not only believed
in the existence of the HIMALAYAN MAHATMAS, but
seemed to be sure of the fact from personal knowledge.
He expressed his entire approbation of Col. Olcott's
work for the resuscitation of Sanskrit in which direction he himself was working hard in his own State.
The party remained at Jammu for a week. On the
last day, they were presented with the *khilat,* which
consisted of an offering to Col. Olcott of seven "cloths"
— technically so called,* and three to each of the rest
— as also an additional purse of two thousand rupees,
which the President receipted for, as before, on behalf

*In point of fact they comprised an embroidered coat (*choga*
red) *"pashminah,"* silk-lined, a Kashmiri square shawl (*rumâl*)
embroidered to the centre, a turban, an embroidered scarf, and
three pieces of Kashmiri fabrics.

of the Society. Before quitting Jammu, the Colonel made over fifteen hundred rupees to the Honorary Secretary of the Head-Quarters House Fund Committee towards the purchase of the Adyar Property, and the remaining rupees one thousand of the Maharajah's cash present, to the Treasurer of the Society, for the Society's general expenses. Col. Olcott had special interviews with His Royal Highness Prince Arama Singh, the youngest son of His Highness the Maha Rajah Saheb, with His Excellency the Diwan, and other high officials of the State, who were all more or less interested in what the President had to say, and professed themselves pleased with his advocacy of Aryan Philosophy. From Jammu to Sialkot the party was provided with State carriages. Thence they proceeded further on their journey. Col. Olcott's visit to the State of Kapurthala, where he was invited by the Diwan, who had specially gone down to Lahore for the purpose, will be found described elsewhere.

DAMODAR K. MAVALANKAR,
Joint Recording Secretary.

INTERVIEW WITH A MAHATMA

[From *The Theosophist*, August, 1884.]

I HAD the pleasure of seeing in several issues of the *Theosophist* articles describing my interview with a Himalayan Mahatma. But I am sorry to see that you have been led or rather misled to form some strange, if not incorrect, notions about the fact, and also regret to find that some positive mistakes have been made by the writer in reporting the matter to you. In order to make the matter more clearly known to you, I beg to write the following few lines and trust they will meet with your approval.

At the time I left home for the Himalayas in search of the Supreme Being, having adopted Brahmacharyashrama, I was quite ignorant of the fact whether there was any such philosophical sect as the Theosophists existing in India, who believed in the existence of the Mahatmas or "superior persons." This and other facts connected with my journey have already been reported to you perfectly right, and so need not be repeated or contradicted. Now I beg to give you the real account of my interview with the Mahatmas.

Before and after I met the so-called Mahatma Kouthumpa, I had the good fortune of seeing in person several other Mahatmas of note, a detailed account of whom, I hope, should time allow, to write to you by and bye. Here I wish to say something about Kouthumpa only.

When I was on my way to Almora from Mansarowar and Kailas, one day I had nothing with me to eat. I was quite at a loss how to get on without food and keep up my life. There being no human habitation in that part of the country, I could expect no help but pray God and take my way patiently on. Between Mansarowar and Taklakhal by the side of a road I observed a tent pitched and several Sadhus, called Chohans,* sitting outside it who numbered near seventeen in all. As to their trimmings, &c., what Babu M. M. Chatterjea reports to you is all correct. When I went to them they entertained me very kindly, and saluted me by uttering "Ram Ram." I returning their salutations, sat down with them, and they entered upon conversation with me on different subjects, asking me first the place I was coming from and whither I was going. There was a chief of them sitting inside the tent and engaged in reading a book. I enquired about his name and the book he was reading from one of his Chelas, who answered me in rather a serious tone, saying that his name was Guru Kouthumpa and the book he was reading was Rigveda. Long before, I had been told by some Pundits of Bengal that the Thibetan Lamas were well-acquainted with the Rigveda. This proved what they had told me. After a short time when his reading was over, he called me in through one of his Chelas, and I went to him.

*The correspondent probably means "the Chutuktus" or the disciples? *Chohans* are the "Masters."

He also bidding me "Ram Ram" received me very gently and courteously and began to talk with me mildly in pure Hindi. He addressed me in words such as follows:— "You should remain here for some time and see the fair at Mansarowar, which is to come off shortly. Here you will have plenty of time and suitable retreats for meditation, &c. I will help you in whatever I can." Having spoken in words as above for some time, I said in reply that what he said was all right, and that I would put up with him by all means, but there was some reason which prevented me from stopping there any longer. He understood my object immediately, and then having given me some secret advice as to my future spiritual welfare bade me farewell. Before this he had come to know that I was hungry that day and so wished me to take some food. He ordered one of his Chelas to supply me with food, which he did immediately. In order to get hot water ready for my ablutions he prepared fire by blowing into a cowdung cake which burst into flames at once. This is a common practice among the Himalayan Lamas. It is also fully explained by M. M. Chatterjea and so need not be repeated.

As long as I was there with the said Lama he never persuaded me to accept Buddhism or any other religion, but only said, "Hinduism is the best religion; you should believe in the Lord Mahadewa — he will do good to you. You are still quite a young man — do not be enticed away by the necromancy of anybody." Having had a conversation with the Mahatma

as described above for about three hours, I at last
taking his leave resumed my journey.

I am neither a Theosophist nor any sectarian, but
am the worshipper of the only "Om." As regards the
Mahatma I personally saw, I dare say that he is a
great Mahatma. By the fulfilment of certain of his
prophecies I am quite convinced of his excellence.
Of all the Himalayan Mahatmas with whom I had an
interview, I never saw a better Hindee speaker than
he. As to his birth-place and the place of his residence, I did not ask him any question. Neither can
I say if he is the Mahatma of the Theosophists. In
short, I beg to ask the leaders of the Theosophic
movement, Col. Olcott and Madame Blavatsky, why
they are entertaining doubts as to his personality, why
do they not refer the matter to the Mahatmas, with
whom they can easily have communication. When
they say they receive instructions from them in petty
affairs, why do they not get them in a matter which
has become a riddle to them. As to the age of the
Mahatma Kouthumpa as I told Babu M. M. Chatterjea and others, he was an elderly looking man.
Cannot the Mahatmas transform themselves into any
age they like? If they can, the assertions of Babu
Damodar cannot be admitted to be true when he says
his Guru was not an old one. When the age of even
a common man cannot be told exactly, how is it possible to be precise about the age of a Mahatma, specially when one believes that the Mahatmas have the
supernatural power of changing their outward appearance and look. It must be admitted that our know-

ledge of them is far from being complete; and there
are several things concerning them which we do not
know.
It is said that

मनुष्याणांसहस्त्रेषु कश्चित्यतितिसिद्धयं ।

यततामपिसिध्यानां कश्चित्मांबोतितत्त्वतः ॥

RAJANI KANT BRAHMACHARI
ALMORA, *3rd June* 1884

Note.— Although the correspondent begins by saying that certain *"incorrect"* notions have crept into the
narrative of his interview with a MAHATMA, I fail to
see a single statement of Babu Mohini M. Chatterjee
contradicted by the Brahmachari. As the former
gentleman is in Europe, he cannot give a reply to the
above letter; but the reader can compare it with
Mohini Babu's statement on pp. 83-86 of Vol. V of
the *Theosophist.** All that the correspondent does now
is that he gives a few *additional* facts.

As regards the Brahmachari's remark about my
statement concerning the MAHATMA's age, the reader
will perceive that the correspondent but repeats, in
other words, to a certain extent, what I have already
said to be the reply of my MASTER (*Vide* page 62,
Vol. V. *Theosophist*, col. 1, para 1.)† I may, however, add that since "intellect moulds the features,"

---

*["The Himalayan Brothers — Do They Exist?"; reprinted
in *Five Years of Theosophy*, pp. 459-69.   — EDS.]
†["A Great Riddle Solved." — EDS.]

many of the comparatively young persons (if *physical* age be taken into account) *look* "elderly," such is the majesty of their appearance. The question has already been discussed at length in the article "Mahatmas and Chelas"* in the last month's *Theosophist*, and in several other writings.

The question put by the correspondent to Col. Olcott and to Mme. Blavatsky, and the advice he offers them, are rather confused. But every reader of the *Theosophist* knows full well that the Founders collect and publish independent testimonies about the existence of the MAHATMAS, not because they have any doubt in the matter, but because they wish to put their case as clearly and as strongly as possible before an enquiring public. Nothing more need be said about it, as every searcher after truth — in whatever department — knows full well the weight and validity of evidence, especially concerning facts which are out of the reach, *at present,* of the *ordinary* run of mankind, although these facts may in the process of higher evolution come more and more within the grasp of a more developed humanity.   — D. K. M.

---

*[An unsigned editorial, probably by H. P. Blavatsky; republished in *Five Years of Theosophy*, pp. 92-95. — EDS.]

LETTER OF H. P. BLAVATSKY TO
DR. HARTMANN.* 1885 TO 1886.

[From *The Path*, February, 1896.]

[NO DATE.]

MY DEAR DOCTOR:—Two words in answer to what the Countess told me. I do myself harm, you say, "in telling everyone that Damodar is in Tibet, when he is only at Benares." You are mistaken. He left Benares toward the middle of May, (ask in Adyar; I cannot say for certain whether it was in May or April) and went off, as everybody knows, to Darjeeling, and thence to the frontier *viâ* Sikkhim. Our Darjeeling Fellows accompanied him a good way. He wrote a last word from there to the office bidding good-bye and saying: "If I am not back by July 21st you may count me as dead." He did not come back, and Olcott was in great grief and wrote to me about two months ago, to ask me whether I knew anything. News had come by some Tibetan pedlars in Darjeeling that a young man of that description, with very long flowing hair, had been found frozen in the (forget the name) pass, stark dead, with twelve rupees in his pockets and his things and hat a few yards off. Olcott was in despair, but Maji told him (and he, D., lived with Maji for some time at Benares,) that he was not dead — she knew it through pilgrims who had returned,

---

*[Written from Würzburg. — EDS.]

though Olcott supposes — which may be also — that she knew it clairvoyantly. Well I know that he is alive, and am almost certain that he is in Tibet — as I am certain also that he will not come back — not for years, at any rate. Who told you he was at Benares? We want him sorely now to refute all Hodgson's guesses and inferences that I simply call lies, as much as my "spy" business and forging — the blackguard: now mind, I do not give myself out as infallible in this case. But I do know what he told me before going away — and at that moment he would not have said a fib, when he wept like a Magdalen. He said, "I go for your sake. If the Maha Chohan is satisfied with my services and my devotion, He may permit me to vindicate you by proving that Masters *do* exist. If I fail no one shall ever see me for years to come, but I will send messages. But I am determined in the meanwhile to make people give up searching for me. I want them to believe I am dead."

This is why I think he must have arranged some trick to spread reports of his death by freezing.

But if the poor boy had indeed met with such an accident — why I think I would commit suicide; for it is out of pure devotion for me that he went.[1] I would never forgive myself for this, for letting him go. That's the truth and only the truth. Don't be harsh,

---

[1]The fact is that Damodar was never asked to go to Tibet, but begged to be permitted to go there, and at last went with permission of H. P. B., on which occasion I accompanied him to the steamer. — H. [Evidently Hartmann. — EDs.]

Doctor — forgive him his faults and mistakes, willing and unwilling.

The poor boy, whether dead or alive, has no happy times now, since he is on probation and this is terrible. I wish you would write to someone at Calcutta to enquire from Darjeeling whether it is so or not. Sinnett will write to you, I think. I wish you would.

Yours ever gratefully,

H. P. B.

Letter CLXXIX*

[Sent from Torre del Greco, July 16, 1885.]

. . . Now that our Damodar is away in Thibet and nothing is known at Adyar about him, and as *Respected* Sir does not care a fig for anything but his own affairs, the Masters find no facility for communicating direct with anyone at Adyar. . . .†

---

*[From *The Letters of H. P. Blavatsky to A. P. Sinnett.*
— Eds.]

†[This letter is unsigned, but is in the handwriting of Babajee, a young Brahman and a probationary chela, who was sent to help H. P. Blavatsky when she went to Europe in 1885. His real name was S. Krishnamachari, but he also called himself Dharbagiri Nath. — Eds.]

DAMODAR K. MAVALANKAR

[Supplement to *The Theosophist*, July, 1886.]

TO relieve the anxiety of a great many friends who have been anxious to learn the fate of our brother Damodar K. Mavalankar, and to dispel the rumours of his death which came by way of Sikkim and Darjeeling, we are very happy to state that we have positive news as late as the 7th of June that he has safely reached his destination, is alive, and under the guardianship of the friends whom he sought. The date of his return, however, is yet uncertain, and will probably remain so for a long time to come.

H. S. OLCOTT
T. SUBBA ROW.

V

Personal Letters

[Written in a less formal style than his articles, Dâmodar's Letters nevertheless contain direct philosophic instruction and many interesting occult hints. The abrupt manner in which he plunges *in medias res* is indicative of the continuously busy life at the Theosophical Headquarters, which allowed time only to carry out the ever present essential task.

The Letters in Part I, written to William Q. Judge in New York, are copied from the originals in the Archives of the Theosophical Society, Point Loma, and have been reproduced literally. In regard to the specially significant Letters II, III, IV, and V, the reader is referred to the prefatory note to "A Hindu Chela's Diary" in the Appendix.

The Letters in Part II were written to A. P. Sinnett in India, and are taken from *The Mahatma Letters to A. P. Sinnett*, Letters CXLIIa and CXLIIb, and from *The Letters of H. P. Blavatsky to A. P. Sinnett*, Letters Xa, CLXXXIX, CXC.

Part III is a Letter to Mrs. Josephine W. Cables, of Rochester, New York, and is reprinted from *The Occult Word* (May-June, 1884) of which she was Editor. — Eds.]

LETTERS TO W. Q. JUDGE

Bombay 5th October 1879.

My dear Mr. Judge,

I am very sorry to hear you write so disparagingly
to Madam Blavatsky about your feelings and the state
of your mind. Is it not surprising to see that a man like
you after having made some progress in the study of
Theosophy should despair at the very moment he is
about to enter the very threshold of true knowledge?
It seems to my mind ridiculously strange that a very
thirsty man should be in quest of water and that when
he has found it he should instead of drinking it, turn
his back against it and fly from the only place where
he can quench his thirst. You have read in "Isis"
various facts to which the noble author attests as having
seen personally. I am positively sure you have so
high an opinion of this awe-inspiring Lady that you will
not hesitate in the least to accept even a tittle of evidence she may bring forward to establish any circumstance which she knows for certain to be a fact. The
more so, because she simply corroborates what was
taught by my forefathers and what is still found in
the ancient Hindu Literature but which is now regarded
as superstition by ignorant men, they being unable
to find the key which opens the box containing these
hidden treasures. But this key you will get, only if
you will continue the study of Theosophy.

In "Isis" the author has shown what powers man

is endowed with and how he can use them. The use
depends upon their development which occultism
teaches us how to cause to effect in us. In order to
show that the study of occult sciences has enabled
certain persons to develope their powers, a few of the
performances of these mysterious personages have
been quoted. She has clearly proved that there live
to this day adepts who have obtained a thorough control
over themselves and over the forces in nature, and
have guarded from time immemorial the sacred writings
of the venerable sages of the past who found out the
Spiritual Powers of man and the only way in which he
can develope them. But have these adepts succeeded
in developing their powers at once when they begun?
Is it possible for a person to get to the top of a house
without using any means by which he can do so? Or
again does it not appear absurd that a man can climb
a tree without proceeding step by step? Do you expect
a child to be a philosopher as soon as it is born? Are
not these illustrations sufficient to convince you that
in order to succeed in any thing you must proceed
gradually? You know any thing rashly done is sure
to be imperfect. In undertaking any thing the first
thing required is perseverance. "Try again" should
ever be our motto. A child will never learn how to walk
if it were never to try to do so, simply because in its
primary attempts it suffers failures and falls every now
and then. But the instinct of the child urges it nevertheless to continue in its efforts until it succeeds. Does
not the same Spirit which gives the child the instinct
illuminate the child after it grows into manhood? Is

it not shameful for every person that, although in
childhood he acts in obedience to the instructions of
the Divine Spirit, he after coming to maturity should
become deaf to the teachings of that Spirit which once
gave him success in his childhood notwithstanding all
the primary failures?   If we understand all these
things why should we not proceed cautiously and patiently? If you see before your eyes a thing which you
were hunting after for a long time, why should you not
try to grasp and tenaciously cling to it?   Should you
give it up simply because you do not succeed for the
first time?   Is all the trouble you took in finding it out
and getting at it to go in vain?   Should you not at such
a trying moment summon the assistance of moral courage?   Is it not degrading for us that we can not *even*
follow the footsteps of our ancestors who discovered
the true path to Spiritual Enlightenment, although
their footprints are so clear that they can be vividly seen
by any one who cares to do so?   How very difficult
would it then have been if the task of discovery had
involved upon us?   Not only are these footprints still
preserved but we can find to this day guides who have
trodden upon these steps and have nearly attained the
same end which these discoverers did.   The question
naturally arises where can these guides be found?
The answer is of course India.   But are they accessible
to all? Can any body employ them as other guides are?
What are their charges for employment?   One answer
is, it is presumed, sufficient to answer all these queries.
The fact that they retire from the busy world necessarily proves that they do not care for any thing

pertaining to it. What else then can induce them to
come over to you to guide you through this path? It
is the proper performance of certain duties which a man
ought to do. But what are these duties is a question
which springs from this answer. If I were to go
minutely into all these details it would take me too long
before I finish this letter and I would therefore curso-
rily glance at what these duties are. We must consider
the whole mankind as one brotherhood for the whole
creation has emanated from that eternally Divine
Principle which is everywhere, is in every thing and in
which is every thing and is therefore the source of all.
We should therefore do all we can to do good to humanity. You know the soul of man is composed of Spirit
and Matter and thus forms a distinct individuality.
Our chief end should be to preserve this individuality
until the Soul is freed of all the Matter that stuck to it
and mixes into that Principle which gives it birth or
rather from which it proceeds. One of the various
things you must do in order to accomplish this is to
leave off as much of worldly consideration as possible.
Your only desire should be to do everything for humanity and not for yourself, i.e., although *you* are in the
world, your *inner man* should be out of it. When you
do this much, you will know other means of accomplishing your aim from the Adepts. You must neither
despair, nor think that there are no adepts simply
because you have as yet seen none. If you have not
met with any, you should know that it is because you
have not properly performed your duties. You would
perhaps think that these personages stop in India

and you have therefore no chance of finding any in America. But then you must remember that for a person whose Spiritual Sight is opened time and space can offer no obstacle. He can travel any distance whenever he pleases in no time. Such men are actually in search of persons who truly and sincerely desire to go to them and study occult Sciences. Why should they not go to you if you are honestly working with that desire? If you produce a certain cause will it not have its effect? Man is endowed with a power by which he can produce a certain cause, but the production of the effect rests with that force in Nature to which the cause is directed. But does this force go against its laws? Certainly not, for if it were to do so, it would be a miracle, but you know that there can be no miracle. If you therefore perform your duties as you ought to do, you will certainly rouse the good Spirits (Forces) in Nature who will compel an Adept to come to you and teach you what you so ardently desire to learn. If you despair after making some progress and learning certain things what should I do? Am I not a beginner? It is only two months that I have been *admitted* into the Society. What I have said above are the aspirations of a Hindu and should be of every person of whatever creed or colour, for castes and races are but the invention of man to suit his convenience. Do not therefore despair but go on with confidence, and success is at hand. If after performing your proper duties you do not meet with an adept you will at least have the consolation of having done what you are in duty bound to do. All your good actions in this world will help you in after-life. I therefore ask of you, my dear brother, to proceed cautiously and patiently with what you have begun. Despair not, and you will shortly trample the foe under your feet. Bear in mind the motto "Try again," and apply it in your case.

I hope you success and conclude

Most truly Yours

DÁMODAR K. MÁVALANKAR.

F. T. S.

II

Bombay 24th January 1880

My dear Sir and brother,

I read with great interest yours of 8th November which I received on the 20th ultimo while I was at Benares. I left this place on the 2nd ultimo with H. P. Blavatsky and Col. Olcott for Allahabad whence I proceeded alone upon my arrival, to Benares to see Pandit Dayanand Saraswati Swámiji, on the business of the Ritual. Col. Olcott and Madam joined me there after about ten days; and when I showed your letter to them, Madam ordered me to write to you all I had personally witnessed at Benares. Having, however, left that place shortly afterwards for Allahabad where I stopped only for two days, I could not find leisure to give you the whole account. After I came to Bombay I was engaged for a long time in doing my work and could not spare time to write to you, for which I hope you will excuse me. I once or twice attempted to do so,

but I did not know what to write. Because if I were
to give you simply an account of what I had seen at
Benares, it might read simply but as a sort of story.
Again I found myself incompetent to add to the account
any reflections of my own. Not that I doubt what I
have seen, but quite the reverse of that. I know that
Madam Blavatsky whom I revere as my Guru, esteem
as my benefactor, and love more than a Mother, and
others whose mere recollection gives my heart a thrill
that makes me quiver with veneration, have done me
favours I am not the least deserving of. I therefore
look down with perfect contempt upon myself when I
see how much they have done for me and what opportunities they had given me for bettering myself, and
how very foolishly I let those opportunities slip by. It
is about six months since I was admitted into the
Society and now I do not think I am a bit better in
any way than I was before. I therefore consider
myself as the lowest of all the Theosophists for although
there may be some (if any, at all) who may be as bad
as myself, they are not yet to be blamed for their actions
as they had no such opportunities of improvement
which I had. Being so very low as I have shown myself
to you, I can not comment upon what I mean to write
to you. I shall simply give you mere facts as they were
personally witnessed by me — Gather what moral you
may from them, I cannot give you my reflections on this
matter for the reasons already stated to you, and because (judging from your letter) I find you are far superior to me in intellect and have made a greater progress.

About a month after I joined the Society I felt as it were a voice within myself whispering to me that Madam Blavatsky is not what she represents herself to be. It then assumed the form of a belief in me which grew so strong within a short time that four or five times I thought of throwing myself at her feet and beg her to reveal herself to me. But then I could not do so because I thought it would be useless, as I knew that I was quite impure and had led too bad a life to be trusted with that secret. I therefore remained silent with the consolation that she herself would confide the secret to me when she would find me worthy of it. I thought it must be some great Indian Adept that had assumed that illusionary form. But there a difficulty occurred to me. I knew that she received letters from her aunts and that she communicated with persons almost in every part of the globe. I could not therefore reconcile my belief, as I thought she would then have to practise the illusion all over the world. Various explanations suggested themselves to me except the right one. I was, however, right (as I have subsequently ascertained) in my original conception that she is some great Indian Adept. At various times I talked to her about these adepts, because that is the only subject I am interested in, although I fear I am not, and shall not be for many years to come or perhaps in this life, worthy of their company. Since I was a child of seven years, my inclination has almost always been in this direction. I always thought of retiring from this world and giving myself up to devotion. I also expressed several times to Madam my intention of retiring from this world and studying this philosophy which alone can make man happy in the true sense of the word. But then she usually asked me what I would do *there* alone. She said that instead of gaining my object I would become perhaps insane by being alone in the jungles without any body to guide me; that I was foolish enough to think that by going into the jungles I could fall in with an adept; and that if I really wanted to gain my object I should have to work in the Society and when the Higher ones whom I dare not mention by any other names, and who had started this Society, would be satisfied with me, they would themselves call me away from the busy world and teach me in private. And when I foolishly asked her many times to give me the names and addresses of some of our Brothers she said to me once: — "One of our Brothers has told me that as you are much after me, I better tell you once for all that I, being a European, have no right to give you any information about them; but if you go on asking Hindus what they know about the matter, you might hear of them; and one of those Higher ones may perhaps throw himself in your way without your knowing him, and will tell you what you should do." Having received these orders I had but to obey and wait; although having an implicit confidence in H. P. Blavatsky I knew that I would have my object fulfilled only through her, and through her alone. I thereupon asked one or two of my Hindu friends, who were inclined in this direction, if they knew any such persons. One of them said he had seen two or three such men but that they were not quite what he thought

"Ráj Yogs." He also told me that he had heard of a man who had appeared several times in Benares but that no body knew where he lived. My disappointment grew bitter and more bitter but I never lost the firm confidence I have that adepts *do* live in India and can *still* be found among us. Shortly afterwards I was ordered to Benares to see Swámiji on that business of the *Ritual.*

A few months before we left Bombay, Pandit Mohunlál Vishnulál Pandea, one of the Councillors of our Society, had written to Madam that there lived in Benares a woman called "Máji" who practised Yog and was his Guru. I had known from Madam that Swámiji also knew that science and that he knows "Máji." Being, however, ordered not to let him know what I knew of him, I could not say to him anything directly but when I made indirect references to these things, he pretended to laugh at me for believing in the powers attained by a Yog. And when I asked him if he knew a woman named "Máji," he replied — "If there be such a woman here at all, she is not known." — Whenever I asked him any thing in regard to these matters, he gave evasive answers. I was disappointed when I saw that all my expectations in going to Benares were but castles in the air. I thought that I had gained nothing except the consolation that I was doing a part of my duty as a Theosophist. Consequently I wrote thus to my most revered Guru: — "As directed by you I have neither let him (Swámiji) know what I know of him nor what my true intentions are. He seems to think that I work in the Society to make money. I have as yet kept him in the dark as regards myself and consequently am

myself groping in the dark — Expecting, however, enlightenment on the subject from you."

Shortly afterwards Madam and Col. Olcott accompanied by two or three European members of our
Society joined me at Benares. To my great surprise,
when asked by Madam, Swámiji mentioned the place
where "Máji" resided and offered to take us there,
adding that he knew her well and that she very often
came to see him. The Europeans that had come to
Benares from Allahabad were Mr. Sinnett, the Editor
of the *"Pioneer"* (a government organ and one of the
most influential newspapers in India), and his wife,
and Mrs. A. Gordon, the writer of the article "Missions
in India" in the January number of the *Theosophist,*
the wife of a Colonel in Bengal, also a Theosophist;
who had come on purpose from Calcutta to Allahabad
— thus crossing all India,— to be *initiated.* They all
wanted to see some great phenomenon performed by
Madam, and especially the former two had come down
to Benares for that purpose, as Madam had refused to
show them any such thing unless permitted by Swámiji.
Swámi having declined to grant the permission asked
for, was consulted by Madam and Col. Olcott as to the
best way of satisfying these two persons, as it was found
that the interests of the Society would be greatly
increased, if the full sympathy of Mr. Sinnett was
secured, who had already done so much for us by
making the Viceroy issue an order published in the
November Number of the *Theosophist,* which set us all
right in the public estimation, and who had made the
Viceroy promise to write to Madam a letter approving

of the plan of the Society, which will be published in the next number. It was then resolved that we should see "Máji" for the purpose. But when we went the next day to her she gave the same reply as Swámiji that it was too sacred a science to be thus treated as a "*Tamásha*" (Show). Madam could not accompany us at that time as she did not feel well, but when we told "Máji" accordingly, she turned a glance of significance at Col. Olcott who returned it, thereby asking her to remain silent, as they alone had then felt Madam's presence near them. "Máji" then said that though she had never visited Europeans, she would herself come to see Madam once or twice before our departure from Benares. Mr. and Mrs. Sinnett being thus disappointed were talking at night about the matter with Madam and Col. Olcott. Mrs. Gordon also formed one of the company. During the course of conversation some one made reference to flowers and immediately afterwards a sound was heard as of something dropping from above. It was found that a number of flowers were thrown by invisible hands on the table around which they were all sitting. When I had gone to Swámiji a short time before the occurrence, I found him in an unusual state, such as he was always in, whenever explaining the Ritual. And I found that the phenomenon exactly corresponded to the time when I saw Swámiji in the strange state of "*Samádhi*" described to you above: "*Samadhi*" being, as you perhaps know, that state when the adept leaves his body. There was therefore no doubt left for me as to what and how it had happened. The next day Mr. and Mrs. Sinnett left for Allahabad and we three with Mrs. Gordon remained at Benares. The next day came "Maji" (who never speaks of herself but as "This body") to see Madam, and I alone was then with them, as Col. Olcott and Mrs. Gordon had gone with Swámiji to see the girls' school. I then gathered from what she said that she had been first in the body of a Fakir who, upon having his hand disabled by a shot he received while he passed the Fortress of Bhurtpore, had to change his body and choose the one that was now "Máji." A girl about seven years of age was dying at that time and so, before her death, this Fakir had entered her body and taken possession of it. "Maji" is not therefore a woman but a real Hindu Fakir in the body of a woman. It is but one by one that I gathered all these particulars. In his former body, this Fakir had studied the Yog science for 65 years, but his study having been arrested and incomplete at the time his body was disabled and consequently unequal to the task he had to perform, he had to choose this other one. In his present body he is 53 years, and consequently the "Inner Máji" is 118 years old. She then asked Madam whether she knew that they had had the same man for their "Guru." But Madam desiring her to give some proofs of what she said to me, she readily furnished them. She said that Madam's Guru was born in Punjab but generally lives in the Southern part of India, and especially in Ceylon. He is about 300 years old and has a companion of about the same age, though both do not appear even forty. In a few centuries he will enter the body of a "*Kshatriya*" (the Warrior caste among the Hindus) and do some great deeds for India, but the time had not yet come. When Madam and Col. Olcott had gone last summer to Karley Caves, they saw a certain Sannyási with a five-legged cow, who took Col. Olcott aside and gave him the Theosophical grip. He had then told Col. Olcott that he was "Maji's" disciple. I communicated this fact on this occasion to "Maji" who laughed and replied that it was none other than Madam's Guru in the Fakir's body, who had given Col. Olcott the grip, and that if we were to see that Fakir again, he would not be able to give us the sign again, as he was for the time being, taken possession of, by Madam's Guru who often performs such things. Then she went home, promising to see us again before our departure.

I must state here that about a fortnight before I left Bombay Madam had asked me how I knew that it was not an Indian adept who took occasional possession of her body and who did all these things which are attributed to her. My inference then is that the real H. P. B. is nothing but either a paralyzed soul or a dead body under the control of some adept. I shall now continue the thread of my account.

"Maji" then came for the second time and on this occasion all of us were present except Swámiji and Madam who came afterwards. Col. Olcott then asked "Maji" some questions about Madam. And "Maji" said that Madam was not what she seems to be. Her interior man had already been twice in a Hindu body and was now in his third. She also said that until that time she had never seen a European but, having got the information from her Guru, about Madam, she had come to see her. I then asked her if the real H. P. B. was still in the body, but she refused to answer that question, and only added that she herself — "Máji" — was inferior to Madam. She then told Col. Olcott that he had once been a young Hindu in the Southern part of India, but had died and had to be reborn again. She then explained to us the meaning of the action of the Fakir in having brought a five-legged cow at Kárli when he saw Col. Olcott there and gave him the Theosophical grip. She said that every person has a right to repeat the Gáyatri Mantram which consists of three "Páds" (Metres) but a Brahmachâri has a right to repeat one "Pád" more while a Yog could repeat as many as he liked and thereby perform wonders. Thus a Yog has a right to repeat a Mantram consisting of five "Páds" which is equal to "Om tat Sat," and as the word "Pád" also means a foot or a leg, he had purposely brought a five-legged cow to signify this meaning. And she moreover said that this symbol was with Madam on her seal-ring, although neither she (Madam) nor any of us had intimated to "Máji" the fact. You will have thus seen how Indian instructions are conveyed by means of symbols and one who can decipher the ancient Aryan symbols will find a vast field to be explored. She first tried to tempt me, trying to make me relinquish my object; but when all this failed, she told me that if I wanted to make any spiritual progress and see any of our Brothers, I must depend entirely for that upon Madam. None else was competent to take me through the right path. If I were to go alone anywhere, I may wander about here and there for years together

but that will be quite useless. I must stop entirely with
Madam and lay my full and only confidence in her.
She told me to work in the Society and practise regularly twice a day what Madam had ordered me to do.
In every respect I must act in obedience to her instructions. Then she told me that I should go once with
Madam to the mountains of Junágad where these adepts
usually live and even if I were not to see any body the
first time, the magnetized air in which they live, will do
me much good — She said that they do not generally
stop in one place but always shift from one place to
another. They however, all meet together on certain
days of the year in a certain place near Bhadrinath in
the Northern part of India, of which you can read in the
January *Theosophist*. She remarked that as India's
sons are becoming more and more wicked, they (these
adepts) have gradually been retiring more and more
toward the north of the Himálaya Mountains. I have
written here as far as I can recollect what "Mâji"
had told us —

You will thus have seen of what a great consequence it is for me to be always with Madam. From
the beginning I felt all that "Mâji" had told me.
Only two or three days after I applied for admission into the Society I said to H. P. B., what I really
felt, that I regarded her as my benefactor, revered
her as my Guru and loved her more than a mother.
Ever since I have assured her of what I then told
her. And now "Mâji" tells me the same thing, streng-
thens my faith and asks me to confide in her (Madam).
And when I afterwards consulted Swámiji in regard

to myself, he, without my telling him a word of what "Maji" had said to me, urged me to do the very same thing, that is to say, to put my faith in H. P. B. All along I have felt and *do still* feel strongly as if I had already once studied this philosophy with Madam and that I must have been once her most obedient and humble disciple. This must have been a fact or else how can you account for the feeling created in me about her only after seeing her not more than three or four times. All my hopes and future plans are therefore centered in her and nothing in the world can shake my confidence in her, especially when two Hindus, who do not speak English and could not have pre-arranged these things, tell me the very same things without previous consultation and what I all along had myself felt. My trip, therefore, to up-country did me one good, that of strengthening my belief which is the chief foundation on which the grand structure is to be built.

Before concluding I shall speak of an incident that happened in my presence at Benares. The night before we left that place seven or eight persons were in the drawing room when I was present. We were all sitting around a table. Madam was talking with me and a Benares Pandit, the writer of the article on "Brahma, Ishwara and Máya" in the October Number of the *Theosophist*. On one side was Col. Olcott talking to a pleader in Benares, who has since joined our Society. Near them was Swámiji sitting silent in his chair. On the other side was Mrs. Gordon talking to Dr. Thibaut, Principal of the Benares College. Near them was a

disciple of Swámiji sitting silent in his seat. In the
course of conversation Mrs. Gordon happened to talk
of flowers. Madam then said to the Benares Pandit
that she would try if any of our Brothers would give
him a sign — And lo! and behold! within two seconds
a shower of flowers at his feet, thrown by invisible
hands. I immediately looked at Swámiji and found that
he looked no better than a dead man. His cheeks were
pale and the flush of life gone. It was evident that his
inner man was not then in his body. I then asked
Madam who had done the phenomenon of flowers,
and her only reply was "One of our Brothers," but
which one she left for me to find out. All of us then
took a flower for ourselves but the smallest of all fell
to the lot of Dr. Thibaut, the Principal of the College.
At the time of going he asked Madam if he could have
another that was lying on the table. When she said,—
"You may take as many as you like, You will have
many more." She repeated this twice or thrice and I
looked up to see from which direction they came. But
I found that they came down directly from the ceiling
and fell right near Dr. Thibaut's feet. All then left
the place and as it was dark outside I took a lamp to
show them the way out. By the time they came in the
outer veranda the light was almost out. Mrs. Gordon
was surprised and wanted to bring another lamp. But
I said that there was no matter with the lamp, but that
it was Madam that was doing something with it. When
Col. Olcott heard the words that thus passed between
us he called back all the visitors who were by this time
near the steps, to see the phenomenon. When they

returned, Madam came out, took the lamp from me, and placed it on the table. Then she said "What is the matter with you, come up," and immediately it shone with an unusual brilliancy. She then said "Go down" and within a short time it was almost dark. Afterwards she brought it up again, thus clearly establishing to the visitors what a Yog can do by his will-power. The next day I asked Swámiji who it was that had twice thrown the flowers the night before. But he first refused to answer my question, saying that I had to do nothing with it. I told him that I wanted to know it, because I could explain it in two ways and I wanted to know which one was correct, viz.,— (1st) that Madam herself did the thing; or (2nd) that some body else did it for her. He replied that even if it were done by some body else, no Yog will do a thing unless he sees the desire in another Yog's mind. I said it was quite true but that I wanted to know which of these was a fact. And then he told me that it was not Madam but some body else that had thrown the flowers. Who that some body was he would not tell me, and it is quite evident he should not tell me when it was done by himself.

I suppose I have sufficiently tired your patience and therefore beg to conclude, especially as I do not see that I have got to write to you any thing more for the present.

Hoping soon to see you here, in whom I take so much interest, I beg to remain, My dear Sir,

Yours in life and *after death*

Dámodar K. Mávalankar F. T. S.

III

PUBLICATION OFFICE OF THE "THEOSOPHIST,"
BREACH CANDY, BOMBAY, INDIA. 14th June 1881.

My dear Judge

I will now begin where I stopped last. I told you there about my being at a certain place where they have their Council. After that I saw .˙. twice or thrice alone on the same business and very rarely he said to me a few words of encouragement and good advice as to how I should go on. Happy were those moments when alone at midnight we thus had conversation! Nothing or no body to disturb us! We were to ourselves during that time. Once he took me to some other place in Ceylon. In that particular village, H. P. B., Col. Olcott and myself were the only three persons that stopped one night, the rest of our party having gone to a further place. We were all busy there initiating people and forming a branch of our Society till about 12 in the night. H. P. B. and Col. Olcott went to bed at about one. As we had to stay in the village only one night we had got down in the Rest House where comfortable accommodation can be had only for two travellers. I had therefore to lay down in an arm-chair in the dining room. I had scarcely locked from inside the door of the room and laid myself in the chair than I heard a faint knock at the door. It was repeated twice before I had time enough to reach the door. I opened it and what a great joy I felt when I saw .˙. again! In a very low whisper he ordered me to dress myself and to follow him. At the back door of the Rest House is the Sea. I followed him as he commanded me to do. He brought me to the back door of the place and we walked about three quarters of an hour by the seashore. Then we turned in the direction of the sea. All around there was water *except the place we were walking upon which was quite dry*!! He was walking in front and I was following him. We thus walked for about seven minutes when we came to a spot that looked like a small island. On the top of the building was a triangular light. From a distance, a person standing on the sea-shore would think it to be an isolated spot which is covered all over by green bushes. There is only one entrance to go inside. And no one can find it out unless the occupant wishes the person to find the way. After we reached the Island we had to go round about for about five minutes before we came in front of the actual building. There is a little garden in front we found one of the Brothers sitting. I had seen him before in the Council Room and it is to him that this place belongs. .˙. seated himself near him and I stood before them. We were there for about half an hour. I was shown a part of the place. How very pleasant it is! And inside this place he has a sort of a small room where the body remains when the *Spirit* moves about. What a charming, delightful spot that is! What a nice smell of roses and various sorts of flowers! I wish I were permitted to visit that place again if I should go to Ceylon another time. The half hour was finished and the time for our leaving the place was near. The master of the place whose name

I do not know, placed his blessing hand over my head
and .˙. and I marched off again. We came back near
the door of the room wherein I was to sleep and he
suddenly disappeared there on the spot. And following
his example as a true disciple I too will now disappear
abruptly until the next mail when I shall resume the
subject.

Yours very truly & Sincerely
Dámodar K. Mávalankar

IV

Secretary's Office of The Theosophical Society
Breach Candy, Bombay, India. 21st June 1881

My dear Judge

In my last letter I omitted to mention to you the
two other places where I was taken before the one
mentioned in my last. But as I am not at liberty to
describe them I shall abstain from doing so for the
present, until I am permitted. I shall only say that one
of them is near Colombo, a private house of .˙. and
the other one near Kandy, a library. I can now think
only of these four places where I was taken while in
Ceylon. Of course, as said before, I saw .˙. and others
on various occasions. One evening after dressing myself for dinner on the Steamer on our way back to Bombay, I took out from my trunk my coat to be put [on]

after dinner. As is my habit, I examined its pockets and put it on my bed. The dinner table was exactly opposite my cabin so that I could easily see any one going in or coming out from there but I saw none; neither did any one else at table. After we finished our dinner I went in and put on the coat. Without thinking I put my hands into my pockets as I usually do and lo! in the right hand one I felt some paper while, when I first examined it, there was nothing inside. I took it out and to my surprise I found a letter addressed to Mme. Blavatsky. I took it nearer to the light and found in the corner the initials .˙. . The cover was open and on it were written in red the words: "For Damodar to read." I then read the letter and saw that it was about the same business. Thinking all the time of this matter I lay down in my bed. Absorbed in deep thought I was startled on the sound of footsteps *in the* cabin which I had locked from inside. I looked behind and there was .˙. again and two others! What a pleasant evening that was! Speaking of various things in regard to knowledge and philosophy for about half an hour! Those were the happiest moments in my life! But that was only for that time and I determined to make myself worthy of enjoying it always!

But enough of it now:

Very truly & Sincerely yours

DÁMODAR K. MÁVALANKAR

V

SECRETARY'S OFFICE OF THE THEOSOPHICAL SOCIETY,
BREACH CANDY, BOMBAY, INDIA.

28th June 1881

My dear Judge

Last time I spoke to you about what happened
to me on my way back to Bombay from Ceylon.
After arriving here you know very well that within a
very few days the "Kitchen row" occurred and there
was a split. Shortly afterwards (Aug. 27 - 1880)
H. P. B. and Col. O. left Bombay for Simla and other
places in the North on the business of the Society
and I was almost alone at the Headquarters. I suppose you know very well that since my leaving off my
caste I have been staying with H. P. B. Mr & Mme.
Coulomb also stayed and have been staying with us
but they are not much interested in these matters.
I worked all alone in H. P. B.'s compartments and
there not a single soul came to disturb me. On the
evening previous to my birthday (in September) I
went as usual for dinner in the evening. The dining
room was just opposite the Bungalow where I had my
table. The outer door of the compound was locked
from inside. We were all three in the dining room.
After dinner we removed to the verandah in H. P. B.'s
Bungalow. A sudden peculiar sensation came over
me and the brilliant moonlight reminded me of my
trip to — where Col. O. & I were magnetised, of which
I think I told you. Presently Mme. C. heard foot-

steps in H.P.B.'s room, and somebody trying to open
the cupboard. I did not hear any such thing but I
did not dare go in as H. P. B. before her departure
had told me not to do so in case I should hear any
noise or voices there. For the same reason I prevented
them from trying to enter there as they wanted to
do for fear there might be some thing. After some
time all that stopped and both of them went to bed.
I went into my writing room the window of which
opens into the verandah where we were sitting after
dinner. And just above the table in front of the
clock was a big triangular note. When I left the
room for dinner there was nothing there as I always
when going in or coming out referred to that clock
and if it had been there before I could not have seen
the figures on the clock and consequently should have
noticed it before. I took it up and opened it and inside was a triangularly folded cap which the Fakirs
and the people in Northern India wear. Inside was
written "To Dámodar" and then were the Initials .˙.
It is a gift I shall always preserve and have it still.
In that place I slept all alone, Mr & Mme. C. sleeping
in the room Miss Bates occupied before, which is in
the opposite bungalow. After that I very often received communications from .˙. and others by post or
in some mysterious way. One night after despatching
the *Theosophist* I went to bed at about one in the
morning. As usual I searched my table and after
putting every thing in order locked the drawers. I
got up in the morning & after taking my bath I
opened the middle drawer of the table & the 1st thing

I saw was a note addressed thus: "Dámodar K. Mavalankar S. By order of ∴." I opened it and it was
written in pure and very high Hindustani so that I
could not understand it and within a few days I got
its translation into English by post. If I were to
mention to you all such communications received by
me I would fill a small volume. I will therefore
mention to you one very important thing which happened within a few days from that time. At about
2 in the morning after finishing my work I locked
the door of the room and lay in my bed. Within
about 2 or 3 minutes I heard H. P. B.'s voice in her
room calling me. I got up with a start and went
in. She said "some persons want to see you" and
after a moment added "Now go out, do not look at
me." Before however I had time to turn my face
I saw her gradually disappear on the spot and from
that very ground rose up the form of ∴. By the
time I had turned back I saw two others dressed
in what I afterwards learned to be Tibetan Clothes.
One of them remained with ∴. in H. P. B.'s room.
The other one I found seated on my bed by the
time I came out. I saluted him & asked him if
he had any orders to give. He said: "If there are
any, they will be told to you, without being asked."
Then he told me to stand still for some time and
began to look at me fixedly. I felt a very pleasant
sensation as if I was getting out of my body. I can
not say now what time passed between that and
what I am now going to relate. But I saw I was
in a peculiar place. It was the upper end of Cashmir

at the foot of the Himalayas. I saw I was taken to
a place where there were only two houses just opposite to each other and no other sign of habitation.
From one of these came out the person who had
written to me the Hindi letter above referred to and
who has been subsequently corresponding with me.
I may mention to you his name since he has allowed
it to be published in Mr Sinnett's book called "The
Occult World" which has just come out. Mr. Sinnett has dedicated the book to this person "Koot
Hoomi ∴ " It was his house. Opposite him stops
∴ Brother K — ordered me to follow him. After
going a short distance of about half a mile we came
to a natural subterranean passage which is under the
Himalayas. The path is very dangerous. There
is a natural causeway on the River Indus which
flows underneath in all its fury. Only one person
can walk on it at a time and one false step seals the
fate of the traveller. Besides this causeway there
are several valleys to be crossed. After walking a
considerable distance through this subterraneous passage we came into an open plain in L —— k. There
is a large massive building thousands of years old.
In front of it is a huge Egyptian Tau. The building
rests on 7 big pillars in the form of pyramids. The
entrance gate has a large triangular arch. Inside are
various apartments. The building is so large that I
think it can easily contain twenty thousand people.
I was shown some of these compartments. This is
the Chief Central Place where all those of our Section
who are found deserving of Initiation into Mysteries

have to go for their final ceremony and stay there the requisite period. I went up with my *Guru* to the Great Hall. The grandeur and serenity of the place is enough to strike any one with awe. The beauty of the Altar which is in the centre and at which every candidate has to take his vows at the time of his Initiation is sure to dazzle the most brilliant eyes. The splendour of the CHIEF's Throne is uncomparable. Every thing is on a geometrical principle & containing various symbols which are explained only to the Initiate. But I cannot say more now as I come now under an obligation of Secresy which K — took from me there. While standing there I do not know what happened but suddenly I got up & found myself in my bed. It was about 8 in the morning. What was that I saw? Was it a dream or a reality? If a reality, how could I traverse the whole of the Himalayas even in my astral body in so short a time? Perplexed with these ideas I was sitting silent when down fell a note on my nose. I opened it and found inside that it was not a dream but that I was taken in some mysterious way in my astral body to the real place of Initiation where I shall be in my body for the Ceremony if I show myself deserving of the blessing. My joy at that moment can be easily conjectured than described — But enough

Very t—— yours,

DÁMODAR K. MÂVALANKAR

VI*

6th September, 1881.

My dear Judge

I have received your favour of the 11th July. You ask me what is my belief about "re-incarnation"? Well, as it is a complicated question, I must give you a plain statement of my full belief.

To begin with, I am a Pantheist and not a Theist or a Deist. I believe that the whole Universe is God. You must however well understand that the word "God" does not convey to me any meaning attached to that word by the Westerns. When I say God, I understand it to be Nature or Universe and no more. Therefore, I might more appropriately be called a "Naturalist." To my mind there is no possibility of the existence of an extra-cosmical Deity. For if there were such a possibility the harmony or equilibrium in nature could not be preserved and the whole Universe instead of being one harmonious whole would be but a Tower of Babel. This harmony can be kept only by the working of the Immutable Laws of Nature. And if the Laws of Nature are Immutable, they must be blind and require no guid-

---

*[Portions of this letter appeared first in *The Platonist*, and later in *The Theosophist*, June, 1884, under the title 'Reincarnation,' and in *The Path*, January, 1896, under the title "Some Views of an Asiatic." The valuable footnotes, signed EDITOR, which Mr. Judge appended in *The Path*, have been added to the present transcription of the original MS.   — EDS.]

ance.* Hence the existence of an extra-cosmical Deity is impossible. This, as far as I can understand, is the Chief teaching and principle of Aryan Philosophy. The Aryan and the Shemite Philosophies differ from each other in this fundamental Idea, viz., that while the former is pantheistic, *i. e.*, not acknowledging the existence of an extra-cosmical God, the latter is Monotheistic, *i. e.*, admitting the existence of an intelligent Creator existing outside the cosmos. How far either of this is true I cannot say. But, as I think the former to be a logical position while the latter merely a matter of blind faith, I accept the former. Now some of the Pantheists recognise the existence of two distinct existences, viz., Matter and Spirit. But thinking deeply over the Subject has led me to the conclusion that this position is not quite logical. For, as far as I can understand, there can be but one Infinite Existence and not two. Call it either Matter or Spirit, anything you like, but it is one and the same. For who can say that this is Spirit and this is Matter? Can you draw any where a line between the two? Take an instance. Ice is a gross form of matter. Suppose it is a little rarefied,

---

*Allowance must be made all through for a lack of complete knowledge of the English language. What is here meant is that the inherent impulse acts according to its own laws without any *extra-cosmic* power meddling with it as a guide. — EDITOR

[Dâmodar himself appends a similar note at this point in the Letter where it appears in *The Theosophist*, and calls the attention of the reader to his article "The Metaphysical Basis af Esoteric Buddhism." See Chapter II of this volume. — EDS.]

you will have water, which you will still call matter. Higher still, you have vapour, but it is still matter. Higher again, it becomes atmosphere, but still it is matter. Furthermore, it becomes ether, but still it is matter, and thus you may go *ad infinitum.* Thus becoming more and more sublimated it will reach its climax of the process of spiritualization. But still it does not become nothing. For if it does, there must come a time when the whole Universe will be nothing. If it is so, it is not infinite as it has an end. If it has an end, it must have a beginning. If it had a beginning, it must have been created and thus we must assume the existence of an extra-cosmical Deity, which, as said above, is not a logical position. Then we thus find logically that this highest sublimated form of matter cannot be nothing. In this case matter has reached that climax of Sublimation or Spiritualization when any further action would make it grosser, not finer. What is commonly understood by the word "Spirit" then is nothing but that highly etherealized form of matter which we with our finite senses can not comprehend. But it is still matter in as much as it is still something and liable to be grosser. Some argue that these terms are adopted to signify the two extreme conditions of matter. But then I can not with my finite senses comprehend where you can draw the line between Matter and Spirit. And the gradations being infinite, I give up this task as hopeless for me, an imperfect finite being. Well then, there is *only one* eternal Infinite Existence, call it either Spirit or Matter. I will however designate it by the latter name as that term is most suited in its common understanding for what I am to state. Matter, as you know, we call *Maya*. Now some say that Matter, when assuming form and shape and being temporary, is illusion and therefore does not really exist. But I do not agree there. In my opinion — and such is that of every rational metaphysician — it is *the only* Existence. And it is called *Maya simply on account of these Transformations.* It is never steady. The Process is ever working. The one Infinite Agglomeration of matter is in some of its modes becoming grosser and grosser, while, in others, becoming more and more sublimated. The Circle is ever turning its round. Nothing goes out of that Circle. Every thing is kept within its bounds by the action of the Centripetal and the Centrifugal Forces. The forms are changing but the *Inner* substance remains the same. You will naturally ask what is the use of our being good or bad, if Nature has her own course? Our souls will be etherealised in their proper time? But then, what is a Soul? Is it material or immaterial? Well it *is* material for me as there is nothing immaterial as said above. Then what is it? Well, as far as I can think, it is an agglomeration of all the attributes together with that something which gives us the consciousness that we are. And just as Thought is Matter, so is every attribute Matter. It might be then asked, will not our souls be etherealised in their proper turn? Well, then take here again the instance of Ice. It is the grossest form of matter. We say it then becomes water. But will it be so unless it comes in contact with heat? Decidedly not. The action of the Centripetal Force is strong and it keeps up together the particles of Ice. It requires the action of Centrifugal Force, which is done by the supply of heat. If that piece of Ice be left in a cold place it will remain so until by accident Sun's rays might penetrate there or in some such way heat might be supplied. Just so then with man. The action of the Centripetal Force keeps us to our gross forms. And if we have to etherealise ourselves we must supply the Centrifugal Force, which is our WILL. And this is the first principle of OCCULTISM. Just as the etherealisation of our Souls is the result of the action of our Will, so is everything else the result of something else. The action of the working of the Circle of Matter is regulated by the Law of Cause and Effect. Nothing can be without it. And everything is at the same time in itself a Cause and an Effect. Take, for instance, heat. It is the cause of the melting of ice into water and at the same time it is the result of some other force. It did not come out of nothing. Then, how can we etherealise ourselves? By studying the action of Causes and Effects and acting accordingly. Or, in other words, by obtaining knowledge of the Forces of Nature — in one word, by studying occultism. You might ask, Can we not rise higher and higher without being Occultists? I reply, decidedly not to that extent to which an Occultist will rise. You will simply desire to rise higher? Well, as said above, this is only the first principle of occultism. And just as one step leads you to

certain progress, more Knowledge will lead you to
a greater progress; for every result must be in proportion to the cause producing it. As said above the
action of matter is always going on. And we are
every instant emitting and attracting various atoms
of matter. Now a person who is not an occultist will
have various desires and unconsciously to himself
he will produce a Cause which will attract to him
such atoms of matter as are not suited for his higher
progress. The same way, when he is emitting others,
he may give them such a tendency that they will mix
with others evilly inclined and thus other Individu-
alities which are thus formed will have to suffer for no
fault of theirs. While an Occultist directs both. He
is the Master of the Situation. He is not guided by
the blind Forces of Nature. He guides them. And
by knowing their action, he produces such conditions
as are favourable to his attaining "Nirvana."* But
what is Nirvana? By Nirvana I do not mean any
locality but a *state*. It is that condition in which we
are so etherealised that instead of being merely a mode
of the one Infinite Existence as at present, we are
merged into Totality or we become THE WHOLE.
There is also another reason why an advanced occultist is superior to one who merely is content with the
first step mentioned above. The more he studies and
understands the action of the Forces of Nature, the
more is he in a position to benefit Humanity. While
the one is merely content with his own advancement

---

*It is said that Buddha attained to Nirvana before he left
this earth, hence he was always free.   — EDITOR

— the other one, the advanced occultist, places his happiness in the good of Humanity which he practically assists and benefits. Perhaps you might ask that as the Universe is evolving, there must come a time when this process of evolution must cease and *in*volution begin; and when the latter process has done her course, everything will be in Nirvana; and therefore what is the use of troubling oneself with the study of Occultism, etc., if we can be just as well in that state? But then there are two reasons why we should do it. The first is, we do not know when the process of involution will begin and perhaps millions and billions of years might pass before everything is in Nirvana, and who knows through how many transformations we may have to pass, for, as said above, Matter is never steady but is ever changing forms. A practical occultist reaches that state in a comparatively very short time. The other reason is — When everything will be in Nirvana, it will not be *me* that attains Nirvana. And here I must state I believe that a man can attain Nirvana only *in this life and no other*. If I do not go to *Nirvana* some time after death, where do I go in the end, you will naturally ask? My reply is that if I do not keep up my Individuality, I lose it. My *Ego* remains; but my Individuality is lost. I lose that something which at present furnishes to me the consciousness that I am Damodar, that I exist as such. My Spiritual Soul or *Ego* if pure and good may be etherealised and reach Nirvana state but it will no longer be the Individuality of Damodar that will attain that state.

Therefore I must keep up that Individuality until
I reach Nirvana state. And how to do it is taught
by occultism. I did not come out of Nothing. The
particles of which I am formed have always existed,
and yet I do not know in what form they existed
before. Probably they have passed through millions
or billions of Transformations.* And why do I not
know it now? Because I did not retain my Individuality. I did not supply the action of the Force
that would not have allowed the disintegration of my
Individuality.† Occultism furnishes that Key. And
if I act up accordingly I may attain Nirvana. But
then I shall not be eternally in that state. For it
is unjust that the actions of a few years should be
rewarded or punished eternally. At the most, how
long can a human life last? Not more than four
hundred years. Would it then be just that my actions of so short a period should be punished or rewarded eternally? For what are even billions of years
compared to eternity? Well, then you might say
what is the use of our attaining Nirvana if we are to
come back again? The reasons are twofold. The

---

*That all the particles of the matter of our universe have
passed through millions of transformations, and been in every
sort of form, is an old assertion of the Adepts. H. P. B. in
Isis Unveiled, and the *Secret Doctrine* points this out as showing
how the Adept may use matter, and it will also bear upon the
protean shapes the astral matter may assume.   — EDITOR

†This word is used to mean the personalities; the person in
any birth. Since the letter was written, *individuality* is much
used to mean the indestructible part.   — EDITOR

first is — I shall be in Nirvana for some time, so long as the action of the Force keeps me there, or, in other words, I shall be there until the completion of the result of my endeavours to attain it, the effect being always in proportion to the Cause. Here again you might ask, but can we not keep up this process *ad infinitum?* Certainly you can not, because the Law of Exhaustion must assert itself.* Everything you do must be to the detriment of another, or, in other words, you exhaust a certain amount of Energy to produce a certain Result. The other reason is that while you are passing through this process of etherealisation you all along give a certain tendency to the particles of which you are formed. This tendency will always assert itself and thus in every Cycle, i. e., in each Circle of your transformation or Re-incarnation, you will have the same advantages which you can always utilise to be soon free, and, by remaining longer in Nirvana State than the generality of Humanity, you are comparatively free.† So every consciousness which has been once fully developed must disintegrate if not preserved by the purity of its successive *Egos* till the attainment of Nirvana

---

*If this be right — and I agree with it — Nirvana has to come to an end, just as Devachan must; and being ended, the individual must return to some manifested plane or world for further work.   — EDITOR

†The comparison made is with the general run of men in all races. They are not free at any time. In the writer's opinion there is a certain amount of freedom in being in Nirvana; but he refers to other and secret doctrines which he does not explain.   — EDITOR

State. Now I believe that the full development of my consciousness as Damodar is possible only upon this earth* and therefore should a person die before his consciousness is developed, he must be reborn on this earth. And this is possible only in two states, viz., if one dies in childhood, or as a congenital idiot. Or there is a third state possible, which is this. Suppose I am studying Occultism and I reach a certain stage where I am able to retain my Individuality suppose my body should be incapacitated for my practical purposes. Then with my Knowledge I can choose any body I like, for, as I said above, Nirvana State is possible of attainment only in this earthly life. I may be in any other body, but my Individuality will be the same as now and I shall know myself as Damodar.

And now I suppose this is sufficient for you. It is very difficult to put such ideas on paper, for the process is tedious. Such things are to be understood intuitionally and therefore our conceptions of them are more ethereal. The first thing I have to do is

*This has always been accepted, that only on earth could we unify the great potential trinity in each, so that we are conscious of the union, and that when that is done, and not before, we may triumph over all illusions, whether of name or form, place or time, or any other. — EDITOR

[It is interesting to note that in the sentence in the text to which this note is appended, Mr. Judge in his *Path* publication uses the name *Krishna* instead of *Dâmodar,* as also at the end of the paragraph. This same substitution is found in *The Theosophist* article, which seems to indicate that Dâmodar himself may have suggested the change. — EDS.]

to materialise my thought, put it into shape and then write down. I have also to think of the objections that might be naturally raised. And therefore in such matters I find it easier to discuss orally than write or speak. I must have missed many points but I have given you the principal ideas so that you may put your questions and I will be most happy to answer them. I must however ask you to hold me alone responsible for any mistakes. I have merely read "Isis Unveiled" and heard H. P. B. talk often with others as also *The Higher Powers* on some few occasions. I have got hints from them. But the subsequent working is entirely of my own making. If you think it good and correct, all credit is due to them — our Brothers — for having got the hints from them and H. P. B. If there are any mistakes, the whole fault rests entirely with me for not having properly understood their teachings. And this would but show that I am greatly lacking in my intuition.

You ask me what my opinion about the West is? Well, to be candid, I can not think very highly of a Theosophical Society that can not go on without the child's toy of a ritual! This very fact itself proves to me that the West is not

[Here the MS. ends abruptly, but it is evident that at most a paragraph or two only have been lost. — Eds.]

LETTERS TO A. P. SINNETT

I

THE THEOSOPHICAL SOCIETY

February, 1881.

With reference to the Rules and Organization of the Society, I beg to make the following suggestions. The points I urge, appear to me very necessary as I have had conversation with many Natives and have a claim to know the Hindu character better than a foreigner can.

A general impression appears to prevail that the Society is a religious sect. This impression owes its origin, I think, to a common belief that the whole Society is devoted to Occultism. As far as I can judge, this is not the case. If it is, the best course to adopt would be to make the entire Society a secret one, and shut its doors against all except those very few who may have shown a determination to devote their whole lives to the study of Occultism. If it is not so, and is based upon the broad Humanitarian principle of Universal Brotherhood, let Occultism, one of its several Branches, be an entirely secret study. From time immemorial this sacred knowledge has been guarded from the vulgar with great care, and because a few of us have had the great fortune to come into contact with some of the custodians of this invaluable treasure, is it right on our part to take advantage of their kindness and vulgarize the secrets they esteem more sacred than even their lives? The world is not yet prepared to hear truth about this subject. By placing the facts before the unprepared general public, we only make a laughing stock of those who have been kind to us and have accepted us as their co-workers for doing good to humanity. By harping too much upon this subject, we have made ourselves in a measure odious in the eyes of the public. We went even to such an extent that, unconsciously to ourselves, we led the public to believe that our Society is under the sole management of the Adepts, while the fact is that the entire executive management is in the hands of the Founders, and our Teachers give us advice only in rare exceptional cases of the greatest emergency. The public saw that they must have misapprehended the facts, since errors in the Management of the Society — some of which could have been very well avoided by the exercise of ordinary common sense — were from time to time exposed. Hence they came to the conclusion that

(1) Either Adepts do not exist at all; or

(2) If they do, they have no connection with our Society, and therefore we are dishonest imposters; or

(3) If they have any connection with the Society, it must be only those of a very low degree, since, under their management, such errors occurred.

With the few noble exceptions who had entire confidence in us, our Native Members came to one of these three conclusions. It is therefore necessary in my opinion that prompt measures should be adopted to remove these suspicions. For this, I see only one alternative:— (1) Either the entire Society should be devoted to occultism, in which case it should be quite as secret as the Masonic or the Rosicrucian Lodge or, (2) Nobody should know anything about occultism except those very few who may have by their conduct shown their determination to devote themselves to its study. The first alternative being found inadvisable by our "Brothers" and positively forbidden, the second remains.

Another important question is that of the admission of Members. Until now, anyone who expressed a desire to join and could get two sponsors was allowed to come into the Society, without our inquiring closely what the motives in joining were. This led to two evil results. People thought or pretended to think that we took in Members simply for their Initiation Fees on which we lived; and many joined out of mere curiosity, as they thought that by paying an Initiation Fee of Rupees Ten, they could see phenomena. And when they were disappointed in this, they turned round on us, and began to revile our CAUSE for which we have been working and to which we have pledged our lives. The best way to remedy this evil would be to exclude this class of persons. The question naturally arises how can this be done, since our Rules are so liberal as to admit every one? But, at the same time our Rules prescribe an Initiation Fee of Rupees Ten. This is too low to keep out the curiosity seekers, who, for the chance of being satisfied, feel they can very well afford to lose such a paltry sum. The fee should therefore be so much increased that those only would join who are really in earnest. We need men of principle and serious purpose. One such man can do more for us than hundreds of phenomena-hunters. The fee should in my judgment be increased to Rs: 200 or Rs: 300. It might be urged that thus we might exclude really good men who may be sincere and earnest but unable to pay. But I think it is preferable to risk the possible loss of one good man than take in a crowd of idlers, one of whom can undo the work of all the former. And yet, even this contingency can be avoided. For, as now we admit some to membership, who appear especially deserving, without their paying their own fees, so could the same thing be done under the proposed change.

DAMODAR K. MAVALANKAR, F. T. S.

Respectfully submitted to the consideration of Mr. Sinnett.

II

Respectfully submitted for the consideration of Mr. Sinnett, under the direct orders of Brother Koot Hoomi.

DAMODAR K. MAVALANKAR.

With the exception of fee — too exaggerated — his views are quite correct. Such is the impression produced upon the native mind. I trust, my dear friend, that you add a paragraph showing the Society in its true light. Listen to your *inner voice*, and oblige me once more,

Yours very faithfully,

K. H.

III

PUBLICATION OFFICE OF THE "THEOSOPHIST,"
BREACH CANDY, BOMBAY, INDIA,
5th June, 1882.

A. P. SINNETT ESQ.,
  ED. "PIONEER"
    SIMLA.

MY DEAR SIR,

When Mme Blavatsky left for Calcutta she left with me (March 30th) a letter for Mr. O'Conor with instructions to forward it to the addressee during the first week of June, if not otherwise ordered. I was accordingly to forward it by to-morrow's mail but I have just been ordered to forward it to you. I therefore enclose it to you now. Please excuse haste — no time to lose — the mail is about to close.

I hope you have received the two telegrams.

Yours
DAMODAR K. M.

IV

PUBLICATION OFFICE OF THE "THEOSOPHIST,"
BREACH CANDY, BOMBAY, INDIA,
26th August, 1882.

A. P. SINNETT ESQ., F. T. S.,
  THE TENDRIL, SIMLA, PUNJAB.

MY DEAR SIR,

It is with the greatest pain and reluctance that I write this letter but I beg of you the indulgence to give this a patient and careful reading.

Last evening Mme. B. received a letter from Mr. Hume, from which she read to me the portion relating to myself. I am accused of being a forger! Mme. B. asked me what Mr. Hume meant for no one could be more surprised at such a groundless charge than she was, for *she* KNOWS *me*. I now remember that about three months ago (I am not sure about the time) a letter was thrown to me at night. I took it up and saw the address. I could distinctly see that the handwriting was familiar to me but it was neither K. H.'s nor M. sahib's, nor Gjwala Khool's. I thought over it and suspected that it was Fern's own signature. I then compared the superscripture with the signature in one of Mr. Fern's letters and found them identical. *Knowing* that even the *chelas* (advanced ones of course) can do such phenomenal things, I said nothing about it except, when forwarding the letter to Mr. Fern I expressed my surprise, or what I do not remember. The address on that letter is now made the pretext for my being called a FORGER!!! Now you know me, Mr. Sinnett, you have seen me, talked with me:— I appeal to your sense of an English gentleman to say whether you consider me *capable* of such an infamy. It is for you to decide what you would call a person who dubs you with the title of a forger for your being merely instrumental in forwarding to him the letter from a mutual friend. My only sin consisted in volunteering to be such a medium of communication. Last year when Mme. B. was so much abused and when it was thought desirable that she should be out of this business as much as possible, *for her sake* I took it upon myself

to be a medium of correspondence between my MAS-
TERS and the Simla Eclectic Theosophists. You
know very well under what circumstances I took this
thing up. But alas! with what result: to be called a
forger or be suspected to be one! Until now I was
proud enough to think that I would not be suspected
of any such infamy at least by persons who now seem
to do so, since all my nearest friends, acquaintances
and all, will give their life to proclaim that I have
never uttered *an untruth even* as yet, and never will.
Well, this proves to me one thing. The world and
especially the several sceptical European races *are not
prepared* and *utterly unfit* for Occultism. Those of our
MASTERS who will have nothing to do with the Europeans are, I say, perfectly right. I care a fig for the
opinion of the outside world. I *know* that I stand like
a mirror before *my* MASTERS. They *do* know me and
They are quite sure that with all my faults I am yet
honest, truthful, sincere, and faithful. Weaknesses I
have many, foremost among which are indiscretion,
imprudence, and still a lingering particle of diffidence
of undertaking any work of serious responsibility. But
THEY *know* I have never played either a "double" or
any game with anyone, much less with *Them*. But
when I am once suspected, I can have nothing to do with
the business. I am a perfect slave of my MASTERS
and if *They* order me I have but to obey. Otherwise
I now positively decline to have anything to do with
the correspondence any of you may have to keep with
Them. Mme. B. has already broken her connection.
I should like to see *what chela* would now volunteer to

do it. I am afraid none. And I do not believe THEY will under the circumstances *compel* any *Chela* to do it. If therefore for want of an intervening channel the communication between THEM and the outside world is at an end, it is neither Their fault nor ours. A cold shoulder ought to be shown to the European world as it well deserves. Of course I do not mean you. If the Europeans have self-respect, we poor Hindoos have too. We never set ourselves up as of *the superior race* but we have some sense in us of self-respect. I see that the cycle is at an end or rather will be in about two months and a half, and this affair must gradually stop. I have too much respect, reverence and love for my MASTERS, to hear THEM talked of as if THEY were so many ignorant babies. And I feel very much for Mme. B. She has been worrying herself for over three years so much so that she has utterly spoiled her constitution. She is unwell and last evening the Doctor said that her whole blood is spoiled. We know what it means. My only hope and prayer is that she may be spared for some time for the sake of the Society. By the Society I mean the Asiatics, for I am firmly convinced that the Europeans have not the stuff in them of Occultists. Of course there are some *very rare exceptions* like you but exceptions only confirm the Rule. I am afraid that if H. P. B. is still worried as she has been, I do not know what may soon happen. I have been trying to induce her to go beyond Darjeeling or some such place for two or three months, where she will neither see nor hear of the world's vilest tricks which has been the chief cause of her ill-health — and then return after she is completely cured. But she says it is better to die when she is almost dead rather than be well and again go through the same process of gradual death. Some day I do not know what news we may learn of her if she is thus persistently ill-treated so mercilessly.

. . . .* of retiring and we shall probably soon have to follow. For you personally I have the highest regard for I believe you to be one of the exceptions mentioned above, but I am compelled to adopt the present course. I have at least one consolation and that is I stand clear before my MASTERS who being clairvoyant can see through me *any time,* and to try to deceive Them when writing or speaking to Them is an useless dodge which can be at once detected.

As if to add insult to injury, Mr. Hume sends to Mme. B. for publication in the *Theosophist* an article about my MASTERS, which, to say the least, is most repulsive to the feelings of us Hindoos!

With the profoundest sympathies and kindest regards for you,

I remain,

Yours truly,

DAMODAR K. MAVALANKAR.

---

*Half a page of the original has been cut out here. — ED.

V

PUBLICATION OFFICE OF THE "THEOSOPHIST,"
BREACH CANDY, BOMBAY, INDIA,
4th September, 1882.

A. P. SINNETT ESQ.,
    THE TENDRIL, SIMLA.

MY DEAR SIR,

I am very sorry to learn that my last long letter has offended you. Personally for you I have always entertained the highest regard, and as Mme. Blavatsky might tell you I have never lost an opportunity to express to her and to others sentiments of great admiration for you on account of your devotion to the Cause of Theosophy and to the Brothers. My last letter was meant not for you but for Mr. Hume; but as I find I have thereby hurt you, I beg to be excused for the same. I wrote it when I was under a feeling of excitement to see the Brothers and Mme. B. talked of so lightly and myself accused in plain language of forgery. But to offend you in any way — you who have all along been doing every thing in your power for the Society — was as far from my mind as to commit a forgery or a murder. I hope therefore that this letter of apology will atone for my unconscious sin. I can assure upon my word that not a single syllable of what I wrote in my last, applied to you personally. Now however that I see my fault in having given way to a feeling of despair and annoyance, I cannot do better than apologise for the same. With kind regards,

Believe me,
Ever yours sincerely,
DAMODAR K. MAVALANKAR.

LETTER TO MRS. CABLES

Secretary's Office of the Theosophical Society,
Adyar (Madras), India, 25th May, '84.

Mrs. Josephine W. Cables, F. T. S.,
40 Ambrose St., Rochester, N. Y., U. S. A.

Dear Madame and Sister, — I have carefully and with pleasure read your letter received two days ago. It should be at first realized that the Mahatmas are constantly and incessantly engaged in the helping of the onward progress of humanity. The higher they rise the more they are united to the more permanent and more ubiquitous. In fact, it is this union which marks the progress. Thus in one sense the real Mahatmas may be said to be almost everywhere, although they may not take cognizance of everything. But at the same time they cannot help giving their attention to where the magnetic attraction draws them; and hence to come under the notice of the Mahatmas depends upon oneself. We must also remember that what we are is the result of what we were, and hence whatever we enjoy or suffer is the just retribution meted out by the law of Karma, which cannot err. To our undeveloped minds various sufferings may look like acts of injustice on the part of nature, but we should not forget that justice is the immutable and fundamental law of nature, and whatever result may appear unjust must be the effect of some remote cause, although the apparent cause and the immediate one may seem to produce an unjust effect — whatever is, is right in nature. It rests with us to so produce the causes as will make our future destiny better, and ensure our future progress, but we cannot meddle with effects. Of course it is possible that while certain causes are operating we may combine to them a cause or set of them as will modify the result; but we must not forget that it is impossible for us to obliterate the causes already produced. Now, if we want to rise higher, we must produce the necessary conditions. In the first place we know that the higher states are more and more ubiquitous. Hence what we must first do is to centre our *manas* (the fifth principle) in those higher ubiquitous states, and this can be done only by constantly disassociating ourselves from the lower desires, &c., which chain us to our narrow personality, and by transferring our consciousness to the *Divine Atma,* and its vehicle (6th and 7th principles) by incessantly cultivating within ourselves the highest aspirations.

The more we succeed in doing that, the more do we obtain knowledge, for the seventh principle is itself absolute knowledge, and by our living in it, as it were, we live in knowledge.

In the second place, we must know that to help purity of thought in ourselves, we must be surrounded by the pure thoughts of others. Hence the more we help others to be pure by education, by teaching them the *Law of Karma* and of *Cosmic Evolution,* the

more we help ourselves, for the purity of others ele-
vates the surrounding objective nature into a more
subjective state, and those subjective currents react
upon us to help us in our higher evolution. Hence
a feeling of *unselfish philanthropy* is an essential
necessity. Also a sense of discrimination and an intellect that can properly understand the operation of
the *Law of Karma* and of *cause* and *effect*. You
will thus see that no interference or recommendation
is necessary, and that for the *Mahatmas* to assist
any one is the result of a purely psychological attraction — an immutable *Law of Nature,* which no
one can override.

I have read carefully the new paper you have
started, and wish you success in the same. The
Theosophical Society affords to every one the best
means of assisting humanity and thereby assisting
himself and whoever increases its sphere of useful-
ness *unselfishly* cannot but be rewarded by the
Mahatmas and *Nature.*

With fraternal regards to all the brothers and
sisters.

Sincerely yours,
DÂMODAR K. MÂVALANKAR

VI

References to Dâmodar

by the

Mahâtmans and H. P. Blavatsky

[The extensive correspondence between the Mahâtmans and the two Englishmen, A. P. Sinnett and A. O. Hume, as well as the many letters written to the latter by H. P. Blavatsky in the early days of the Theosophical Society, contain many references to a large number of those most closely connected with the work of the Society, outstanding among whom was Dâmodar.

This Chapter is devoted to relevant passages from these Letters. A large number of short references have been omitted, which simply mention Dâmodar as transmitting messages and letters from the Mahâtmans and H. P. Blavatsky by occult means and otherwise; and one or two other unimportant references which are not comprehensible without long explanations.

Signatures are herein given as they appear at the end of the Letters quoted from. Chronological arrangement has been followed according to the latest information published by Mrs. Margaret Conger and Miss Mary K. Neff.

—Eds.]

PART I

QUOTATIONS FROM "THE MAHATMA LETTERS TO A. P. SINNETT"

LETTER VIII

[Received at Bombay. Feb. 20, 1881.]

. . . I wrote a few words in the Maratha boy's letter, only to show you that he was obeying *orders* in submitting his views to you. Apart from his exaggerated idea about *huge fees*, his letter is in a way worth considering. For Damodar is a Hindu — and knows the mind of his people at Bombay; though the Bombay Hindus are about as unspiritual a group as can be found in all India. But, like the devoted enthusiastic lad he is, he jumped after the misty form of his own ideas even before I could give them the right direction. . . .   — K. H.

LETTER CXXXIV

[Sent from Dehra Dun. Nov. 4, 1881.
Received at Allahabad. Nov. (?) 1881.]

. . . Adetyarom B. wrote a foolish letter to Damodar and Benemadhab writes a foolish request to Mr. Sinnett.

. . . I will be pleased if Mr. Sinnett says, to everyone of those who may address him with similar pretensions the following: "The 'Brothers' desire me to in-form one and all of you, *natives*, that unless a man is prepared to become a thorough theosophist *i. e.* to do as D. Mavalankar did,— give up entirely caste, his old superstitions and show himself a true reformer (especially in the case of child marriage) he will remain simply a member of the Society with no hope whatever of ever hearing from us. . . ."

— H. P. BLAVATSKY

LETTER XLIII

[Received at Allahabad. 1882.]

. . . As you have already been notified by Damodar thro' the D——, I did not call you a chela — examine your letter to assure yourself of it — I but jokingly asked O. the question whether he recognised in you the stuff of which chelas are made. . . . — M.

LETTER XLVIII

[Received at Allahabad. March 3, 1882.]

. . . Bhavani Shanker is with O., and he is stronger and fitter in many a way more than Damodar or even our mutual "female" friend. . . .   — K. H.

LETTER LXXXVIII

[Received at Allahabad. March 11, 1882.]

. . . My good friend — it is very easy for us to give phenomenal proofs when we have necessary conditions. For instance — Olcott's magnetism after six years of purification is intensely sympathetic with ours — physically and morally is constantly becoming more

so. Damodar and Bhavani Rao being congenitally sympathetic their auras help — instead of repelling and impeding phenomenal experiments. After a time you may become so — it depends on yourself. To force phenomena in the presence of difficulties magnetic and other is forbidden, as strictly for a bank cashier to disburse money which is only entrusted to him. . . .
— K. H.

Letter XI

[Received at Allahabad. June 30, 1882.]

. . . Yes I am quite ready to look over your 50 or 60 pages and make notes on the margins: have them set up by all means and send them to me either through little "Deb" or Damodar and Djual Kul will transmit them. . . . — K. H.

Letter XVI

[Received at Simla. July, 1882.]

. . . Olcott is on his way to Lanka and Damodar packed up to Poona for a month, his foolish austerities and hard work having broken down his physical constitution. I will have to look after him, and perhaps, to take him away, if it comes to the worst. . . .
— K. H.

Letter XXX

[Received at Simla. Aug., 1882.]

. . . None of our *Upasika* or *Yu-posah*, neither H. P. B. nor O., nor even Damodar, nor any of them can be incriminated. . . . — K. H.

Letter XXXII

[Received at Simla. (Aug. or Sept.) 1882.]

. . . Since we have mixed ourselves with the outside world, we have no right to suppress the personal opinion of its individual members, nor eschew their criticisms, however unfavourable to us — hence the positive order to H. P. B. to publish Mr. Hume's article. Only, as we would have the world see both sides of the question, we have also allowed the joint protest* of Deb, Subba Row, Damodar and a few other chelas — to follow his criticism of ourselves and our System in the Theosophist. . . . — K. H.

Letter LXXXIII

[Received at London. (Sept. or Oct.) 1883.]

I am advised to request that, for the future, communications intended for me may be sent thro' either Damodar or Henry Olcott. Madam B's discretion is not improving in ratio with her physiological enfeeblement. — K. H.

Letter CXXVIII

Indian Telegraph.

To	From
Station Adyar Madras	Station Jammoo
To	From
Person Madame Blavatsky	Person Colonel Olcott
Editor of the Theosophist.	

*[See Ch. IV, 'A Protest.' — Eds.]

Damodar left before dawn at about eight o'clock letters from him and Koothumi found on my table — Don't say whether return or not — Damodar bids us all farewell conditionally and says brother theosophists should all feel encouraged knowing that he has found the blessed masters and been called by them. The dear boys recent developments astonishing Hooney bids me await orders.

Madras 25-11-83. Hour 17.30.

LETTER CXXIX

Class P.　　　INDIAN TELEGRAPH.　　Local No. 48

To	From
Station Adyar Madras	Station Jummar
To	From
Person Madame Blavatsky	Person Col. Olcott

The	Masters	have
taken	Damodar	return
not	promised	

We will send him back. K. H.

Adyar 25-11-83. Hour 10.15.

LETTER LV

[Received at Elberfeld. (Sept. or Oct.) 1884.]

. . . It would be well also to burn wood-fires in the rooms now and then, and carry about as fumigators open vessels (braziers?) with burning wood. You might also ask Damodar to send you some bundles of incense-sticks for you to use for this purpose. These are helps, but the best of all means to drive out unwelcome guests of this sort, is to live purely in deed and thought. . . .

. . . I can now send my occasional instructions and letters with any certainty only thro' Damodar. But before I can do even so much the Soc. especially the H. Qrs. will have to pass first thro' the coming crisis. . . .   — K. H.

LETTER LXIII

[Received at London. Oct., 1884.]

. . . My letters *must not* be published, in the manner you suggest, but on the contrary if you save Djual K. trouble copies of some should be sent to the Literary Committee at Adyar — about which Damodar has written to you — so that with the assistance of S. Y. K. Charya, Djual K., Subba Row and the Secret Committee (from which H. P. B. was purposely excluded by us to avoid new suspicions and calumnies) they might be able to utilise the information for the realization of the object with which the Committee was started, as explained by Damodar in the letter written by him under orders. . . .   — K. H.

LETTER CXXXVIII

[Sent from Adyar. March 17, 1885.]

. . . Happy Damodar! He went to the land of Bliss, to Tibet and must now be far away in the regions of our Masters. No one will ever see him now, I expect. . . .   — H. P. BLAVATSKY

LETTER LXV

[Received at London, Mar. 27, 1885.]

. . . They declined (though the reason they gave was another one) — to receive our instructions through Subba Row and Damodar, the latter of whom is hated by Messrs. L. Fox and Hartmann.   Subba R. resigned and Damodar went to Tibet.   Are our Hindus to be blamed for this? . . .   — K. H.

PART II

QUOTATIONS FROM "THE LETTERS OF
H. P. BLAVATSKY TO A. P. SINNETT"

LETTER VII

[Received at Allahabad. Nov., 1881.]

. . . The Disinherited wants to write to you he says — if you permit him — through Damodar. The Boss said something about going to see Damodar. But D —— does not say a word. . . . — H. P. BLAVATSKY

LETTER XX

[Sent from Bombay. Dec. 7, 1881.
Received at Allahabad. Dec., 1881.]

. . . The *Theosophist* not out yet and we are the 8th to-day! Why? Because *without me* all went topsy-turvy and 2,000 Rupees of subscription money spent for what — better ask the wind. Damodar is as loony as a March hare. . . .   — H. P. B.

LETTER Xc

[Received at Simla. June 4, 1882.]

. . . As for O'Conor's letter it is such a stupid transparent thing for me that it is not worth talking about. I did receive his letter *one hour later* than E.'s for Mrs. Gordon; and with it orders to do about it as I liked, to either answer it or not but *to hold my tongue* as to the fact of my having received it until further developments. I left it with Damodar and Deb on March 30th with instructions. And to prove it *to you* — (about others I do not care) let me, my dear Boss, set your heart at ease. I happened to write to you about this O'Conor's letter on Friday — (at Madras) the Disinherited having advised me to do so. I sent my letter Friday. On Saturday, at 1.35 p.m. I received your telegram with your enquiry about O'Conor's letter. I answered as I *was ordered* and wrote to you that I should telegraph to Damodar in whose possession I left my answer to O'Conor to send it to you immediately. I sent the telegram on Saturday evening, but whether sent or not that night, it reached Damodar but Sunday when it was too late to send you a *registered* letter as he always does. Well, he sent it on Monday and you must have received it. Do not send it to O'Conor. I will have nothing to do with Mrs. Scott's friends now. I will have no more *tests*, no more *insults*, no more *humiliation* and *explanation*. Tear it after showing it to Mr. Hume. You are at liberty to show him also *this letter*. If your friends and sceptics will insist that, after receiving your telegram of enquiry I had time between Saturday and Monday to send to my "confederate" Damodar instructions, well show them the telegram he received from me on Sunday. This will prove, at least, that he had O'Conor's answer in his possession ever since March.   — H. P. BLAVATSKY

LETTER XD

To	*From*
Malabar Hill	Madras St. Thome

To	*From*
Damodar K. Mavalankar	H. P. Blavatsky

c/o Theosophical Society,
Breach Candy

Letter	to	Oconor
given	you	March
thirty	send	Sinnett.

By Malabar Hill: 4-6-82.

LETTER XIV

[Sent from Bombay. Aug. 4, 1882.]

. . . Poor Damodar is still at Poona, but is all right now in health. The brothers picked him up and even endowed him with such a mesmeric force that he cured several desperate cases (one *blindness* in a boy) in a few days. Whether it will last or not I do not know. But the Poona Fellows craved for something phenomenal and he gave it to them. . . .

— H. P. BLAVATSKY

LETTER XVI

[Sent from Bombay. Aug. 26, 1882.]

. . . Damodar will write to Fern to decline receiving his letters to M. henceforth. He will not run the risk of being called a *forger*, and impostor and what not. *Damodar a deceiver!!* I may as well suspect Olcott or yourself of forgery or deceit as him. I won't have him insulted and that's all. . . . — H. P. B.

Letter XXV

[Sent from 'Ooty.' Aug. 23, 1883. Rec'd. at London. Oct. 1883.]

. . . Then about "Uncle Sam's" complaint — what the devil do *I* know about office doings? What have *I* to do with the business management of Damodar which is Olcott's business. He sent to Ward this *printed* notice as he did to thousands, and as Olcott is an American business man, so is Ward, and it is not for a *Yankee* to kick at sharp business as they call it. I was furiously *ashamed* when I received your letter and Ward's telegram. But I felt I was a fool; for Olcott, whom I blew up and skinned for it (he has just arrived here to form an Anglo-Indian Branch) says they send such printed compliments to everyone and Damodar did not know at that time that I had or rather was going to receive these 20 rupees Mr. Ward sent, enclosed in a private and even *non*-registered to me. Of course he ought to make a difference, but he does not because he is a boy and was not brought up for office business, and shall S. Ward think bad or any worse of me for it? Did I not send him the whole last year the *Theosophist,* and forbade Damodar to even ask the money for it. . . . — H. P. Blavatsky

Letter XXVII

[Sent from Adyar. Sept. 27, 1883. Rec'd. at London. Nov., 1883.]

. . . I would be happy to find *one* member in your L. L.* doing unremunerated one fourth of the work done by Damodar or Balloi Babu. . . .

— H. P. Blavatsky

*[London Lodge. — Eds.]

Letter XXIX

[Sent from Madras. Nov. 17, 1883.
Received at London. Dec., 1883.]

. . . Most extraordinary phenomena took place among the travellers — Olcott, Brown, Damodar and two Madrassee secretaries. Damodar has so developed that he can get out of his body at will. They sent him on the 10th to me, giving him a message and asking him to tell me to telegraph to them the message back as a sure sign he was indeed in his astral body. At the same hour Coulomb heard his voice in my room and I saw and heard him, and telegraphed what he had asked me immediately. You will find it in the *Supplement*. Then Brown puts letters and questions under Damodar's pillow and receives answers a few minutes later, in K. H.'s handwriting and his usual paper and from my Boss too. Now they will say that it is Damodar the third *humourist* an "Oriental" one this once. Olcott saw K. H. at last and so will Brown at Jammu — D. K. says. . . . — H. P. Blavatsky

Letter XXX

[Sent from Adyar. Nov. 24 (26?), 1883.
Received at London. Dec., 1883.]

. . . Well there's news again. Day before yesterday I received telegram from Jummar from Olcott "Damodar taken away by the Masters." Disappeared!! I thought and feared as much though it *is* strange for it is hardly four years he is chela. I send you both telegrams from Olcott and Mr. Brown's second one. Why should Brown be so favoured — is what I cannot understand. He may be a good man, but what the devil has *he* done [of] so holy and good! That's all I know about him that it seems to be K. H.'s second visit *personally* to him. He is expected here or in the neighbourhood by two chelas who have come from Mysore to meet Him. He is going somewhere to the Buddhists of the Southern Church. Shall *we* see him? I do not know. But there's a commotion here among the chelas. Well strange things are taking place. Earthquakes, and blue and green sun; Damodar spirited away and Mahatma coming. And now what *shall* we do in the office *without* Damodar! . . .

— H. P. BLAVATSKY

LETTER XXXI

[Sent from Madras. Jan. 25, 1884.
Received at London. Feb., 1884.]

. . . Ragonath Row and Subba Row are to take charge of the *Theosophist* and Damodar and a new chela who will be sent here in my absence. . . .

— H. P. BLAVATSKY

LETTER XLIV

[Sent from Torre del Greco. June 21, 1885.]

. . . The only friend I have in life and death is poor little exiled Bowajee D. Nath in Europe; and poor dear Damodar — in Tibet. . . .   — H. P. B.

LETTER XLVI

[Sent from Würzburg. Aug. 19, 1885.]

. . . Alexis Coulomb's handwriting is naturally like mine. We know all how Damodar was once deceived by an order written *in my handwriting* to go upstairs and seek for me in my bedroom in Bombay when I was at Allahabad. It was a trick of M. Coulomb, who thought it good fun to deceive him, "a chela" — and had prepared a semblance of myself lying on my bed, and having startled Damodar — laughed at him for three days. . . . And if he could imitate so well my handwriting in a note why could he not copy (he had four years to study and do it) every scrap and note of mine to Mme. Coulomb on identical paper and make any interpolations he liked? . . . I have seen Coulomb copying one of such scraps of mine, at his table, in a scene shown to me by Master in the Astral light.

— H. P. BLAVATSKY

LETTER CXIX

[Sent from Würzburg. Oct., 1885.]

. . . Well you say you got that "impression" while reading some matter among the *Secret Doctrine* (in Dharbagiri's writing). I looked over carefully page by page and found nothing in D. N.'s writing, but in Damodar's which you probably mistook. It is about what the Earth (and other planets) does during "obscuration"? Is it this? For if so, then I can tell you that Damodar wrote it *under dictation* — but you have not understood the meaning quite correctly. . . .

— H. P. BLAVATSKY

LETTER L

[Sent from Würzburg. Oct. 9, 1885.]

. . . He [D. N.] had heard from some one in Paris *whom he won't name but whom I suspect*, that Mr. Sinnett had said while in Paris that all the Hindus at Hᵈ. Qᵗʳ. were *liars;* and that made him desperate, for he then thought that every word he said to Mr. Sinnett would be regarded as a lie. Now I feel sure Mr. Sinnett said nothing of the kind and if he has, he did not mean to include in that category our friend D. N. . . . his return to his Master depends upon the restoration of the T. S.'s previous *status:* unless the Society begins again to run smoothly, at least in appearance, he has *to remain exiled* — as he says — for it appears that his Master — Mahatma K. H. holds him, Damodar, and Subba Row responsible for the two thirds of Mr. Hodgson's "mayas" — he says. It is *they,* who, irritated and insulted at his appearance at Adyar, regarding his (Hodgson's) cross-examination and talk about the *Masters* — degrading to themselves and blasphemous with regard to Masters; instead of being frank with H. and telling him openly that there were many things they could not tell him — went on to work to augment his perplexity, allowed him to suggest things without contradicting them, and threw him out of the saddle altogether. You see, Hodgson counted without his host: he had no idea of the character of the true Hindu — especially of a chela — of his ferocious veneration for things sacred, of his reserve and exclusiveness in *religious* matters; and they (our Hindus) whom even *I* had never heard pronounce or mention one of the Masters *by name* — were goaded into fury in hearing Hodgson make so cheap of those names — speaking laughingly of "K. H.", and "M." — etc. with the Oakleys. And it is unfortunate *me* who now pays for all! . . .*   — H. P. BLAVATSKY

LETTER LIV

[Sent from Würzburg. 1885 (?1886)]

. . . I have a number of diagrams with reference to the evolution of the septenary globes and Cosmogony of Esoteric Buddhism, made by Djual Khool and Sarma for me to explain to you, and Hume during the first year of the Simla teaching; and several of them I had copied by a Parsee, a good draughtsman of the School of Arts at Bombay, who could not do them well — and then, I copied them from D. Kh.'s with Tibetan signs and names, translating them and doing it the best I could — since I did not want to give the originals out to a stranger and you could not have understood them — and gave them to Olcott to be copied and one of them — the one I sent to Hume I believe — *was* copied by Coulomb who is a very good draughtsman — *too* good unfortunately.† I remember how well he *copied* the few lines in English, a remark by D. K. on the cosmogony — in a way that I was astonished: it was a *perfect* copy of D. K.'s writing,

---

*[See *The Letters of H. P. Blavatsky to A. P. Sinnett*, pp. 157-8 for further description of the attitude of a Hindû chela when trying to defend his Teacher.   — EDS.]

†[Cf. Letter XLVI, page 304 of this volume.   — EDS.]

grammatical mistakes, and all. Neither Olcott, nor I, nor Damodar, ever made a secret of such copies. . . .*

LETTER LXV

[Sent from Würzburg. Jan., 1886.]

. . . You have perhaps heard, that Hurrissingjee (Thakur of Baunagar's cousin) took it into his head to build a shrine for the portraits of the two Masters and meant to spend over it 10,000 rupees. He several times asked Master; He would not answer. Then he asked Olcott, who bothered Mah. K. H. through Damodar, as I had refused point blank to put *such* questions to Masters. Then the Mahatma answered "Let him talk with the chelas about it I do not care" or something to that effect. Well Damodar and Chundra Coosho I think and others went to work to make a plan of the shrine. Even the dirty Coulomb, was called in for his draughtsman's capacities. We were in Europe then. But as soon as we were gone came the Coulomb row. When we returned, Hurrissingjee, to show that the exposure had no effect on him, wanted to *sell a village* and build the shrine *quand même*. The day after my return Mahatma told me to write to Hurrissingjee that He expressly *forbid* spending such amount of money. That it was useless and foolish. So I wrote. Then came the anniversary and Hurrissingjee sent a delegate for himself as he was sick. When

---

*This letter was unsigned, but it is in H. P. B.'s handwriting.   — EDS.]

the superlatively idiotic idea of a Temple of Humanity or Universal Brotherhood came into Olcott's pumpkin, the delegate, when the others were subscribing, was asked by Olcott and he said (in full convention in the *Pandala* before hundreds of people) "I believe His Highness wants to subscribe Rs. 1,000 — " I said to Olcott "too much — it's a shame" — but he pitched into me for my trouble and as I was then sitting there in the light of a prisoner in dock — I shut up. Well; Olcott came one day and said, "Do ask Master to permit me to have money (generally) subscribed for the Temple." So I sent his temple and himself to a hot place and said *I would not.* Then he went to Damodar, and D.—— asked I think, for two or three days after I heard through Damodar that the prohibition to Hurrissingjee of spending money on such flapdoodles had been removed and that Hurrissingjee *had* a letter to that effect. . . .   — H. P. B.

Letter LXXVII

[Sent from Würzburg. Feb. 16, 1886.]

. . . I never said, what he charges me with, either to the Coulomb or Damodar. Both were told by a party wronged by Mohini of that affair, one that happened *before* Mohini had even heard of the Theos. Soc. But, as Coulomb will swear to anything against me, and that Damodar is not there to answer it — hence Mr. Bowaji's *safe charges* against me, whom HE HATES — well in a way he did not conceal before the Countess. . . .   — H. P. Blavatsky

APPENDIX

A Hindu Chela's Diary

NOTES ON "A HINDU CHELA'S DIARY"

THE series called "A Hindu Chela's Diary" was published by William Q. Judge in four parts in *The Path*, beginning in June, 1886. It was a specially attractive and significant feature in his then recently started magazine, and has commanded the attention of earnest Theosophical aspirants for light and wisdom ever since. It contains rare glimpses of the relationship between an 'accepted chela' and his Guru described as plainly as was permissible by one who was receiving instruction while living a normal and very busy life in the outer world.

W. Q. Judge did not publish the name of the Hindû chela whose experiences are described in the 'Diary,' but from the Letters addressed to Judge and preserved in the archives of the Theosophical Society (Point Loma) which are reproduced in Chapter V of this volume, it is clear that the chela was none other than Dâmodar K. Mâvalankar.

Comparison of the contents of the above-mentioned letters with the contents of the 'Diary' shows that the latter was far more than a mere record of certain events in their natural order. It was a piece of skilful literary workmanship, in which facts described in the letters and others not mentioned therein were woven into a record of enthralling interest. Certain incidents described in the 'Diary' are omitted or only casually referred to in the letters, and *vice versa.*

In regard to the authorship, the letters are of course by Dâmodar, and are plain statements of fact, including the real names of persons mentioned written as from one chela to another with open heart and profound sincerity and impersonality. As to the 'Diary,' we have no definite evidence of authorship. It may have been written entirely by Dâmodar from his own recollections modified sufficiently to conceal his personality, but it seems more likely that W. Q. Judge compiled and reconstructed the material supplied by Dâmodar, for at the end of the 'Diary' the editor ("Trans.") says he was left with discretion to give out certain matters. Probably there was another letter (or letters) now lost, from which Judge derived information, because Dâmodar refers in one place to a fact (the Council Room) evidently familiar to Judge but not previously mentioned in the letters. W. Q. Judge received the letters more than five years before he published the 'Diary.' Dâmodar says on January 24, 1880, that he was admitted into the Society about six months earlier, and the writer of the 'Diary' says that it is about seven months since he began to listen to *Kunala*. Who was Kunala?

This leads to the question of identification of the Hindû names given in the 'Diary' with the names given in the letters, an easy task in nearly every case.

"A certain X," living at Benares was Mâji or Mâjji. Swâmiji K. was Pandit Dayânand Saraswâti Swâmiji. Vishnurama was Pandit Mohunlâl Vishnulâl Pandea. The English 'officer' is A. P. Sinnett. The Rest House "in B." is in Ceylon. Kunala is certainly H. P. Blavatsky, but the name also appears in connexion with some occult experiences in Ceylon, where 'Kunala' appears to have been overshadowed by, or at least taken on the appearance of, one of the Masters, probably the Mahâtman Morya, H. P. Blavatsky's Guru, who is said to spend much of his time in Ceylon. 'Nilakant' in one place is also H. P. Blavatsky, but in the other two references may be Dâmodar himself. The latter are the two occult letters received by the chela. They are prefaced by the word 'Nilakant' as if addressing him by name.   — C. J. RYAN

A HINDU CHELA'S DIARY[1]

IN the month of December he arrived at Benares, on what
he hoped would be his last pilgrimage. As much as I
am able to decipher of this curious manuscript, written in
a mixture of Tamil — the South Indian language — with
Mahratta, which, as you know, is entirely dissimilar, shows
that he had made many pilgrimages to India's sacred
places, whether by mere impulse or upon actual direction, I
know not. If he had been only any ordinary religiously
disposed Hindu we might be able to come to some judgment
hereupon, for the pilgrimages might have been made in order
to gain merit, but as he must long ago have risen above the
flowery chains of even the Vedas, we cannot really tell for
what reason these journeys were made. Although, as you
know, I have long had possession of these papers, the time
had not until now seemed ripe to give them out. He had,
when I received them, already long passed away from these
busy scenes to those far busier, and now I give you liberty
to print the fragmentary tale without description of his
person. These people are, you know, not disposed to have
accurate descriptions of themselves floating about. They
being real disciples, never like to say that they are, a manner
quite contrary to that of those famed professors of occult
science who opportunely or inopportunely declare their
supposed chelaship from the house top.
* * * "Twice before have I seen these silent temples standing by the rolling flood of sacred Ganges. They have not

---

1. The original MS. of this Diary as far as it goes is in our
possession. The few introductory lines are by the friend who
communicated the matter to us. — [Ed.]

changed, but in me what changes have occurred! And yet
that cannot be, for the I changeth not, but only the veil
wrapped about, is either torn away or more closely and
thickly folded round to the disguising of the reality. * * *
It is now seven months since I began to use the privilege of
listening to Kunâla. Each time before, that I came to see
him, implacable fate drove me back. It was Karma, the
just law, which compels when we would not, that prevented
me. Had I faltered then and returned to the life then even
so far in the past, my fate in this incarnation would have
been sealed — and he would have said nothing. Why?
Happy was I that I knew the silence would have not indicated in him any loss of interest in my welfare, but only that
the same Karma prevented interference. Very soon after
first seeing him I felt that he was not what he appeared
exteriorly to be. Then the feeling grew into a belief within
a short time so strong that four or five times I thought of
throwing myself at his feet and begging him to reveal himself to me. But I thought that was useless, as I knew that
I was quite impure and could not be trusted with that secret.
If I remained silent I thought that he would confide to me
whenever he found me worthy of it. I thought he must be
some great Hindu Adept who had assumed that illusionary
form. But there this difficulty arose, for I knew that he
received letters from various relatives in different parts,
and this would compel him to practice the illusion all over
the globe, for some of those relatives were in other countries,
where he had been too. Various explanations suggested
themselves to me. * * * I was right in my original conception of Kunâla that he is some great Indian Adept. Of
this subject I constantly talked with him since ——— although I fear I am not, and perhaps shall not be in this life
worthy of their company. My inclination has always been

in this direction. I always thought of retiring from this
world and giving myself up to devotion. To Kunâla I
often expressed this intention, so that I might study this
philosophy, which alone can make man happy in this world.
But then he usually asked me what I would do *there* alone?
He said that instead of gaining my object I might perhaps
become insane by being left alone in the jungles with no one
to guide me; that I was foolish enough to think that by
going into the jungles I could fall in with an adept; and
that if I really wanted to gain my object I should have to
work in the reform in and through which I had met so
many good men and himself also, and when the Higher
Ones, whom I dare not mention by any other names, were
satisfied with me they themselves would call me away from
the busy world and teach me in private. And when I
foolishly asked him many times to give me the names and
addresses of some of those Higher Ones he said once to me:
'One of our Brothers has told me that as you are so much
after me I had better tell you once for all that I have no
right to give you any information about them, but if you
go on asking Hindus you meet what they know about the
matter you might hear of them, and one of those Higher
Ones may perhaps throw himself in your way without your
knowing him, and will tell you what you should do.' These
were orders, and I knew I must wait, and still I knew that
through Kunâla only would I have my object fulfilled. * * *

"I then asked one or two of my own countrymen, and
one of them said he had seen two or three such men, but
that they were not quite what he thought to be *'Raj Yogs.'*
He also said he had heard of a man who had appeared
several times in Benares, but that nobody knew where he
lived. My disappointment grew more bitter, but I never
lost the firm confidence that Adepts do live in India and

can still be found among us. No doubt too there are a few
in other countries, else why had Kunâla been to them.
* * * In consequence of a letter from Vishnurama, who
said that a certain X[2] lived in Benares, and that Swamiji K
knew him. However, for certain reasons I could not address Swamiji K directly, and when I asked him if *he* knew
X he replied: "If there be such a man here at all he is
not known." Thus evasively on many occasions he answered me, and I saw that all my expectations in going to
Benares were only airy castles. I thought I had gained
only the consolation that I was doing a part of my duty.
So I wrote again to Nilakant: "As directed by you I have
neither let him know what I know of him nor what my
own intentions are. He seems to think that in this I am
working to make money, and as yet I have kept him in
the dark as regards myself, and am myself groping in the
dark. Expecting enlightenment from you, etc." * * * The
other day Nilakant came suddenly here and I met Sw. K.
and him together, when to my surprise K at once mentioned
X, saying he knew him well and that he often came to see
him, and then he offered to take us there. But just as we
were going, arrived at the place an English officer who had
done Kunâla a service in some past time. He had in some
way heard of X and was permitted to come. Such are the
complications of Karma. It was absolutely necessary that
he should go too, although no doubt his European education
would never permit him to more than half accept the
doctrine of Karma, so interwoven backward and forwards
in our lives, both those now, that past and that to come.
At the interview with X, I could gain nothing, and so we
came away. The next day came X to see us. He never
speaks of himself, but as 'this body.' He told me that he

2. I find it impossible to decipher this name.

had first been in the body of a Fakir, who, upon having his
hand disabled by a shot he received while he passed the
fortress of Bhurtpore, had to change his body and choose
another, the one he was now in. A child of about seven
years of age was dying at that time, and so, before the complete physical death, this Fakir had entered the body and
afterwards used it as his own. He is, therefore, doubly not
what he seems to be. As a Fakir he had studied Yoga
science for 65 years, but that study having been arrested
at the time he was disabled, leaving him unequal to the
task he had to perform, he had to choose this other one. In
his present body he is 53 years, and consequently the inner
X is 118 years old. * * * In the night I heard him talking
with Kunâla, and found that each had the same Guru, who
himself is a very great Adept, whose age is 300 years,
although in appearance he seems to be only 40.[3] He will
in a few centuries enter the body of a *Kshatriya*,[4] and do
some great deeds for India, but the time had not yet come."

"Yesterday I went with Kunâla to look at the vast and
curious temples left here by our forefathers. Some are in
ruins, and others only showing the waste of time. What a
difference between my appreciation of these buildings now,
with Kunâla to point out meanings I never saw, and that
which I had when I saw them upon my first pilgrimage,
made so many years ago with my father." * * * * *

A large portion of the MS. here, although written in the
same characters as the rest, has evidently been altered in
some way by the writer, so as to furnish clues meant for
himself. It might be deciphered by a little effort, but I

3. There is a peculiarity in this, that all accounts of Cagli-
ostro, St. Germain and other Adepts, give the apparent age as
forty only. — [ED.]

4. The warrior caste of India. — [ED.]

must respect his desire to keep those parts of it which are
thus changed, inviolate. It seems that some matters are here
jotted down relating to secret things, or at least, to things
that he desired should not be understood at a glance. So I
will write out what small portion of it as might be easily
told without breaking any confidences.

It is apparent that he had often been before to the holy
city of Benares, and had merely seen it as a place of pilgrimage for the religious. Then, in his sight, those famous
temples were only temples. But now he found, under the
instruction of Kunâla, that every really ancient building
in the whole collection had been constructed with the view
to putting into imperishable stone, the symbols of a very
ancient religion. Kunâla, he says, told him, that although
the temples were made when no supposition of the ordinary people of those eras leaned toward the idea that nations
could ever arise who would be ignorant of the truths then
universally known, or that darkness would envelop the intellect of men, there were many Adepts then well known to the
rulers and to the people. They were not yet driven by
inexorable fate to places remote from civilization, but lived
in the temples, and while not holding temporal power, they
exercised a moral sway which was far greater than any
sovereignty of earth.[5] And they knew that the time would

5. In the ancient Aztec civilization in Mexico, the Sacerdotal
order was very numerous. At the head of the whole establish-
ment were two high priests, elected from the order, solely for
their qualifications, as shown by their previous conduct in a
subordinate station. They were equal in dignity and inferior
only to the sovereign, who rarely acted without their advice in
weighty matters of private concern. (Sahagun *Hist. de Nueva
Espana, lib. 2; lib. 3 cap. 9 — Torq. Mon. Ind. lib. 8 cap. 20;
lib. 9, cap. 3, 56*; cited by Prescott in *vol. 1, Conq. Mex. p. 66*).

come when the heavy influence of the dark age would make
men to have long forgotten even that such beings had existed, or that any doctrines other than the doctrine based on
the material rights of *mine* and *thine,* had ever been held. If
the teachings were left simply to either paper or papyrus
or parchment, they would be easily lost, because of that decay
which is natural to vegetable or animal membrane. But
stone lasts, in an easy climate, for ages. So these Adepts,
some of them here and there being really themselves Maha
Rajahs,[6] caused the temples to be built in forms, and with
such symbolic ornaments, that future races might decipher
doctrines from them. In this, great wisdom, he says, is
apparent, for to have carved them with sentences in the
prevailing language would have defeated the object, since
languages also change, and as great a muddle would have
resulted as in the case of the Egyptian hieroglyphics, unless
a key stone had also been prepared; but that itself might
be lost, or in its own turn be unintelligible. The ideas underneath symbols do not alter, no matter what might be the
language, and symbols are clear immortally, because they are
founded in nature itself. In respect to this part of the
matter, he writes down that Kunâla informed him that
the language used then was not Sanscrit, but a far older
one now altogether unknown in the world.

From a detached sentence in the MS., it is shadowed
out that Kunâla referred to a curious building put up
many years ago in another part of India and now visible,
by which he illustrated the difference between an intelligent
construction and unintelligent one. This building was the
product of the brain of a Chandala,[7] who had been enriched

6. King or Ruler. — [ED.]

7. A low caste man, *e. g.,* a sweeper. Such a building can
now be seen at Bijapur, India. — [ED.]

through a curious freak. The Rajah had been told upon some event occurring, by his astrologers, that he must give an immense sum of money to the first person he saw next day, they intending to present themselves at an early hour. Next day, at an [un]usually early season, the Rajah arose, looked out of the window, and beheld this Chandala. Calling his astrologers and council together and the poor sweeper into his presence, he presented him with lacs upon lacs of rupees, and with the money the Chandala built a granite building having immense monolithic chains hanging down from its four corners. Its only symbology was, the change of the chains of fate; from poor low caste to high rich low caste. Without the story the building tells us nothing.

But the symbols of the temple, not only those carved on them, but also their conjuncture, need no story nor knowledge of any historical events. Such is the substance of what he writes down as told him by Kunâla. He says also that this symbology extends not only to doctrines and cosmology, but also to laws of the human constitution, spiritual and material. The explanation of this portion, is contained in the altered and cryptic parts of the MS. He then goes on:

* * * "Yesterday, just after sunset, while Kunâla and X were talking, Kunâla suddenly seemed to go into an unusual condition, and about ten minutes afterwards a large quantity of malwa flowers fell upon us from the ceiling.

"I must now go to ——— and do that piece of business which he ordered done. My duty is clear enough, but how am I to know if I shall perform it properly. * * * When I was there and after I had finished my work and was preparing to return here, a wandering fakir met me and asked if he could find from me the proper road to Karli. I directed him, and he then put to me some questions that looked as if he knew what had been my business; he also had a very significant look upon his face, and several of his questions were apparently directed to getting me to tell him a few things Kunâla had told me just before leaving Benares with an injunction of secrecy. The questions did not on the face show that, but were in the nature of inquiries regarding such matters, that if I had not been careful, I would have violated the injunction. He then left me saying: 'you do not know me but we may see each other.' * * * I got back last night and saw only X, to whom I related the incident with the fakir, and he said that, 'it was none other than Kunâla himself using that fakir's body who had said those things, and if you were to see that fakir again he would not remember you and would not be able to repeat his questions, as he was for the time being taken possession of for the purpose, by Kunâla, who often performs such things.' I then asked him if in that case Kunâla had really entered the fakir's body, as I have a strange reluctance toward asking Kunâla such questions, and X replied that if I meant to ask if he had really and in fact entered the fakir's person, the answer was no, but that if I meant to ask if Kunâla had overcome that fakir's senses, substituting his own, the answer was, yes; leaving me to make my own conclusions. * * * I was fortunate enough yesterday to be shown the process pursued in either entering an empty body, or in using one which has its own occupant. I found that in both cases it was the same, and the information was also conveyed that a Bhut[8] goes through just the same road in taking command of the body or senses of those unfortunate women of my country who sometimes are possessed by them. And the Bhut also sometimes gets into possession

---

8. An obsessing astral shell. The Hindus consider them to be the reliquiæ of deceased persons. — [ED.]

DÂMODAR

of a part only of the obsessed person's body, such as an arm
or a hand, and this they do by influencing that part of the
brain that has relation with that arm or hand; in the same
way with the tongue and other organs of speech. With
any person but Kunâla I would not have allowed my own
body to be made use of for the experiment. But I felt perfectly safe, that he would not only let me in again, but also
that he would not permit any stranger, man or gandharba,[9]
to come in after him. We went to ——— and he * *
The feeling was that I had suddenly stepped out into freedom. He was beside me and at first I thought he had but
begun. But he directed me to look, and there on the mat
I saw my body, apparently unconscious. As I looked
* * * the body of myself, opened its eyes and arose. It
was then superior to me, for Kunâla's informing power
moved and directed it. It seemed to even speak to me.
Around it, attracted to it by those magnetic influences,
wavered and moved astral shapes, that vainly tried to whisper in the ear or to enter by the same road. In vain! They
seemed to be pressed away by the air or surroundings of
Kunâla. Turning to look at him, and expecting to see him
in a state of samadhi, he was smiling as if nothing, or at
the very most, but a part, of his power had been taken away
* * * another instant and I was again myself, the mat
felt cool to my touch, the bhuts were gone, and Kunâla
bade me rise.

"He has told me to go to the mountains of ——— where
——— and ——— usually live, and that even if I were not
to see any body the first time, the magnetized air in which
they live would do me much good. They do not generally
stop in one place, but always shift from one place to an-

---

9. Nature spirit or elemental. — [Ed.]

other. They, however, all meet together on certain days of the year in a certain place near Bhadrinath, in the northern part of India. He reminded me that as India's sons are becoming more and more wicked, those adepts have gradually been retiring more and more toward the north, to the Himálaya mountains. * * * Of what a great consequence is it for me to be always with Kunâla. And now X tells me this same thing that I have always felt. All along I have felt and do still feel strongly that I have been once his most obedient and humble disciple in a former existence. All my hopes and future plans are therefore centred in him. My journey therefore to up country has done me one good, that of strengthening my belief, which is the chief foundation on which the grand structure is to be built. * * * As I was walking past the end of Ramalinga's compound holding a small lamp of European make, and while there was no wind, the light three several times fell low. I could not account for it. Both Kunâla and X were far away. But in another moment, the light suddenly went out altogether, and as I stopped, the voice of revered Kunâla, who I supposed was many miles away, spoke to me, and I found him standing there. For one hour we talked; and he gave me good advice, although I had not asked it — thus it is always that when I go fearlessly forward and ask for nothing I get help at an actual critical moment — he then blessed me and went away. Nor could I dare to look in what direction. In that conversation, I spoke of the light going down and wanted an explanation, but he said I had nothing to do with it. I then said I wanted to know, as I could explain it in two ways, viz: 1st, that he did it himself, or 2d, that some one else did it for him. He replied, that even if it were done by somebody else, *no Yogee will do a thing unless he sees the de-*

sire in another Yogee's mind.[10]   The significance of this drove out of my mind all wish to know *who* did it, whether himself, or an elemental or another person, for it is of more importance for me to know even a part of the laws governing such a thing, than it is to know who puts those laws into operation. Even some blind concatenation of nature might put such natural forces in effect in accordance with the same laws, so that a knowledge that nature did it would be no knowledge of any consequence.

*"I have always felt and still feel strongly that I have already once studied this sacred philosophy with Kunâla, and that I must have been, in a previous life, his most obedient and humble disciple. This must have been a fact, or else how to account for the feelings created in me when I first met him, although no special or remarkable circumstances were connected with that event. All my hopes and plans are centred in him, and nothing in the world can shake my confidence in him especially when several of my Brahmin acquaintances tell me the same things without previous consultation. * * *

"I went to the great festival of Durga yesterday, and spent nearly the whole day looking in the vast crowd of

---

10. This sentence is of great importance. The Occidental mind delights much more in effects, personalities and authority, than in seeking for causes, just as many Theosophists have with persistency sought to know when and where Madame Blavatsky did some feat in magic, rather than in looking for causes or laws governing the production of phenomena. In this italicized sentence is the clue to many things, for those who can see. — [ED.]

*[A footnote to the title of the section appearing in *The Path* for August, 1886, reads:

"In reply to several inquiries as to the meaning of *Chela,* we answer that it here means an accepted disciple of an Adept. The word, in general, means, *Disciple.*"   — EDS.]

men, women, children and mendicants for some of Kunâla's friends, for he once told me to never be sure that they were not near me, but I found none who seemed to answer my ideas. As I stood by the ghaut at the river side thinking that perhaps I was left alone to try my patience, an old and apparently very decrepit Bairagee plucked my sleeve and said: 'Never expect to see any one, but always be ready to answer if they speak to you; it is not wise to peer outside of yourself for the great followers of Vasudeva: look rather within.'

"This amazed me, as I was expecting him to beg or to ask me for information. Before my wits returned, he had with a few steps mingled with a group of people, and in vain searched I for him: he had disappeared. But the lesson is not lost.

"To-morrow I return to I———.

"Very wearying indeed in a bodily sense was the work of last week and especially of last evening, and upon laying down on my mat last night after continuing work far into the night I fell quickly sound asleep. I had been sleeping some hour or two when with a start I awoke to find myself in perfect solitude and only the horrid howling of the jackals in the jungle to disturb me. The moon was brightly shining and I walked over to the window of this European modeled house threw it open and looked out. Finding that sleep had departed, I began again on those palm leaves. Just after I had begun, a tap arrested my attention and I opened the door. Overjoyed was I then to see Kunâla standing there, once more unexpected.

" 'Put on your turban and come with me,' he said and turned away.

"Thrusting my feet into my sandals, and catching up my turban, I hurried after him, afraid that the master would get beyond me, and I remain unfortunate at losing some golden opportunity.

"He walked out into the jungle and turned into an unfrequented path. The jackals seemed to recede into the distance; now and then in the mango trees overhead, the flying foxes rustled here and there, while I could distinctly hear the singular creeping noise made by a startled snake as it drew itself hurriedly away over the leaves. Fear was not in my breast for master was in front. He at last came to a spot that seemed bare of trees, and bending down, seemed to press his hand into the grass. I then saw that a trap door or entrance to a stairway very curiously contrived, was there. Stairs went down into the earth. He went down and I could but follow. The door closed behind me, yet it was not dark. Plenty of light was there, but where it came from I cared not then nor can I now, tell. It reminded me of our old weird tales told us in youth of pilgrims going down to the land of the Devas where, although no sun was seen, there was plenty of light.

"At the bottom of the stairs was a passage. Here I saw people but they did not speak to me and appeared not to even see me although their eyes were directed at me. Kunâla said nothing but walked on to the end, where there was a room in which were many men looking as grand as he does but two more awful, one of whom sat at the extreme end."

*   *   *   *   *   *   *

[Here there is a confused mass of symbols and ciphers which I confess I cannot decipher, and even if I had the ability to do so, I would check myself, because I surmise that it is his own way of jotting down for his own remembrance, what occurred in that room. Nor do I think that even a plain reading of it would give the sense to any one but the writer himself, for this reason, that it is quite evidently fragmentary. For instance, I find among the rest, a sort of notation of a division of states or planes: whether of consciousness, of animated, or of elemental life, I cannot tell; and in each division are hieroglyphs that might stand for animals, or denizens of the astral world, or for anything else — even for ideas only, so I will proceed at the place of his returning.]

"Once more I got out into the passage, but never to my knowledge went up those steps, and in a moment more was I again at my door. It was as I left it, and on the table I found the palm leaves as I dropped them, except that beside them was a note in Kunâla's hand, which read:

" 'Nilakant — strive not yet to think too deeply on those things you have just seen. Let the lessons sink deep into your heart, and they will have their own fruition. To-morrow I will see you.' * * * *

"What a very great blessing is mine to have had Kunâla's company for so many days even as we went to ———. Very rarely however he said a few words of encouragement and good advice as to how I should go on. He seems to leave me as to that to pick my own way. This is right, I think, because otherwise one would never get any individual strength or power of discrimination. Happy were those moments, when alone at midnight, we then had conversation. How true I then found the words of the Agroushada Parakshai to be:

" 'Listen while the Sudra sleeps like the dog under his hut, while the Vaysa dreams of the treasures that he is hoarding up, while the Rajah sleeps among his women. This is the moment when just men, who are not under the dominion of their flesh, commence the study of the sciences.' [11]

---

11. See Agroushada Parakshai, 2d book, 23d dialogue. — [ED.]

"The midnight hour must have powers of a peculiar nature. And I learned yesterday from glancing into an Englishman's book, that even those semi barbarians speak of that time as 'the witching hour,' and it is told me that among them 'witching' means to have magic power. * * *

"We stopped at the Rest House in B——— yesterday evening, but found it occupied and so we remained in the porch for the night. But once more I was to be blessed by another visit with Kunâla to some of his friends whom I revere and who will I hope bless me too.

"When every one had quieted down he told me to go with him to the sea which was not far away. We walked for about three quarters of an hour by the seashore, and then entered as if into the sea. At first a slight fear came into me, but I saw that a path seemed to be there, although water was all around us. He in front and I following, we went for about seven minutes, when we came to a small island; on it was a building and on top of that a triangular light. From the sea shore, the island would seem like an isolated spot covered all over by green bushes. There is only one entrance to go inside. And no one can find it out unless the occupant wishes the seeker to find the way. On the island we had to go round about for some space before we came in front of the actual building. There is a little garden in front and there was sitting another friend of Kunâla with the same expression of the eyes as he has. I also recognized him as one of those who was in the room underground. Kunâla seated himself and I stood before them. We stayed an hour and saw a portion of the place. How very pleasant it is! And inside he has a small room where he leaves his body when he himself moves about in other places. What a charming spot, and what a delightful smell of roses and various sorts of flowers! How I should wish to visit that place often. But I cannot indulge in such idle dreams, nor in that sort of covetousness. The master of the place put his blessing hand upon my head, and we went away back to the Rest House and to the morrow full of struggles and of encounters with men who do not see the light, nor hear the great voice of the future; who are bound up in sorrow because they are firmly attached to objects of sense. But all are my brothers and I must go on trying to do the master's work which is only in fact the work of the Real Self which is All and in All.

"I have been going over that message I received just after returning from the underground room, about not thinking yet too deeply upon what I saw there, but to let the lessons sink deep into my heart. Can it be true — must it not indeed be true — that we have periods in our development when rest must be taken for the physical brain in order to give it time as a much less comprehensive machine than these English college professors say it is, to assimilate what it has received, while at the same time the real brain — as we might say, the spiritual brain — is carrying on as busily as ever all the trains of thought cut off from the head. Of course this is contrary to this modern science we hear so much about now as about to be introduced into all Asia, but it is perfectly consistent for me.

"To reconsider the situation: I went with Kunâla to this underground place, and there saw and heard most instructive and solemn things. I return to my room and begin to puzzle over them all, to revolve and re-revolve them in my mind, with a view to clearing all up and finding out what all may mean. But I am interrupted by a note from Kunâla directing me to stop this puzzling, and to let all I saw sink deep into my heart. Every word of his I regard with respect, and consider to hold a meaning, being never used by him with carelessness. So when he says, to let it sink into my 'heart,' in the very same sentence where he refers to my thinking part — the mind — why he must mean to separate my heart from my mind and to give to the heart a larger and greater power.

"Well, I obeyed the injunction, made myself, as far as I could, forget what I saw and what puzzled me and thought of other things. Presently, after a few days while one afternoon thinking over an episode related in the *Vishnu Purana*,[12] I happened to look up at an old house I was passing and stopped to examine a curious device on the porch; as I did this, it seemed as if either the device, or the house, or the circumstance itself, small as it was, opened up at once several avenues of thought about the underground room, made them all clear, showed me the conclusion as vividly as a well demonstrated and fully illustrated proposition, to my intense delight. Now could I perceive with plainness, that those few days which seemed perhaps wasted because withdrawn from contemplation of that scene and its lessons, had been with great advantage used by the spiritual man in unraveling the tangled skein, while the much praised brain had remained in idleness. All at once the *flash* came and with it knowledge.[13]   But I must not depend upon these flashes, I must give the brain and its governor, the material to work with.   *   *   *   *   *   *

"Last night just as I was about to go to rest, the voice of Kunâla called me from outside and there I went at once.

12. An ancient Hindu book full of tales as well as doctrines.
— [ED.]

13. These *flashes* of thought are not unknown even in the scientific world, as, where in such a moment of lunacy, it was revealed to an English scientist, that there must be iron in the sun; and Edison gets his ideas thus. — [ED.]

Looking steadily at me he said: 'we want to see you,' and as he spoke he gradually changed, or disappeared, or was absorbed, into the form of another man with awe-inspiring face and eyes, whose form apparently rose up from the material of Kunâla's body. At the same moment two others stood there also, dressed in the Tibetan costume; and one of them went into my room from which I had emerged. After saluting them reverently, and not knowing their object, I said to the greatest,

" 'Have you any orders to give?'

" 'If there are any they will be told to you without being asked,' he replied, 'stand still where you are.'

"Then he began to look at me fixedly. I felt a very pleasant sensation as if I was getting out of my body. I cannot tell now what time passed between that and what I am now to put down here. But I saw I was in a peculiar place. It was the upper end of ——— at the foot of the ——— range. Here was a place where there were only two houses just opposite to each other, and no other sign of habitation; from one of these came out the old faquir I saw at the Durga festival, but how changed, and yet the same: then so old, so repulsive; now so young, so glorious, so beautiful. He smiled upon me benignly and said:

" 'Never expect to see anyone, but always be ready to answer if they speak to you; it is not wise to peer outside of yourself for the great followers of Vasudeva: look rather within.'

"The very words of the poor faquir!

"He then directed me to follow him.

"After going a short distance, of about half a mile or so, we came to a natural subterranean passage which is under the ——— range. The path is very dangerous; the River ——— flows underneath in all the fury of pent up waters,

and a natural causeway exists upon which you may pass;
only one person at a time can go there and one false step
seals the fate of the traveller. Besides this causeway, there
are several valleys to be crossed. After walking a considerable distance through this subterranean passage we came
into an open plain in L———K. There stands a large massive building thousands of years old. In front of it is a huge
Egyptian Tau. The building rests on seven big pillars
each in the form of a pyramid. The entrance gate has a
large triangular arch, and inside are various apartments. The
building is so large that I think it can easily contain twenty
thousand people. Some of the rooms were shown to me.

"This must be the central place for all those belonging
to the ——— class, to go for initiation and stay the requisite
period.

"Then we entered the great hall with my guide in front.
He was youthful in form but in his eyes was the glance of
ages. * * * * The grandeur and serenity of this place
strikes the heart with awe. In the centre was what we
would call an altar, but it must only be the place where
focuses all the power, the intention, the knowledge and the
influence of the assembly. For the seat, or place, or throne,
occupied by the chief ——— the highest ——— has around
it an indescribable glory, consisting of an effulgence which
seemed to radiate from the one who occupied it. The surroundings of the throne were not gorgeous, nor was the spot
itself in any way decorated — all the added magnificence was
due altogether to the aura which emanated from Him sitting
there. And over his head I thought I saw as I stood there,
three golden triangles in the air above — Yes, they were
there and seemed to glow with an unearthly brilliance that
betokened their inspired origin. But neither they nor the
light pervading the place, were produced by any mechanical

means. As I looked about me I saw that others had a triangle, some two, and all with that peculiar brilliant light."

[Here again occurs a mass of symbols. It is apparent that just at this spot he desires to jot down the points of the initiation which he wished to remember. And I have to admit that I am not competent to elucidate their meaning. That must be left to our intuitions and possibly future experience in our own case.]

        *   *   *   *

"14th day of the new moon. The events of the night in the hall of initiation gave me much concern. Was it a dream? Am I self deluded? Can it be that I imagined all this? Such were the unworthy questions which flew behind each other across my mind for days after. Kunâla does not refer to the subject and I cannot put the question. Nor will I. I am determined, that, come what will, the solution must be reached by me, or given me voluntarily.

"Of what use to me will all the teachings and all the symbols be, if I cannot rise to that plane of penetrating knowledge, by which I shall myself, by myself, be able to solve this riddle, and know to discriminate the true from the false and the illusory? If I am unable to cut asunder these questioning doubts, these bonds of ignorance, it is proof that not yet have I risen to the plane situated above these doubts.   * * * *   Last night after all day chasing through my mental sky, these swift destroyers of stability — mental birds of passage — I lay down upon the bed, and as I did so, into my hearing fell these words:

" 'Anxiety is the foe of knowledge; like unto a veil it falls down before the soul's eye; entertain it, and the veil only thicker grows; cast it out, and the sun of truth may dissipate the cloudy veil.'

"Admitting that truth; I determined to prohibit all anxiety. Well I knew that the prohibition issued from the depths of my heart, for that was master's voice, and confidence in his wisdom, the self commanding nature of the words themselves, compelled me to complete reliance on the instruction. No sooner was the resolution formed, than down upon my face fell something which I seized at once in my hand. Lighting a lamp, before me was a note in the well known writing. Opening it, I read:

" 'Nilakant. It was no dream. All was real, and more, that by your waking consciousness could not be retained, happened there. Reflect upon it all as reality, and from the slightest circumstance draw whatever lesson, whatever amount of knowledge you can. Never forget that your spiritual progress goes on quite often to yourself unknown. Two out of many hindrances to memory are anxiety and selfishness. Anxiety is a barrier constructed out of harsh and bitter materials. Selfishness is a fiery darkness that will burn up the memory's matrix. Bring then, to bear upon this other memory of yours, the peaceful stillness of contentment and the vivifying rain of benevolence.' "[14] * * * *

14. The careful student will remember that Jacob Bœhme speaks of the "harsh and bitter anguish of nature which is the principle that produces bones and all corporification." So here the master, it appears, tells the fortunate chela, that in the spiritual and mental world, anxiety, harsh and bitter, raises a veil before us and prevents us from using our memory. He refers, it would seem, to the other memory above the ordinary. The correctness and value of what was said in this, must be admitted when we reflect that, after all, the whole process of development is the process of *getting back the memory of the past.* And that too is the teaching found in pure Buddhism as well also as in its corrupted form. — [ED.]

[I leave out here, as well as in other places, mere notes of journeys and various small matters, very probably of no interest.]

"In last month's passage across the hills near V———, I was irresistibly drawn to examine a deserted building, which I at first took for a grain holder, or something like that. It was of stone, square, with no openings, no windows, no door. From what could be seen outside, it might have been the ruins of a strong, stone foundation for some old building, gateway or tower. Kunâla stood not far off and looked over it, and later on he asked me for my ideas about the place. All I could say, was, that although it seemed to be solid, I was thinking that perhaps it might be hollow.

" 'Yes,' said he, 'it is hollow. It is one of the places once made by Yogees to go into deep trance in. If used by a chela (a disciple) his teacher kept watch over it so that no one might intrude. But when an adept wants to use it for laying his body away in while he travels about in his real, though perhaps to some unseen, form, other means of protection were often taken which were just as secure as the presence of the teacher of the disciple.' 'Well,' I said, 'it must be that just now no one's body is inside there.'

" 'Do not reach that conclusion nor the other either. It may be occupied and it may not.'

"Then we journeyed on, while he told me of the benevolence of not only Brahmin Yogees, but also of Buddhist. No differences can be observed by the true disciple in any other disciple who is perhaps of a different faith. All pursue truth. Roads differ but the goal of all remains alike."

* * * "Repeated three times: 'Time ripens and dissolves all beings in the great self, but he who knows into what time itself is dissolved, he is the knower of the Veda.'

"What is to be understood, not only by this, but also by its being three times repeated?

"There were three shrines there. Over the door was a picture which I saw a moment, and which for a moment seemed to blaze out with light like fire. Fixed upon my mind its outlines grew, then disappeared, when I had passed the threshold. Inside, again its image came before my eyes. Seeming to allure me, it faded out, and then again returned. It remained impressed upon me, seemed imbued with life and intention to present itself for my own criticism. When I began to analyze it, it would fade, and then when I was fearful of not doing my duty or of being disrespectful to those beings, it returned as if to demand attention. Its description:

"A human heart that has at its centre a small spark — the spark expands and the heart disappears — while a deep pulsation seems to pass through me. At once identity is confused, I grasp at myself; and again the heart reappears with the spark increased to a large fiery space. Once more that deep movement; then sounds (7); they fade. All this in a picture? Yes! for in that picture there is life; there might be intelligence. It is similar to that picture I saw in Tibet on my first journey, where the living moon rises and passes across the view. Where was I? No, not afterwards! It was in the hall. Again that all pervading sound. It seems to bear me like a river. Then it ceased,— a soundless sound. Then once more the picture; here is Pranava.[15] But between the heart and the Pranava is a mighty bow with arrows ready, and tightly strung for use. Next is a shrine, with the Pranava over it, shut fast, no key and no keyhole. On its sides emblems of human passions. The

---

15. The mystic syllable OM. — [Ed.]

door of the shrine opens and I think within I will see the truth. No! another door? a shrine again. It opens too and then another, brightly flashing is seen there. Like the heart, it makes itself one with me. Irresistible desire to approach it comes within me, and it absorbs the whole picture.

" 'Break through the shrine of Brahman; use the doctrine of the teacher.' "16

[There is no connection here of this exhortation with any person, and very probably it is something that was said either by himself, in soliloquy, or by some voice or person to him.

I must end here, as I find great rents and spaces in the notes. He must have ceased to put down further things he saw or did in his real inner life, and you will very surely agree, that if he had progressed by that time to what the last portions would indicate, he could not set down his reflections thereon, or any memorandum of facts. We, however, can never tell what was his reason. He might have been told not to do so, or might have lacked the opportunity.

There was much all through these pages that related to his daily family life, not interesting to you; records of conversations; worldly affairs; items of money and regarding appointments, journeys and meetings with friends. But they show of course that he was all this time living through his set work with men, and often harassed by care as well as comforted by his family and regardful of them. All of that I left out, because I supposed that while it would probably interest you, yet I was left with discretion to give

---

16. There is some reference here apparently to the Upanishad, for they contain a teacher's directions to break through all shrines until the last one is reached. — [ED.]

only what seemed to relate to the period marked at its beginning, by his meetings with M————, and at the end by this last remarkable scene, the details of which we can only imagine. And likewise were of necessity omitted very much that is sufficiently unintelligible in its symbolism to be secure from revelation. Honestly have I tried to unlock the doors of the ciphers, for no prohibition came with their possession, but all that I could refine from its enfolding obscurity is given to you.

As he would say, let us salute each other and the last shrine of Brahman; Om, hari, Om!   TRANS.]

CPSIA information can be obtained
at www.ICGtesting.com
Printed in the USA
BVHW070821080120
568938BV00024B/1114/P